Goldwin Smith

The Empire

A Series of Letters

Goldwin Smith

The Empire
A Series of Letters

ISBN/EAN: 9783337320898

Printed in Europe, USA, Canada, Australia, Japan

Cover: Foto ©ninafisch / pixelio.de

More available books at **www.hansebooks.com**

THE EMPIRE.

A SERIES OF LETTERS

PUBLISHED IN

"THE DAILY NEWS," 1862, 1863.

BY

GOLDWIN SMITH.

Oxford and London:

JOHN HENRY AND JAMES PARKER.

1863.

CONTENTS.

THE EMPIRE.

THE following series of Letters appeared, with
two exceptions, in *The Daily News*, (1862,
1863). My best thanks are due to the Editor of
that journal for the readiness with which he admitted them into his columns. He always lends
a generous protection to independent thought, the
salt without which all our liberties would lose
their savour.

I did not intend, when the letters were written,
to reprint them in that form; but when I tried
to put the matter of them into a more regular
shape, I found that the discussion which ran
through the series had followed the main lines
of thought, and that in attempting to be more
methodical I only became less clear.

Most of the letters, however, have been revised;
some have been amplified, partly by taking up
into them defences of their arguments which
originally appeared in short supplementary letters; to some, more appropriate titles have been
given. The order of subjects has been substituted
for the order of dates, but the dates have been

retained, because in some cases they point to the occasions on which the letters were written.

The first of the series, with the article of *The Times* appended, stands as it was. *The Times'* article is most valuable, because it gives the reader, on the best possible authority, the dominant view of the question, and the arguments by which that view is supported. We may be sure that we have in it the reasons which mainly govern official men in maintaining the present system. It is rather personal in its language, but I dare say its personality will not shock the reader any more than it hurts me. Vituperation, indeed, when used in controversy, sometimes helps us to a judgment: it is the surest proof that on the side on which it is used the arguments are exhausted and the case is complete.

The first letter was occasioned by the affair of the "Trent," which revealed the danger of the present connexion between Canada and England. The shadow of that danger still falls upon these pages. But it is hoped that no argument will be found in them which can fairly be ascribed to panic, or which reason would, on that account, refuse to consider in the calmest hour. To reason, of course, all arguments must be addressed. It would be vain to address them to tyrannical and insensate pride. It would have been vain to argue with a Roman or a Spanish despot about the expediency of cutting off a part of his over-grown dominions, though to the eyes of any man in his senses that expediency might have been most clear.

I am not careful to defend myself against the charge of being wanting in patriotism if I suggest that the strength and wealth of England might be increased by resigning useless dependencies. No Englishman, whose interest lies wholly in England, ought to be very careful to defend him-self against the charge of seeking, in the dis-cussion of public questions, any object but the happiness and greatness of his country.

I am as little careful to defend myself against the charge of being sordid if I argue against the needless expenditure of public money. Public money is spent by ambitious politicians; it is mainly made by peasants and artisans, who have no share in the pleasures of ambition. Nor are a cheap policy and a great policy opposed to each other. A truly great policy is generally cheap, because it has the moral forces on its side. Eco-nomy follows it unsought, just as in individual men loftiness of aim, though not studious of parsimony, is generally attended by simplicity of life. The expense of aimless bluster is enormous, and so is the expense of making littleness pass for greatness.

The term Empire is here taken in a wide sense, as including all that the nation holds beyond its own shores and waters by arms or in the way of dominion, as opposed to that natural influence which a great power, though confining itself to its own territories, always exercises in the world. In the case of our Empire this definition will embrace a motley mass of British Colonies, conquered Colonies of other European nations, conquered territories in India, military and maritime stations, and protectorates, including our practical protectorate of Turkey, as well as our legal protectorate of the Ionian Islands. These various dependencies stand in the most various relations to the Imperial country, some, such as India, being under our absolute dominion; while others, such as Canada, are in truth free nations dependent upon us only in name. The reasons, or alleged reasons, for retaining them are also of the most various kinds. In some cases they are political, in some military, in some commercial, in some diplomatic. Frequently these various reasons are blended together, but in different proportions. The pride of Empire, however, runs through the whole, and so does the notion that extent of territory is the extent of power. In the case of the Turkish protectorate this notion presents itself, as it were, in an inverted form, the fear that the power of Russia will increase as its territory advances being our motive for supporting the declining Empire of the Turks.

The arguments of the Letters will not be found, if candidly viewed, to be tainted by any chimerical theory of an approaching millennium, or of a reign of universal peace. No cession is advocated or suggested of any place supposed to be a source of military strength to us, except on the ground that the place is not really a source of military strength, but of weakness. Nor, it is hoped, is any language used which can impugn the duty incumbent upon England not only of placing her own shores beyond the ignominious danger of attack and maintaining her own honour on every just occasion, but of using the strength which Providence has given her to vindicate the violated rights of nations and to defend the oppressed against the oppressor. For my part, indeed, I do not shrink from frankly avowing that while I cordially repudiate propagandism, whether on the side of revolution or reaction, as unjustifiable in itself and fraught with eventual mischief to every good cause, I equally repudiate the doctrine of non-intervention, if by that doctrine is meant the tame sufferance of high-handed wrong in the community of nations. I believe that the complacent enunciation of this doctrine by English statesmen is a symptom that, owing to the multitude of her useless dependencies, and the consequent dispersion and exhaustion of her forces, the power of England is beginning to decline. If flatterers of the national pride, in the exercise of their calling, deny this, it may nevertheless be true.

It is quite consistent with these views to believe, and to rejoice in the belief, that whatever sage reflections may be made upon the unchangeable wickedness of human nature, the tendency of nations to aggressive war has greatly diminished since the history of the world began. No civilized nation would now set forth, as barbarous nations did, in the mere lust of conquest, nakedly avowed, to invade and despoil another. Men have not become angels; but their motives for remaining at peace have gained strength, and their motives for going to war have been weakened. With a single exception, it may be said that no nation in the civilized world at present shews any tendency to attack any other nation.

Wars are going on, and more are likely to ensue, but they arise from other causes than rapacity and the love of aggrandizement. The Italians desire to get rid of the Austrians and the French; the Poles to get rid of the Russians; the Greek, the Serb, the Albanian, the Rouman, and the Bulgarian to get rid of the Turk. These are struggles for liberty, not for empire, and they threaten the peace of no one but the tyrant. Passion and prejudice may say, and possibly believe, that the Federal States of America are fighting for Empire: but cooler observers will not fail to see that a struggle for the maintenance of national unity is a totally different thing from a struggle for Empire; and that it no more betrays disordered ambition in the case of the American Commonwealth, than it did in the case of the English aristocracy when they put down the rebellion in Ireland, or when they resisted as treason the agitation for Repeal. Aggressive tendencies, no doubt, linger in some of the military Governments of civilized nations, though they have subsided in the nations which those Governments oppress. To some extent such tendencies linger even in the Government of England; but the conquerors among our statesmen are compelled to find a distant vent for their love of glory in attacks on Afghans and Chinese: and to induce the nation to indulge them even in these minor imitations of the great scourges of humanity, they are compelled to provide some pretext of self-defence, which does homage to the general ascendancy of the moral rule.

The only exception to the unaggressive tendency of civilized nations at the present time is France. In the breasts of the French people, there seems too much reason to fear, the delirious passion for glory and aggrandizement excited by the conquests of Napoleon is not yet extinct. It is partly owing to this cause, as well as to a want of political self-control, that the nation has rendered up its liberties into the hands of a military despot, who promises domination abroad as a compensation for the loss of freedom, and of dignity with freedom, at home. The religious and moral convictions of the people were too completely prostrated by the Revolution and its consequences, to be able at present to contend with much effect against a dominant passion. The clergy, bigots without faith, are only eager to make their Church popular by pandering to the impulse of the hour. Commercial connexions have begun to exert a real and beneficent influence in favour of peace; but this influence extends only to a part of the people: it does not touch the soldiery: nor is there any constitutional assembly through which it can effectually control the military despot, should his personal interest or temper lead him to declare for war. We may hope that the aggressive disposition of the French people will presently pass away; that the increase of wealth, the experience of tranquillity, the growing power of commercial connexions, the rise of a rational religion, of which symptoms may be discerned by observant eyes, the restoration, for which some brave and generous spirits are struggling, of constitutional checks upon the military government, these and all-healing time, will at length give the spirit of peace the victory over the spirit of war. Even while the present evil lasts, we are bound to remember that it owes its existence to the unjustifiable attacks made by the kings and nobles of Europe on revolutionary France, without which Napoleon, his conquests, and the craving for military glory which they have excited, would have never been. But at present it is vain, and worse than vain, to deny that from this quarter a danger hangs over the peace and civilization of the world. The friends of peace

as well as the friends of liberty in France are
heartily grateful to this country for putting herself into a resolute attitude of self-defence. They
know that the sight of the means to do ill deeds
may in certain contingencies cause ill deeds to
be done.

The way, however, to guard against this danger
while it lasts, is apparently to cultivate, not
clandestine connexions, such as might give just
umbrage to France, but frank amity with other
nations, and among the rest with Spain, a nation
which, if we will be kind to her and respect her
honour, has not a single inducement to be our
enemy, and the strongest of all possible inducements to be our friend.

It must be admitted, to state the case fairly,
that while some of the old causes of war have
died out, or declined, two new causes, though of
a secondary kind, have come into being in modern
times. The first of these causes is connected with
the progress of civilization itself. It arises from
a re-action of the adventurous and self-devoting
spirit of man, against the dull prosaic tenor of
peaceful society and of commercial and industrial life. It will not be allayed by the acquisition of wealth, nor by the increase of material
enjoyments. It will be allayed only when the

chivalrous instincts of mankind find some better satisfaction than that which is afforded by the romance, the peril, and the pageantry of war. There is something, indeed, in the character of a soldier, in its best form, which the world could scarcely afford at present to let die.

The second cause is an accidental result of the order of modern society, generally favourable to peace, which divides the functions of the states-man from those of the soldier. If ambitious Ministers were called upon, like the Chiefs and Kings of former times, themselves to face death in the field, instead of issuing their orders to others to face it for them, they might, under the present circumstances of the world, sometimes be less ready than they are to go to war. As it is, they sit safely at home and earn a reputation for courage and spirit, by lavishing the blood of the brave. The remedy for this in a constitu-tional country is, that the representatives of the nation, while they are always ready to drag small criminals to their bar, should also have the honesty and firmness to call to account the authors of unjust and calamitous wars.

It is another proof of the decline of aggressive tendencies among nations, that a great wish has lately been shewn by England, and by other

nations following her example, to establish a
purely defensive force of citizens, incapable of
acting out of their own country, in place of that
kind of armament which serves the purposes of
aggressive war. The movement is at present in
its infancy, and its results are crude; probably
it will go through several failures before it at-
tains success; but it is too deep, too widely
spread, and too reasonable to permit us to think
that it will die.

There is nothing chimerical either, or savour-
ing of millenarian fancies, in the hope that from
the progress of reason and still more from the progress of liberty, open dealing between nations will
at no distant time supersede secret diplomacy, and
put an end to the existence of the brotherhood of
intriguers whom secret diplomacy harbours, and
who, through the powers thus put into their
hands, have often been able, with very mean
abilities, to make themselves great scourges of
mankind. In this case another great source of
war will become extinct.

Adam Smith, in stating the reasons why we
must despair of getting rid of our useless dependencies, does not hesitate to mention as the
strongest reason of all, "that such sacrifices are
always contrary to the private interest of the

governing part of the nation, who would thereby be deprived of the disposal of many places of trust and profit, of many opportunities of acquiring wealth and distinction which the possession of the most turbulent, and to the great body of the people the most unprofitable, province seldom fails to afford." It is hoped that in the following letters the influence of great establishments, enlisting a number of interests as well as a number of prejudices, has not been overstated: but it would be senseless not to take notice of this influence among the causes which, independently of reason and the public good, stand in the way of any retrenchment of our Empire, and which the intelligence and the will of the nation must be exerted to overcome.

It is not our soldiers, however, nor the officers of our Army, that have an interest in retaining the outlying dependencies of an Empire spreading over the globe. On them this Empire entails constant banishment, often in unhealthy climates, and all the discomfort of a wandering life. They might guard England without sacrificing all the comforts of a settled habitation, and all the happiness of home. More than this, it is in fact to the extent of the Empire that they must attribute the wretched inadequacy of their pay.

b

An officer of the Navy is very ill paid compared with other professions, and considering the. hardships and dangers he has to undergo : an officer of the Army, taking into account the purchase of commissions and steps, can often hardly be said to be paid at all. Yet the public expects these men not only to face the shot, and to allow themselves to be tossed to and fro all over the globe, but to devote themselves to the science of their profession with the ardour of a lawyer or a physician cheered on by the prospect of ten thousand a-year. If they ask for justice, they are summarily told that " things are done on a great scale ;" and if they lay their heads together to press their claims, they are. told that their conduct savours of " insubordination :" as though a man could not ask for his just wages and yet do his duty to his employers. Nevertheless, though our soldiers and sailors, at least the officers of our Army and Navy, are ill paid, our establishments are the most expensive in the world. And it is the extent of the Empire that makes them expensive. A soldier in a Colony or Dependency costs double as much as a soldier at home, besides all the incidental expenses, such as the cost of Colonial fortifications, and the sudden transmission of troops to distant points

attendant upon outlying and dangerous possessions. The tax-payers of this country will never
consent, nor can they be in reason called upon
to consent, to pay more money for the Army and
Navy than they pay at present. On the contrary, they are demanding, and will continue to
demand, retrenchments; and the question will
be whether those retrenchments shall be made by
cutting down the services, or by putting bounds
to an unreasoning and aimless ambition.

If it is objected that the tendency of these
Letters is only to destroy, and that they build up
nothing in the place of the Colonial Empire
which they pull down, the commonplace answer
must be given, that to remove an evil is to do
a good. "He that taketh away weights from the
motions," said Pym, in a speech for the removal
of grievances, "doth the same as he that addeth
wings." What shall we give to England in place
of her useless dependencies? What shall we give
to a man in place of his heavy burden, or of his
dangerous disease? What but unencumbered
strength and the vigour of reviving health?

The leading idea which it is desired that the
reader should carry with him through the Letters
is this, that great changes have come over the
world since the time when our Empire was

formed and our Imperial policy was adopted;
and that, the world being changed, it is at least
a fair subject for inquiry whether our policy
ought to remain the same. What was wisdom
in our fathers, regard being had to the circumstances of their days, may be utter folly in us.

The most obvious of these changes, and the one
which bears most directly on the policy of our
Imperial system, is the fall of protection and the
progress of free trade. If the victory of free
trade is not yet universal, it may be said, among
the most civilized nations, to be general. Its
final triumph is no longer doubtful; and even
where it has not yet received the homage of legal
submission, its influence is felt in an enhanced
sense of the blessings of commerce and in the
increase of all those feelings of sociability and
good-will which commercial intercourse produces
among nations.

The introduction of free trade, however, if it
is the most obvious, is not the only change
affecting the value of extended Empire and the
policy of retaining it which the world has undergone during the momentous epoch of revolutionary transition, political, social, and religious,
in the midst of which we live. Nations buried
in the tomb of feudalism and Church authority,

have risen, or are rising again, to the life of free
institutions and liberty of conscience. That which
half a century ago was hopeless and abject decrepitude, the safe mark of injustice and insult,
is now hope and vigour, of which aggressors
will soon find it necessary to beware. At the
same time, the fierce hatred which the religious
divisions of the sixteenth century put between
Christian nations, and which has so long made
the prosperity and strength of each seem the
calamity and weakness of all the rest, begins to
sink with the dogmatic establishments in which
it has been embodied and by whose mutual antipathies it has been fed. Those who hope to see
Christendom one day reconciled in liberty, as it
has been divided by false authority, may reckon
this as not the least of the reasons for expecting
a decline in the motives for aggressive war.

If, in the midst of the vast revolution which
is going on over the world, the almost invisible
filaments of political connexion which still bind
England to her Colonies should at length cease
to exist, and if she were to find that a few military positions no longer answered the purpose
for which they had been occupied or repaid the
money which they cost, history a century hence
would probably not number this amongst the

greatest events of an eventful age, nor give it so
large a space in her record as she will give to
other things of which England itself is now the
scene.

I have been warned, in the course of the discussion, that Professors are not Statesmen. I heartily acknowledge it; and perhaps the observation
may be extended not without pertinency or advantage to journalists as well as to Professors.
I hope it will be found that in these pages I have
confined myself to the discussion of general principles, and that I have not presumed to trench
on administrative, much less on military or naval questions. But perhaps our Statesmen would
not command our confidence less, even in their
administrative capacity, if we could see from
their policy or speeches that they had in view
things of which a student of history cannot fail
to be sensible, — the peculiar character of the
age in which they act, and the nature of the
tremendous forces which are heaving the world
around them, and with which they are called
upon to deal. That they have not these things
in view is almost proved by their constant reference to diplomatic arrangements founded on no
principle and utterly obsolete; by their attempts
to galvanize the Ottoman Empire as a necessary

part of their "European system," on which they
have wasted so much blood and money, and are
wasting so much money still; and by the zeal
with which they labour to propagate a transition
phase of English Monarchy as the eternal and
universal order of the world. Of the great religious movement going on around them, the
movement of the Second Reformation, they seem,
in the same manner, judging from their Church
policy, to take no heed.

They have themselves, under the impulse of
the general movement, just given the signal in
their own country for a revolution, the scope of
which they seem, if it is not presumptuous to
say so, but imperfectly to apprehend; a revolution
which in its consequences is likely to have a great
effect upon the present among other questions.
They have all concurred in promising a large extension of the suffrage; and this promise, in whatever spirit and with whatever object it may have
been made, must before long be performed. The
result will in all probability be, that Parliament
will become much more democratic. Perhaps
democratic assemblies may not be more moderate in their policy than aristocratic assemblies, when solid objects of desire are in view;
but they certainly are not so willing to pay

money or incur danger for the sake of mere fancies, still less of mere "responsibility." And if the Empire or any parts of it do not yield strength or profit, if they yield nothing but peril and expense, we may feel pretty confident that a democratic assembly will be inclined to lay a rude hand on them; and that those who have summoned such an assembly into being will do well to set this part of their house in order before it comes.

When we look at this immense and complicated mass of Empire, of establishments, of diplomatic connexions, rivalries, and guarantees; when we think of the movements which are going on both in this country and the world around us; and when we consider the ephemeral nature of our administrations; even those whose faith in English statesmen is the strongest may be tempted to ask whether the helm is really in their hands and the compass really before their eyes, or whether the ship is drifting before the wind and tide to an unknown shore.

G. S.

March 4, 1863.

THE EMPIRE.

I.
COLONIAL EMANCIPATION.

TO THE EDITOR OF THE "DAILY NEWS."

SIR,—Ought not the narrow escape we have had of a war in defence of Canada to lead the nation to think seriously not only of the reduction of Colonial expenditure, but of Colonial Emancipation? England has long promised herself the honour of becoming the mother of free nations. Is it not time that this promise should be fulfilled?

If there had been a war with the United States, the "Trent" would have been the occasion, but Canada would have been the cause. It is because we have a dependency on that continent, easily assailable, and which, because it is a dependency, it is thought not immoral to assail, that the idea of a quarrel with England rises in the minds of the Americans whenever their temper or the desire of relief from internal difficulties leads them to think of a foreign war.

It was generally assumed that the war would have been short and easy. In defence of England all wars would be short and easy; but the best judges seem to think that a war would be by no means short or easy if waged in defence of Canada against a power with

B

an immense population close at hand, and able to put an overwhelming force upon the Lakes.

There is but one way to make Canada impregnable, and that is to fence her round with the majesty of an independent nation. To invade and conquer an independent nation, without provocation, is an act from which, in the present state of opinion, even the Americans[a] would recoil. The manifest unwillingness of the Canadians to be annexed was a greater tower of strength on the late occasion than our arms or theirs.

To protect dependent Colonies we not only burden our overtaxed people with gratuitous taxation, but scatter our forces, naval as well as military, over the globe, leaving the heart of England open to a sudden blow. What do we gain in return? What is the use of our appointing Governors of Colonies, except to the circle of men who make Governing Colonies their profession? The time was when the universal prevalence of commercial monopoly made it well worth our while to hold Colonies in dependence for the sake of commanding their trade. But that time is gone. Trade is everywhere free, or becoming free; and this expensive and perilous connexion has entirely survived its sole legitimate cause. It is time that we should recognise the change that has come over the world.

We have, in fact, long felt that the Colonies did nothing for us. We now are very naturally beginning

---

[a] "Even the Americans" as they were, while their Government was filled with the aggressive insolence of the Southern slave-owner. I know not what reason we have for believing that a Government representing the industrious and thrifty citizens of the North is likely to be military and aggressive.

to grumble at being put to the expense of doing any-thing for them. If they are to do nothing for us, and we are to do nothing for them, where is the use of con-tinuing the connexion ?

We vaguely dream of making institutions for the colonies after the model of our own. The history of our own institutions ought to teach us that constitutions are not made, but grow ; and that, to be strong and re-spected, they must be developed by a nation itself out of the elements of its own character and circumstances, not imposed on it, however benevolently, from without. We vaguely dream—some at least, vaguely dream—of propagating constitutional monarchy and aristocracy over our colonial empire. A glance at the history of constitutional monarchy and aristocracy ought to shew us that they are the modified offspring of feudalism, native to the feudal soil, and as incapable of being transplanted to a land of small estates and social equality as the trees of the tropics are of being trans-planted to Canadian snows.

We are keeping the Colonies in a perpetual state of political infancy, and preventing the gristle of their frames from being matured and hardened into bone. Not only so—not only do we retard their political de-velopment, but we actually give it a wrong bias, and that in a direction which perhaps is not generally sus-pected. We are making them extravagantly demo-cratic. Their nominal subjection to the British Crown masks the want of a conservative element in their in-stitutions, and makes them feel free to plunge with impunity into all the excesses of universal suffrage.

In case they ultimately part from us violently (as, if emancipation is too long delayed, they must) this fatal bias will be aggravated. America was flung into her wild democracy partly by the force with which she parted from monarchy and aristocracy at her revolution.

In the same manner we are overlaying the religion of the Colonies with a feeble Anglicanism, the creature of historical accidents in this country, and incapable of permanently forming the spiritual life of a new nation [b].

[b] I speak of Anglicanism as a religion propagated, established, and fettered by the State. Mr. Wakefield, one of the founders of the Church-of-England Colony of Canterbury, and a strong advocate of the Establishment of a Colonial Episcopate on a free principle, says in his "View of the Art of Colonization," (p. 164):—"After the Wesleyans I should award the first rank in point of efficiency to the two Churches of Scotland, but especially to the Free Church, but merely because in the colonies it is becoming the only Church of Scotland. Next come Independents, Baptists, and other dissenters from the Church of England. Then the Roman Catholics, whose lower position arises from the poverty of the great bulk of the Catholic emigrants, and last of all figures the Church of England, which, considering the numbers and wealth of her people at home, and her vast influence accordingly, can offer no excuse for neglecting her colonial people, save one only, that in consequence of her connexion with the State, she is, in the colonies, subject to the Colonial Office, and therefore necessarily devoid of energy and enterprise."

Of the Free Church of the Wesleyan Methodists Mr. Wakefield says:—"Oh! but this is not a church? Isn't it? At any rate it has all the proportions of one. It has a profound and minute system of government, which comprehends the largest and takes care of the smallest objects of a Church. It has zeal, talents, funds, order, and method, a strict discipline, and a conspicuous success. But our concern with it is only in the Colonies. There, it does not wait, as the other Churches do, till there is a call for its services, and then only exhibit its inefficiency; but it goes before settlement; it leads colonization; it penetrates into settlements where there is no religion at all, and gathers

Our presence in Canada artificially preserves from
absorption the French Canadian element, an antediluvian relic of old French society with its torpor and
bigotry, utterly without value for the purposes of modern civilisation[c].

into its fold many of those whom the other Churches utterly neglect.
This Church alone never acts on the principle that anything is good
enough for the Colonies. Whether it sends forth its clergy to the back-
woods of North America, the solitary plains of South Africa, the wild
bush of Tasmania and Australia, or the forests and fern plains of New
Zealand, it sends men of devoted purpose and first-rate ability. It
selects its missionaries with as much care as the Propaganda of Rome.
It rules them with an authority that is always in full operation; with
a far-stretching arm, and a hand of steel. It supplies them with the
means of devoting themselves to their calling. Accordingly it succeeds
in what it attempts. It does not attempt to supply the higher classes
of emigrants with religious observances and teaching. It does this for
its own people, who are nearly all of the middle or poorer classes; and,
above all, it seeks, and picks up, and cherishes, and humanizes the basest
and most brutish of the emigrant population. In the Colonies generally, it is the antagonist, frequently the conqueror, of drunkenness,
which is the chief bane of low Colonial life. It makes war upon idle-
ness, roguery, dirt, obscenity, and debauchery. In the Convict Colonies,
and those who are infected by them, it is the great antagonist of Downing-street, whose polluting emigration it counteracts, by snatching
some and guarding others from the pestilence of convict contamination.
If it had the power which the Church of England has in our legislature,
it would put a stop to the shame of Convict Colonization, open and dis-
guised. For it is truly a Colonizing Church: it knows that in Colonization, as you sow, so shall you reap: it acts on this belief with vigour
and constancy of purpose that put the other Churches to shame, and
with a degree of success that is admirable, considering that its first
'centenary' was only held the other day." It is really as a free Church
that the Church of England has achieved her success in our dependent
Colonies as well as in the independent States of America.

    [c] I speak, of course, of the institutions, not of the people, whose qua-
lities may be invaluable in tempering the character of the Anglo-Saxon
race. We artificially preserved the old French laws and, with them,
the old social system by the "Quebec Act," passed to cut off the Cana-

That connexion with the Colonies, which is really a part of our greatness—the connexion of blood, sympathy, and ideas—will not be affected by political separation. And when our Colonies are nations, something in the nature of a great Anglo-Saxon federation may, in substance if not in form, spontaneously arise out of affinity and mutual affection.

It is difficult to say whether the West Indies are to be classed among Colonies or Dependencies. Since we washed our hands of slavery, they have become a mere burden; and they will as certainly be a perpetual source of embroilment with the Confederate States (if the Confederates achieve independence) as our northern possessions have been with the Old Confederation.

The case of military dependencies, such as Gibraltar, Malta, and the Ionian Islands, is, of course, distinct from that of Colonies: yet it has been to a great extent affected by the same alteration of circumstances, especially by the triumph of free trade. We have no need now to post ourselves in arms all over the globe, in order to make way for our trade, or to thrust an iron bar into the jaws of the Mediterranean to keep it open to our goods. Trade has become its own protection, and all waters are, or soon will be, open, where there is a consumer requiring the goods which the producer brings.

There is not the same fear which there was at the

dians from the rebellious English of the American colonies. All the other political and social elements in North America have been absorbed with remarkable rapidity and completeness by the Anglo-Saxon, as has been remarked by De Tocqueville. If old French tenures and old French endowments are good things, modern society must be an aberration.

height of French domination, lest the Mediterranean should become a French lake. A revived Spain, a revived Italy, and in course of time a revived Greece, will take good care of that.

On the other hand, the revival of the Spanish power, under comparatively liberal institutions, which even the Tory *Quarterly* now admits, will render Gibraltar every day a more dangerous and expensive possession. We won that place fairly in war ; but Spain, to which while in our hands it is a standing insult, may as fairly try to win it back again. It seems to be admitted that since the vast improvement of guns and naval batteries it could not stand a naval siege [d]. To hold it securely, therefore, we must remain masters of the Mediterranean, and to do this, we must undergo the enormous expense of coping with the Mediterranean powers in their own waters, at the same time that we keep up a sufficient force to protect our own coasts. With railroads, France, lying between us and our Mediterranean fleet, can fight us with the same crews, first in the Mediterranean, and a few days afterwards in the Channel.

We have no longer, as when our flag was planted on the rock of Gibraltar, to deal with the decrepitude of the old Spanish monarchy, and we must not bear ourselves as if we had.

.The Ionian Islands are not a permanent property, but a temporary trust. If this great England of ours only knew how much it would add to her greatness to do one signal act of moderation !

[d] So it was said after the destruction of Sweaborg.

I do not say that we should hastily throw up anything; but I do say that since what we call our Empire
was formed the world is changed, and that we ought to
take practical note of the change. I say, too, that the
greatness of England really lies not in her Empire, but
in herself.

India, of course, stands on a peculiar footing. There,
all cant apart, we have not only taken up a position
from which it is difficult to recede, but assumed responsibilities which we are bound, if we can, to discharge.
Whether the dominion of that country, as distinguished
from the enjoyment of its trade, for the sake of which
our dominion was originally acquired, adds to our real
strength or wealth, seems at least open to doubt. It
is indeed something—it is much—to have displayed on
that great theatre the qualities of an Imperial race.
But when we come to actual advantages, a perennial
supply of old Indians spending Indian pensions at
Bath and Cheltenham seems the main item on the side
of profit; while, on the side of loss, we must place
a heavy annual expenditure of our best blood, wasted
in Indian warfare, or by Indian disease; the paralysing
sense of our weak point, and the loss of dignity and
force thence resulting to our diplomacy in Europe;
and not only the Sikh and Affghan, but in a great
measure the Russian war.

The crucial question probably is, whether the English can convert India from a dependency into a Colony,
by settling in it, taking the place of the Mahometans,
its last conquerors, and permanently forming the governing and civilising class. If the climate or any

other cause forbids this, the days of our dominion are numbered. No country, much less a poor country as India on the average is, can afford permanently to pay exile price for its establishments. The taxation required to give all the servants of the State double pay and pensions would surely produce revolts; and to be always suppressing revolts in blood would be a prospect which we should hardly desire to encounter. The horrors of the Sepoy mutiny cancelled the work of all our Indian missionaries ten times over.

Whether our dominion in India propagates Christianity is a question, the answer to which must be taken from facts, not from those who subsist, however meritoriously, by the missionary establishments. It is high time that the balance should be struck between the expenditure and the results, in order that we may be quite sure that we are not wasting in India that which might bear good fruit at home. But if you look to history, I think you will find that the great conversions of the heathen have been made, not by the clergy of a conquering power, but by missionaries, in the full sense of the term, throwing themselves into a heathen nation, and offering to it in their own persons, unalloyed, the highest example of the religion which they preached. The religion of conquerors is seldom a welcome gift; and the English in India are sure to be always worse than the English in England, and by their vices to discredit their religion.

To revert, however, to the case of the Colonies proper. The policy of our statesmen towards them has, no doubt, of late years been high-minded and sagacious, favourable to self-government, and therefore, theoretically, favourable to emancipation. But actually to take the decisive step of emancipating a Colony will be difficult for them unless they are strongly supported, and even pressed, by public opinion. Our governments, under the party system, are ephemeral, and cannot exercise much foresight; they are hampered by routine, the fetters of which it is hard for them, in their brief tenure of power, to break; they are trammelled, not by the love of patronage, which few of our public men lack the dignity to disregard, but by the strong claims of political friends who stand ready for each Colonial Governorship as it falls vacant. Most of them are also probably unwilling, as servants of a monarchy, with aristocratic connexions, to ratify democracy in the Colonies, while they find themselves unable to construct any other kind of constitution.

It is not to be expected that an inch of the Empire will be given up by the present Premier[e]. Though youthful in bodily vigour, he is old in ideas, and unconscious of the great moral and material changes which have taken place in Europe since he first entered public life. But he will be succeeded, probably, by statesmen more imbued with the ideas and alive to the exigencies of our own age: and depend upon it,

[e] Since this was written, the adherents of Lord Palmerston as well as the writer have been surprised by the determination of his Government to cede the Ionian Islands. The words in the text, which were justified, it is believed, at the time when they were written, by the bearing of the Government, are now joyfully withdrawn.

such statesmen will be disposed to retrench our Empire,
in order to add to our security and greatness.

I am, &c.

GOLDWIN SMITH.

Jan. 27, 1862.

To the above letter the following reply was made
by *The Times* in a leading article, Feb. 4, 1862.

" EXPERIENCE has taught us that there are certain fallacies
which reappear at intervals like comets of short period, give
a feeble glare for a week or two, and then vanish. As a
general rule, we do not think it necessary to note their re-
currence. The 'psychological law' which causes a certain
number of men to fancy themselves capable of great political
discoveries, always insures the reiteration of the same shallow
theories and the same commonplace arguments. Among the
oldest discussions of this kind is that which relates to the alleged inutility of colonies. It has been handed down through
the *doctrinaires* of two or three generations, and in our time
has enjoyed almost as much favour as the projects for general disarmament or for equalizing the political rights of
the sexes. But for the last few years its popularity with
' thinkers ' seems to have declined. These gifted persons
have been forced to acquiesce in the prejudice of their coun-
trymen, which is against the destruction of the British Empire. The immense increase of the national commerce which
has followed the founding of the Australian colonies, and the
more recent development of those in North America, have
satisfied the country that it has not been a loser by them.

" Nor are Englishmen generally indifferent to the spectacle
which the Empire now presents. To have established communities in every region of the globe, and to find them uni-
formly prosperous, and desirous of maintaining their con-

nexion with the mother country and each other, is a triumph of enterprise and civilization of which few among us fail to be proud.

"So completely has the destruction of this noble fabric ceased to be an idea of any class of men who can influence the country, that when we find it from time to time reproduced by some narrow-minded and illiterate politician, we are content to pass it over in silence as not worth discussing. But the subject has been just brought forward by a gentleman who is officially entitled to notice. Mr. Goldwin Smith, Professor of Modern History at Oxford, has addressed a letter to a contemporary, in which he advocates the dismemberment of Queen Victoria's dominions as a policy to be carried out thoroughly and with as little delay as possible. Now, though the opinions of Mr. Smith as an individual may carry little weight, yet a Professorship of History at Oxford is a public function, and the opinions promulgated under its shelter are likely to receive notice even when they bear such evident marks of perversity as the letter of Mr. Smith. It is not always safe to count on the weakness of a bad argument. We know from experience that though not one Englishman in a hundred sided with the Peace Society, yet so old and able a ruler as the Emperor Nicholas was firmly convinced that Manchester would never allow England to go to war. So when we find that a person who may be held to speak with some authority, as teaching history and politics in the first English University, advocates the giving up of Canada and India, Gibraltar and the Ionian Islands, declares that England has relatively declined to such an extent as to make the retention of her possessions impossible, and expresses a belief that the death of Lord Palmerston will be the signal for the abandonment of these ancient provinces and garrisons, we feel bound to protest against such statements, as likely to mislead opinion in foreign countries, among the populations of India, and among the discontented factions of one or two of our dependencies. Should any of

our foreign contemporaries, however, labour under this delusion, we can assure them that, in this country at least,
Professors of History do not count for statesmen, and that
the habit of propounding political theories to young men
who cannot contradict them¹, without the responsibility
of enforcing them in public life, is not reckoned the surest
way to acquire practical views either of philosophy or
politics. It would seem that the uprising of the British American people to defend their connexion with England, and
the enthusiasm they have shewn for the honour of our common flag, are no merits in the eyes of some among us. Those
who are talking continually about ' our American brethren,'
meaning thereby the people of the Federal States, have no
word of good-will for their own fellow-subjects who, placed
in a position of great danger, did not shrink from accepting
in our cause any quarrel which the violence of their neighbours might force upon them. The late events in Canada
are taken as a theme by Mr. Smith, and he sees in them,
not as others do, reason for pride and gratification, but
matter which should cause us to ' think seriously.' The
result of his own ' serious thinking ' is that the British
Empire is about to be broken up by revolt or foreign
war, unless we forestall our adversaries by breaking it up
ourselves. We have had, he tells us, ' a narrow escape '
of a war in defence of Canada. To protect dependent
colonies we burden our people with taxation. What
do we gain in return? ' What is the use of appointing
governors of colonies, except to the circle of men who
make governing colonies their profession ?' ' This extensive
and perilous connexion'—namely, that between the mother
country and the colonies—' has entirely survived its sole
legitimate cause,' which the writer declares was the monopoly
of the colonial trade. ' We now are very naturally beginning

¹ I may be permitted to say that such is not my "habit." My
habit is to propound my political theories to those who *can* contradict
them, as I have done on the present occasion.

to grumble at being put to the expense of doing anything for them. If they are to do nothing for us, and we are to do nothing for them, where is the use of continuing the connexion?' On the sentiment and style of this sentence we need make no comment. Nor does the argument call for much notice. Mr. Smith falls into an error of which no one conversant with the mercantile affairs of this country could be guilty. So far from the foundation and maintenance of colonies being of no advantage to England, it can be proved by figures that our export trade has grown up and is now in a great measure supported by the settlements which Englishmen of past or present days have made in distant regions of the globe. Commercial monopoly has nothing at all to do with the benefits which a country like England receives from its colonies. Those benefits depend on the fact that every emigrant becomes a far more productive customer when set down on a new soil than when he was struggling for existence at home. He immediately obtains the means of comfort and even of luxury. His ideas of both are formed from what he has seen and envied in his own country. His wants are those of Englishmen. He naturally becomes a large consumer of English productions. English manufactures, though not of the purest taste, English eatables and drinkables, though sometimes far from delicate or wholesome, are exported in immense quantities to supply what is really a piece of England in the New World or at the Antipodes. The wants of the colonist are not only larger than those of the German or Russian, the Mexican or the Brazilian, but they differ in kind, and the difference is in our favour. France, with her artistic industry and the wines which she alone can supply, may be more cosmopolitan and more independent of special markets. But the statistics of Australian, Canadian, and Indian trade prove that even now the British settlements abroad are large elements in England's mercantile greatness.

"This the whole world sees and acknowledges. Not even

the conquest and re-conquest of India have excited more
admiration of late years among foreign nations than the
colonization of Australia.   Every French traveller breaks
forth into raptures at the prosperity of Melbourne, and regrets that the Orleans Government did not assert its right
to the islands of New Zealand.   Yet it is but a few years
since the colonies of Australia were denounced as failures,
and philosophers of Mr. Smith's school declared that the
attempt to renew the experiment of America must end in
ruin.   Australia has grown up and now takes our manufactures by millions.   The truth is that there is no wiser policy
for a country like ours than to take possession of the waste
places of the earth, and give our crowded populations the
power of settling in them under our own laws, modified, if
need be, to suit their particular exigencies.   Men will not
flock readily to a country where there is a strange or distrusted Government, nor will they so readily choose a land
disfigured by slavery and mob law as one which still cherishes
a feeling of loyalty to the Sovereign and of attachment to the
institutions of their native country.   We will venture to say
that, of those who once had misgivings as to the policy of
retaining Canada, nine out of ten are by this time convinced
of their error, and are prepared to give her all the assistance
she may require, either for maintaining her allegiance to this
country, or for working out her independence, whenever she is
able and willing to do so.   It is true that Canada numbers as
large a population as the Confederate States in 1786 ; but
when the American colonies revolted there was no powerful
empire on their borders ready to absorb them into the gulf
of democracy, and no one has elsewhere depicted in stronger
colours than Mr. Smith himself the extreme pain and reluctance with which they realized the necessity of separation
from the British Crown.   As to the question of military expenses, that will, we think, be settled by the united good
sense of Englishmen and colonists.   Doubtless money has been
wasted, as in the Caffre wars at the Cape ; but more re-

cently the duty of self-defence has been acknowledged by every colony of importance. This journal has for years lost no opportunity of inculcating on the people of Canada and the Cape the necessity of a military organization of their own. The example of our own Volunteers has had a powerful effect, and the demonstration just made in Canada shews that henceforth those provinces need not draw largely on the resources of England for their defence.

"It is also as well to remind the Professor that the colonists have rights as well as ourselves. They are British subjects, and as long as they choose to remain so the mother country has no right to deprive them of their heritage. That they are contented with their position Mr. Smith does not deny, though, like the public-house orator who claimed credit for being the first to apprise his audience that they were downtrodden and oppressed, he informs them that they suffer great evils by their connexion with us. The provision for the wants of members of the Church of England in the colonies is denounced as ' overlaying the religion of the colonies with a feeble Anglicanism, the creature of historical accidents in this country, and incapable of permanently forming the spiritual life of a new nation.' The attachment of the French Canadians to the English Government is thus requited :— ' Our presence in Canada artificially preserves the French Canadian element, an antediluvian relic of old French society, with its torpor and bigotry, utterly without value for the purposes of modern civilization.'

"But if the greater colonies are to be abandoned both for their sake and ours, to save them from constitutional monarchy and Anglicanism, and to save ourselves from bankruptcy, India and the Mediterranean garrisons must be given up for other reasons. Gibraltar, we are told, cannot be much longer held against the Spaniards. ' The revival of the Spanish power will render Gibraltar every day a more dangerous and expensive possession. . . . It seems to be admitted that since the vast improvement of guns and naval batteries it could not

stand a naval siege. . . . We have no longer, as when our flag
was planted on the Rock of Gibraltar, to deal with the decrepitude of the old Spanish monarchy, and we must not bear
ourselves as if we had.' In other words, Gibraltar must be
given up, because England can no longer hold it from Spain.
For similar reasons the surrender of Malta and the Ionian
Islands is desirable, because we cannot 'undergo the enormous expense of coping with the Mediterranean Powers in
their own waters.' As for India, the only profit of which
Mr. Smith considers to be ' a perennial supply of old Indians
spending Indian pensions at Bath and Cheltenham,' the prospect is a series of revolts which will soon cause the days of
our dominion to be numbered. It is almost an insult to our
readers to repeat such stuff as all this, but when we reflect on
the ignorance of nations respecting each other, and more particularly the incredible opinions which prevail in regard to
British power and policy, we feel that it is as well not to pass
it over. It is no uncommon thing to find matter equally
worthless reproduced abroad as the utterance of English opinion. Even the ' Discussion Forum' occupied the attention
of the French police long before the people who walked along
Fleet-street daily knew of its existence. So we may as well
declare at once, for the benefit of Americans and Spaniards,
Russians and Ionians, Sikhs and Sepoys, that England has no
thought of abandoning her transmarine possessions. If they
read Mr. Smith's letter, they will find he admits ' it is not to
be expected that an inch of the Empire will be given up by
the present Premier,' who is too ' old in ideas' to recognise
the 'exigencies' which the Professor has discovered. And
when the hopeful event of Lord Palmerston's resignation or
demise takes place they will be much disappointed if they
expect that he will be succeeded by statesmen ' disposed to
retrench our empire.' So far from believing in her own decline, England believes that she was never more powerful
than now, or more capable of holding what she has won. To
the people of the colonies we would say that, as long as they

shew the goodwill to the mother country and the loyalty to the Crown which now prevail, no party in this country will ever dare to deprive them of the birthright of British citizenship. No party, we believe, in this country desires to keep them against their will; nor do we pretend to deny that the time must come when they will no longer require our aid, and when it will be better for both that they should set up for themselves. In the meantime, whatever their race or religion, their rights are secure; and, if the letter which we have drawn from its obscurity be read in Quebec or Montreal, we would ask the French Canadians to believe that it in no way represents the opinions of any class of Englishmen, but only the fancies of one morbid mind."

II.

COLONIAL EMANCIPATION.

TO THE EDITOR OF THE "DAILY NEWS."

Sir,—I have watched with interest, and I trust with an open mind, the debate to which my last letter to you on this subject has given rise in the press. It leads me to hope that the question has taken hold upon the public attention, and that the nation will exercise in this grave and urgent matter the deliberation and forecast which a part of the governing class, under the tuition of *The Times*, seems to have almost abjured. The leading journal has indeed waged war against "thinkers" for a quarter of a century, with no questionable success. The politicians over whose minds it has exercised an almost undisputed sway have, under its most skilful treatment, become "animals" of small "discourse," "looking" neither "before" nor "after," priding themselves on their "common sense," and taking common sense to consist in eschewing thought, and exaggerating the casual notion or passion of the hour. Their perilous tampering with the tremendous question of Parliamentary Reform was the natural result of such a training. I am most willing to be called a "thinker," or, if possible, worse names, if I can contribute even in the slightest degree towards inducing however small a section of the public to exercise fore-

cast in politics, to study our position in the community
of nations, its changes, and its necessities; to mark the
ways of Providence, and subdue ambition to them; and
to lay, by deliberate action on intelligible principles,
the solid foundations of happiness and greatness.

I know the place of "thinkers" and "professors" in
political discussion; I know that not to them, but to
"statesmen," belongs the ultimate decision, the paramount responsibility, and therefore the highest honour;
though I do not feel inclined to class among "statesmen" literary men playing the man of action on paper,
and flattering prejudices which they despise by sneer-
ing at their own kind.

Not every man of business or every party leader,
however, is a statesman in such a sense that we can
look to him for the settlement of this question. Men
of business with their hands full of office-work seldom originate great reforms. On every subject where
popular prejudice is strong, the lips of a party-leader,
to whose party popularity is the breath of life, are inevitably sealed. Organic change requires preparation
and foresight. We had thirteen Colonial Secretaries in
twenty years; and the far-reaching wisdom which looks
to the fruit of distant years can hardly be expected
from the Minister of an hour. The nation may trust, if
ever a nation could trust, its public servants for the able
and upright management of its current business; but
it must think for itself.

The Times is quite right in saying that the uselessness of dependent Colonies, except under the reign of
commercial protection, is a fallacy which has been

handed down through the *doctrinaires* of two or three generations. And no doubt this great public instructor on economical subjects knows that the first of these *doctrinaires* who " gave a feeble glare for a week or two and then vanished," who "defended their shallow theories with commonplace arguments," whose views "have enjoyed almost as much favour as the projects for general disarmament or for equalizing the political rights of the sexes," and whose ideas, though "reproduced from time to time by narrow-minded and illiterate politicians," the great organ of " prejudice" is content to pass over in silence as not worth discussing, was the "thinker" and "professor" Adam Smith. Colonial Emancipation dawned upon the same mind and at the same time as Free Trade. Of course Adam Smith could not be expected, when founding a new science, before his discoveries had been verified by experience, and with the prejudices and passions of all the world against him, to speak so boldly as he would speak now. He did not speak so boldly as he would speak now even upon some parts of the free-trade theory itself. But his real sentiments appear in words the import of which is not to be mistaken. " To propose," he says, " that Great Britain should voluntarily give up all authority over her Colonies, and leave them to elect their own magistrates, to enact their own laws, and to make peace and war as they might think proper, would be to propose such a measure as never was, and never will be, adopted by any nation in the world. No nation ever voluntarily gave up the dominion of any province, how troublesome soever it might be to govern it, and how small soever the re-

venue which it afforded might be in proportion to the
expense which it occasioned. Such sacrifices, though
they might frequently be agreeable to the interest, are
always mortifying to the pride of any nation; and,
- what is perhaps of still greater consequence, they are
always contrary to the private interest of the governing
part of it, who would thereby be deprived of the disposal of many places of trust and profit, of many opportunities of acquiring wealth and distinction, which
the possession of the most turbulent and, to the great
body of the people, the most unprofitable province
seldom fails to afford. The most visionary enthusiast
would scarce be capable of proposing such a measure,
with any serious hopes at least of its ever being
adopted. If it were adopted, however, Great Britain
would not only be immediately freed from the whole
annual expense of the peace establishment of the Colonies, but might settle with them such a treaty of commerce as would effectually secure to her a free trade,
more advantageous to the great body of the people,
though less so to the merchants, than the monopoly
which she at present enjoys. By thus parting good
friends, the natural affection of the Colonies to the
mother country, which perhaps our late dissensions have
wellnigh extinguished, would quickly revive. It might
dispose them not only to respect, for whole centuries,
that treaty of commerce which they had concluded
with us at parting, but to favour us in war as well as
in trade, and, instead of turbulent and factious subjects, to become our most faithful, affectionate, and
generous allies; and the same sort of parental affection

on the one side, and filial respect on the other, might revive between Great Britain and her Colonies, which used to subsist between those of ancient Greece and the mother city from which they descended[a]."

Adam Smith wrote after the commencement of the quarrel with the North American Colonists, too late to control, if reason could have controlled, the passions which were hurrying the Nation into a disastrous and ignominious war. The mother country and the Colonies parted, not as the *doctrinaire* would have had them part, by mutual consent, in the fullness of maternal and filial affection, with a treaty of commerce and an enduring alliance between the kindred nations; but as practical wisdom and self-complacent "prejudice" willed that they should part, after a bloody and ruinous struggle, made doubly aliens to each other by the broken tie of blood, with retaliatory restrictions upon commerce, and enduring hate. Yet even so the emancipation of the Colony, by the increase of trade and productive energy which independence brought, repaid even to the mother country the cost of the war; and so far was the power of England from sinking under the blow, as the ignorance of her enemies hoped and the ignorance of her statesmen feared, that she was able before many years were over to stand alone against the world in arms.

The two columns through which the article of *The Times* against my letter ran, contained not a single relevant argument or fact of any description. So far as the article was a defence of anything, and not

[a] Wealth of Nations, bk. iv. ch. 7.

merely an attack on me, it was a defence not of our
system of keeping the Colonies in a state of dependence,
but of Colonization; which is about as much to the
point as a defence of happiness and virtue. Those
who wish to know how the nation is guided will find
in this article an instructive specimen of the way in
which "statesmen" who are not "thinkers" deliberate
on a great practical question. The perusal will assist
the reflecting reader to determine whether the absence
of thought is the real root of national greatness.

The value of our export trade to the Colonies—on
which *The Times* dilated with so much display of its
own knowledge of "figures," and so much contempt
for my "mercantile ignorance"—is obviously quite
beside the question, unless it can be shewn that the
continuance of this trade depends on the continuance
of the political connexion.

"Before the American Revolution," says Mr. Herman
Merivale, in his well-known work on Colonization, "we
possessed Colonies even more extensive and valuable
than at present. Yet the trade with those Colonies,
though a thriving one, never seems to have been in
a wholly satisfactory state. It was subject, like all other
trades involved in prohibitions, to the fluctuations arising
from that uncertainty of supply and demand which is
produced by monopoly. And during the latter years
of the connection, mutual jealousies and antipathies,
more powerful even than self-interest, nearly reduced
it to ruin. As soon as the connection was severed what
was the consequence? Did the industrious Colonists
become 'sluggish foreigners,' and cease to supply goods

fast enough to meet the cravings of the Liverpool and London markets? Was our profitable colonial trade turned into a losing foreign trade? All the world knows, on the contrary, that the commerce between the mother country and the Colony was but a peddling traffic, compared to that vast international intercourse, the greatest the world has ever known, which grew up between them when they had exchanged the tie of subjection for that of equality;"—equality which, as Mr. Merivale says in the words of a Greek poet, is "the surest bond between friends, between states, and between allies."

But figures, as it happens, prove that *The Times*, in estimating the value of our export trade to the Colonies so highly as it does in comparison with our export trade to foreign countries, is the victim of a great though not uncommon error. Our exports in 1861 were,—

To foreign countries £82,854,000
To the East Indies, Ceylon, Singapore, and Hong
   Kong (which are not British Colonies, but
   only dependencies)   19,656,000
To the British Colonies in North
   America   3,696,000
To Australia   10,701,000
To the West Indies   .   .   2,463,000
                           16,860,000

Thus the export trade to the British Colonies[b] was

---

[b] The Cape of Good Hope is treated in Parliamentary returns not as a colony but as a military and maritime station, like Gibraltar and Malta. The exports to it were £1,986,000.

less by three millions than that to India and China, while it was only about one-fifth part of that to foreign countries.

Not only so, but the export trade to foreign countries has been increasing much more rapidly and steadily than that to the British Colonies, although the markets in Australia have been multiplying so fast. The foreign trade has increased forty millions since 1847, the Colonial trade only ten millions.

The export trade to the North American Colonies is actually a declining trade, the average for the five years ending in 1856 having been £4,189,600; that for the five succeeding years, to 1861, having been £3,705,400; so that upon the last five years there was an average fall of about half a million; and, to crown all, this decline has taken place under the operation of protective duties imposed on our manufactures by the Canadian Legislature, "without the slightest justifi-· cation," as *The Times* in a later article says, though it holds me up to reprobation for not flattering the Canadians. I have not flattered the Canadians, but I have said in effect that they are ripe and worthy to be a great nation.

Thus *The Times* when it speaks of "the immense increase of the national commerce which has followed the more recent development of the Colonies in North America," makes a speculative statement which experience unfortunately does not confirm.

If the profits of the Canadian trade for this year are set against the costs of military and naval defence, they will cut but a poor figure. The United States, though they are at war and we are on doubtful terms with them, will nevertheless be this year a source of great profit to us. Our greatest and most loyal Colony will be, in a pecuniary point of view, not a profit but a loss.

Our people will not like this. They will cry out, with *The Times* at their head [c], that the Canadians must pay their own military expenses. The Canadians will perhaps reply, as the people of New Zealand do, that it is an Imperial question; that they are brought into peril as our dependency and on our account; and that they must have a voice in our foreign policy if they are to pay for our wars. Then there will be an altercation, in which *The Times* will do its best to inflame and exaggerate the anger of our people. And so we shall have a rupture, part from our great Colony in anger, and lose the glory of having been the first nation in history to confer independence spontaneously and deliberately on a daughter State.

"Figures" are equally against *The Times* in its argument from colonial emigration. "Men will not flock readily to a country where there is a strange or distrusted government, nor will they so readily choose a land disfigured by slavery and mob-law as one which still cherishes a feeling of loyalty towards the Sovereign and of attachment to the institutions of their mother country." This is a plausible and loyal hypothesis; but the fact is that, in ordinary years, for one British emigrant that goes to our Colonies two go to the United States.

[c] It need hardly be said that this anticipation has since been signally fulfilled.

Thus *The Times* seems to have been quite right when it said, on the 2nd of September last, "We are not aware of any single advantage which Canada gives us, and which in time of peace we have not from the United States." The feeling which the Canadians have shewn since this sentence was written against the people of the United States, however valuable it may be thought in itself, does not change the economical facts.

Well-informed men will scarcely require me to support my assertion that the monopoly of the Colonial trade was formerly the great object of our Colonial empire, though it is so positively contradicted by *The Times*. Adam Smith [d] shews that in respect of military force "all the European Colonies of America have, without exception, been a cause rather of weakness than of strength to their respective mother countries;" and that in respect to the other of the two common advantages of empire, revenue furnished for the support of the Home Government, all the European Colonies except those of Spain and Portugal "have been a source to their respective mother countries not of revenue but of expense." The advantages, he proceeds, "of such Colonies to their respective mother countries consist altogether in those peculiar advantages which are supposed to result from provinces of so very peculiar a nature as the European Colonies of America; and the exclusive trade, it is acknowledged, is the sole source of all these peculiar advantages." Lord Sheffield at the time with the dispute with the Americans said, "The only use of the American Colonies is the monopoly

[d] Wealth of Nations, bk. iv. ch. 7.

of their consumption and the carriage of their produce." Pitt at the same time embodied the views of
the statesmen of those days as to the use of Colonial
dependencies in his famous declaration, "That the Colonists had no right without the consent of Parliament to
manufacture even a nail of a horseshoe." The statesmen of those days were ignorant of political economy,
the light of which had then barely dawned, but they
were not devoid of sense; and their policy, though it
was not enlightened, had substantial advantages in
view. It was adapted to a universal reign of monopoly, and they would themselves have discarded it
under the reign of free trade.

The Times itself pronounces, after all, that "the
time may come when it will be better for both parties
that the Colonies should set up for themselves." Is it
treason, then, to look forward deliberately to that time,
and to endeavour to ascertain its signs and note the
moment when it has arrived? Is no policy but that
of "drifting" worthy of a great nation? Is all foresight the badge of "*doctrinaires*" and "thinkers," and
only blindness wise? Is emancipation a criminal "dismemberment of the dominions of Queen Victoria,"
unless it be brought about, as in the case of the dominions of George III., by a calamitous rupture and
perhaps a disastrous war?

I should be ashamed to fill your columns by answering mere appeals to blind and tyrannical passion. *The
Times* seems really to think that, under its tutorship,
the English nation has been reduced to the arrogant
fatuity of an Eastern despot, who answers all honest

counsel with the bowstring. Indeed, though I can imagine an Eastern despot bursting into a rage at being told that he had grown weaker, I can scarcely imagine even an Eastern despot bursting into a rage at being told that a neighbouring power had grown stronger. We are to be forbidden, under pain of personal denunciation, to note the revival of Spain, because it implies that England has "relatively declined!" An Imperial nation may give itself over, as well as an Emperor, to its sycophants, and, intoxicated by their incense, may rush as blindly on its doom.

There is only one sentence in the article of *The Times* which calls for any further notice. It is that in which the inhabitants of the Ionian Islands are told, in conjunction with "Sikhs and Sepoys," and in no ambiguous manner, that whatever may be the rights of the question between us and them, we mean to apply to them the law of the strong. I trust *The Times* will find no "class" or "section" of Englishmen who are not "morbid" enough to feel deeply dishonoured and humiliated by having this said in their name. We, the great crusaders against slavery, refuse our sympathy to the Free States of America in their struggle against the slave-owners of the South, because they are fighting for "empire," while the South is fighting for "independence." And shall we avow, in language worthy of a besotted Turk, that, in our dealings with the weak, empire shall be our paramount object, and that not only "independence," but justice, shall hold a secondary place?

I have had worthier opponents than *The Times* in

journalists who, while they denounce my views pretty strongly, at least see that a momentous practical question is in issue, and that an honest attempt has been made to bring it before the public mind. But the arguments of these writers appear to me to resolve themselves in the main into the fear of losing "glory" and "prestige," and sinking into an "insular position."

As to the "glory which a country is supposed to derive from an extensive Colonial Empire," Sir G. C. Lewis, in his Essay on the Government of Dependencies, says [e], "We will merely remark upon this imagined advantage, that a nation derives no true glory from any possession which produces no assignable advantage to itself or to other communities. If a country possesses a dependency from which it derives no public revenue, no military or naval strength, and no commercial advantages or facilities for emigration, which it would not equally enjoy though the dependency were independent, and if, moreover, the dependency suffers the evils which are almost inevitable consequences of its political condition, such a possession cannot justly be called glorious." Glory is the halo that gathers round true greatness: round figments it will not gather, or it will not shine long.

"Prestige" goes with real strength, and with real strength alone. What would be thought of a general who should occupy more ground than he could cover, exhaust his resources, and wear out his men before the day of battle, in order to gain "prestige" in the eyes of his opponent? What was our "prestige" in America

[e] Chap. vi. p. 239.

worth when, "to the disgrace of our diplomacy," as *The Times* says, "we compromised the frontier and the future of Canada by submitting to the Ashburton treaty?" The moral of this event is not effaced because, when the Americans have a great rebellion on their hands, we have succeeded, with the opinion and interests of all Europe to back us, in extorting reparation for a flagrant wrong.

"Prestige" is a French word, which I find rendered in the dictionary "illusion," "juggling trick," "imposture." The ablest of my critics tells me in good plain English that what he thinks so valuable and wishes so much to preserve is "apparent power." "Is, then, Mr. Goldwin Smith really persuaded that England, deprived of her Colonies and of India, would wear before the world the same air of grandeur with which she is now invested? Grant all he writes as to the worthlessness of this dependent Empire calculated in money, and it has still to be shewn that the augmentation of wealth and strength which he promises us from its sacrifice is likely to impose on mankind as majestically as does at present the possession of merely apparent power [f]." When we can see through the "appearance" of power, and coolly own to ourselves that we do see through it, will not our enemies have the sense to do the same? Wooden artillery has been useful as a stratagem in war; but I never heard that it was useful, or that anything was risked by a wise Commander to preserve it, after the enemy had found out that it was wooden.

[f] *Saturday Review*, Feb. 8, 1862.

England is not the first nation that has possessed "apparent power" on a grand scale. Rome possessed it, and imposed most "majestically" on mankind at the moment when she was tottering to her fall. Spain possessed it to an extent that filled the heart of the world with awe : but bold spirits soon found out that the power of Spain was "apparent."

Not "apparent power," but most apparent weakness, is the true name for territories scattered over the globe, known to yield neither revenue nor military force to the possessors, and, from the moral feebleness which besets all dependencies, unprovided with any effective means of self-defence.

The Times indeed tells us that "the duty of self-defence has been acknowledged by every Colony of importance." But we have only to go back a few months to find in the columns of the same journal that " acknowledged" is not the same as " performed." " The old feeling of dependence on the one side," said *The Times* on the 20th July last, "and the old belief in the duty of military protection on the other, are giving way but slowly, and the consequence is that while the English merchant has not a single advantage in his dealings with a Colony, the English taxpayer is expected to furnish the Colonists with army, navy, packet service, a great part of their government, and a little of their religion."

An appeal is made to a French writer, M. Mignet, who, it seems, holds that England was intended by Nature to be a second-rate power, and that she is a first-rate power only by virtue of the scattering of

D

her forces all over the globe. I venture to submit that M. Mignet is mistaken, and that Nature intended England to be a first-rate power when she cast the hearts and limbs of Englishmen in such a mould, and placed them in this island, with a climate bracing yet not ungenial; with a soil which at once makes a wholesome demand on labour and well rewards it; broad and rich enough for the husbandman, though the natural home of the mariner; furnished for its political course alike with the stability of agriculture and the activity of trade; and divided from the nations of the mainland by a protecting yet not an estranging sea. I submit that the reality of power lies in this nation itself, and that the rest is an illusion. If I mistake not, my critic is of the same mind. If I mistake not, he knows that in imagining the Empire of England to be her strength, M. Mignet dreams. But he fears to exchange an unsound for a sound policy, lest the dream should be disturbed. Suppose one day, while we are pursuing the unsound policy, M. Mignet and other Frenchmen should awake!

Is "apparent power" really the object which the statesmen, in their imperial policy, pursue? Is this all that we gain by submitting to an immense taxation? Do our people pay in the solid elements of strength and prosperity as well as in security, and receive in return "apparent power"? It has been said that history is little more than a record of the miseries inflicted on the many by the passions of a few. Perhaps this is not the less true because the "few," instead of being feudal lords, are now the Clubs and *The Times.*

I do not admit that the emancipation of the Colonies would reduce England to an insular position. She would differ from any other island in being the heart and centre of a great confederacy of states belonging to her own race. Each of these would have its own government, and contribute by comparative experience and emulation to the political progress of the whole ; but they might be bound together not only by sympathy but by alliance, and not only by alliance, but to some extent by mutual civic rights. As regards the position of England in Europe, I contend that she would become not more, but less insular, when disencumbered of her distant dependencies. Why cannot she now speak the one word of " spirited foreign policy" that is worth speaking—the word that would set Italy free ? Because her armies and fleets are scattered, and she is in fear for her dependencies all over the globe. It will scarcely be said that our country was very insular in the time of Elizabeth, when she was the head of Protestantism in Europe ; or in the time of the Commonwealth, when under the safeguard of her power the Huguenot and the Vaudois, in the midst of persecutors thirsting for their blood, worshipped God in peace. If the Protector were here now, he would no doubt have a "spirited policy." It would not be his old policy, but one adapted to these times. Yet I doubt whether it would be one of " apparent power."

I am accused of neglecting " sentiment," and looking only to advantage. I reply that political confederations are not religious communities, and that reciprocal advantage, not sentiment, must be their basis, if they are intended to endure. None but a cynic would despise sentiment: none but a fool would build on it. If it be true that we derive no advantage from Canada which we do not equally derive from the United States, this is practically decisive. And therefore it is satisfactory to know that the Prince of Wales was as heartily welcomed by the people of the United States as he was by the Canadians; and that consequently "sentiment" does not cease with political connexion.

The most candid of my opponents, avowing that the political character of the Colonies is being injured under the present system, and that they are plunging into wild excesses of democracy, says that, still, to emancipate them instead of trying to set their politics right, would be to give up a problem which we are bound to solve. How the problem is to be solved he does not attempt to say. But I submit to him that the solution is clear. Nations, like men, are intended by nature to form their own character by self-exertion and self-control. They have in them the faculties of political life, which they must develop, as we did, by their own efforts. Every hour that an adult Colony is kept in leading strings, a mischief is done to its political character from which it may hereafter recover no doubt, but at the expense of great suffering and disaster.

I cordially agree with *The Times* that "the Colonists have rights as well as ourselves." They have a right above all, even if they do not know it themselves, to be released from the childish thraldom which, if it is prolonged, will be fatal to their hope of attaining the manly strength and stature of great nations.

It is difficult to see on what grounds, either of reason or experience, we base our notions about the beneficent tutelage of a home government. Reason tells us that the people of a Colony, if equally intelligent, educated, and moral with those of the mother country, ought to be equally capable of governing themselves. And experience tells us that the most successful Colonies in history have been founded by refugees. How much did the home government of the Stuarts do for the Puritan founders of New England?

When my critics speak of " *our* fagging steadily on at the problem of Colonial Government until it is solved," they use the current language expressive of the common idea. The common idea both among ourselves and among the Colonists is, that England herself is constantly engaged, with the wisdom of all her sages and the light of all her political experience, in conducting the political education of the Colonies. The fact is, that England is occupied with her own concerns. The tutelage of the Colonies is not exercised even by Parliament in any practical sense. It has been delegated wholly to the Colonial Office, and the Colonial Office generally speaking is the permanent Under-Secretary, — the "Mr. Mother Country" of satirical writers on Colonial subjects, who, as he has all the trouble and none of the glory, is likely, if his nature is human, to be content with administering his vast and motley empire according to established routine, and is not likely gratuitously to undertake problems with which the imperial genius of a Charlemagne might have feared to cope.

The Colonial Office, a pure bureaucracy based upon no constituency, and not practically amenable in its ordinary administration to the free public opinion of this country, is a solecism in English institutions. So far from being England, it is not even English.

I pointed out, not as a ground for hasty action (which indeed I expressly repudiated) but for deliberation, the bearing of certain great changes which have recently taken place in the world, such as the extension of free trade and the revival of Spain and Italy, on the value and the security of some of our military and naval dependencies. I presume there is nothing very injurious to the national honour in suggesting that an outlying dependency has become less secure, when our peaceful population is called under arms to protect our own country from invasion, and when Defence Commissions are inquiring of our merchants what would be the effect on trade if the French were in possession of London.

I will point to one other change of circumstances, most happy in itself, which, if I mistake not, will increase the difficulty of holding distant dependencies of whatever kind. To hold such dependencies we must have a large standing army; and a large standing army can only be raised, except at intolerable expense, from a population unprosperous enough to drive them to enlist. Miserable Ireland used to furnish two-fifths of our soldiers; now Ireland is in a fair way to be no longer miserable. Highland wretchedness, which was another recruiting-ground, is gone long ago. The repeal of the corn laws has told heavily against recruiting amongst our own peasantry. In the last war, England had to go into an evil market and hire German mercenaries to fight her battles. Yet this conveys no permanent warning; it seems to be taken as a transient accident, or a passing fit of perversity among the people.

Not only are soldiers growing scarce, but public feeling seems now to be rebelling against that arbitrary treatment of the soldier, when he has enlisted, which is as necessary to the maintenance of a standing army as the power of cheap enlistment. The people fix first on military flogging, because it is most before their eyes. Hereafter, moved by some tale of the soldier's wretchedness in tropical dependencies, of suicide, or reckless crime committed in despair, they may check the power of the government to send soldiers into compulsory exile, and to keep them there. In that case let the Secretary for War tell us how much it would cost to keep men voluntarily under the standard in the dependencies.

Those who foretell these difficulties do not create them, any more than the barometer creates the storm. And to rail at the barometer instead of preparing for the storm is hardly the part of wisdom or of greatness.

I am accused of "not shewing common patriotism." My object certainly was not to shew "common patriotism," of which there is a perennial current from more eloquent pens. These topics can have an interest only for those who wish to look through "common patriotism" to the real and abiding sources of our country's greatness. That the masters of that statecraft, the object of which is "apparent power," should be a little angry, is not surprising; but, let me observe, people are sometimes angry, or affect to be angry, not only when they are told new and unpalatable truths, but when they are told their own thoughts.—I am, &c.,

GOLDWIN SMITH.

Feb. 14, 1862.

III.

COLONIAL GOVERNMENT*.

Sir,—I have just read the speech of the Duke of Newcastle, the Secretary of State for the Colonies, at the Australian Anniversary Dinner [b]. He enters into a defence of the present connexion between the Mother Country and the Colonies; and whether we look to his office or to his character, the importance of his words on this subject can hardly be overrated. We may be sure that from him we shall have the truth.

The Duke dwells upon the greatness of the Colonial trade as triumphantly proving that "the Colonies are still of some advantage, even in a low pecuniary aspect, to the commercial welfare of the Mother Country." But, as has been said before, arguments drawn from the amount of the Colonial trade prove nothing, unless it can be shewn that the prosperity of the trade in some way depends on the continuance of the political connexion. The immense increase of our trade with the United States since the severance of their political connexion with the Mother Country proves that the reverse is the truth. The defenders of the system of dependency seem always unwilling to face this fact.

* This letter stands in place of the original postscript to No. II.
[b] Reported in *The Daily News*, Thursday, Feb. 13, 1862.

To prove that our dominion over the Colonies is real and effective, not a phantom of self-deluding pride, the Duke mentions one instance in which a Colonial legislature altered a money bill on his "venturing to express an opinion, without interposing the authority of the Crown, that it would not be wise or just to pass it." Suppose the Colonial Legislature, notwithstanding his gentle whisper of disapproval, had passed the bill, would he have ventured then to interpose the authority of the Crown? That is the real test of the reality of his dominion. Christopher Sly the Tinker might possibly persuade the Emperor of All the Russias to desist from an objectionable course of action, if his reasons were good, and if he had a persuasive tongue. But this would not prove that the Emperor of All the Russias was subject to the dominion of Christopher Sly. The Secretary of State gives advice to the Colonies: so do our newspapers, and probably with at least as much effect. The newspapers, if their advice is disregarded, have no veto: neither, I apprehend, has the Secretary of State.

The Legislature of Canada, in defiance of the Colonial Secretary's expostulations, laid a heavy protective duty on British goods, whereby they not only did the greatest injustice to their fellow-subjects in this country, who were all the time being taxed for their protection; but gave to the winds the settled commercial policy of the Empire. Did the Home Government dare to use the veto of the Crown? No, they signified their dissent and their submission.

In like manner, when the same Legislature resolved

to contravene the policy of the Empire in the highest
matter of all, the matter of religion, by secularizing
lands which the British Legislature had reserved for
the maintenance of the Established Church, did the
Home Government, seeing so vital a principle at stake,
dare to assert its power? As in the other case, it
surrendered; and the Colonial Secretary who has recorded the transaction congratulates himself on having
escaped, by the promptitude and grace with which the
surrender was performed, the awkward alternative of
having an Act of the Canadian Legislature passed in
direct contravention of the Act of the Imperial Parliament securing the endowments to the Church. He
thinks indeed that, had such an Act been passed, he
would have put the veto of the Crown on it. In that
case we should have been drawn into a contest with the
Canadians for the theoretic right of forbidding that
which we did not mean or dare to prevent, just as we
were drawn by the statesmen of former times into
a contest with the Americans, in effect for the theoretic
right of taxing them, when it was admitted that we
could not exercise the power. The Governor General
of Canada was directed by the Home Government, in
hauling down the Imperial colours, to tell the Canadian
Parliament that "in coming to this conclusion, Her
Majesty's Government had been mainly influenced by
the consideration, that great as in their judgment
would be the advantages which would result from
leaving undisturbed the existing arrangement, by which
a certain portion of the public lands of Canada were
made available for the purpose of creating a fund for

the religious instruction of the inhabitants of the Province, still the question whether that arrangement was to be maintained was one so exclusively affecting the people of Canada, that its decision ought not to be withdrawn from the Provincial Legislature, to which it properly belongs to regulate all matters concerning the domestic interests of the Province ᶜ." If the question of a Religious Establishment and of the relation between Church and State is a Provincial question, what question is Imperial? If on this subject the Home Government at once gives way, on what subject will it make a stand?

The Duke of Newcastle tells us that the Colonists are adopting the laws, the law courts, and the legal processes of this Country. But the independent States of America have equally adopted, or rather they have kept as a part of their English heritage, our laws, our courts, our forms of legal procedure. The decisions of our great judges are cited and the authority of our great jurists is invoked before their tribunals with as much respect as if they were the nominal liegemen of an office in Downing-street. And surely there is a charm and a value in this free homage to our law and its great expositors which does not belong to the constrained submission of provinces still dependent on the Crown.

The Duke goes on to say with proud satisfaction that the Australian Colonists have "the same institutions generally" as the Mother Country. He adds the qualifying words "as far as they are adapted to a new country like Australia." But a further qualification, of the

ᶜ Earl Grey on Colonial Policy, vol. i. p. 254.

most momentous kind, will be found in his own speech.
For he proceeds to express his wish "that when the
power of self-government had been granted to the
Colonists they had been less adventurous in the use of
it, and had been less precipitate in applying manhood
suffrage to a country where the population was constantly moving, and where those established rights and
interests were not to be found which might prove
a check to it in other countries." The Duke regrets
this, but "he does not despair."

If the institutions of the Colonies are directly opposed
to those of the Mother Country in religion, in politics,
and in trade; if, while we have an Established Church,
they have none; if, while we have a high electoral qualification, and an aristocratic Parliament, they have manhood suffrage and democratic assemblies; if, while we
proclaim Free Trade as the principle of our commercial
system, they pass measures of Protection, in what does
"the unity of the Empire" consist? What is the frame
that it would be such treason to "dismember?"

The Duke of Newcastle indeed owns with perfect
frankness that the power of the Crown even to put
down rebellion in the Colonies is gone. The subjects
of Her Majesty there have the remarkable liberty, which
is not shared by her other subjects, of renouncing their
allegiance whenever they see fit. The Duke trusts
"that the day will never come when the Mother Country will make an effort to retain her Colonies by force."
He trusts "the day will never return when a single red-
coat will point a bayonet or fire a shot in hostility to
the Colonies if they wish to separate from the Mother

Country." If a Colony, in a moment of exasperation at some act of the Colonial Office or the Governor, thinks proper to shew Her Majesty's representative, with Colonial frankness and heartiness, to the door, not a finger is to be moved to vindicate the honour of the Crown. Surely these are singular liegemen of the Empire, and the "dominion" held over them is one of an unprecedented kind.

Two attributes of Imperial power indeed we still retain. Our Privy Council still drags Colonial causes to its distant and expensive Court of Appeal. Our Mint still deranges Colonial currency by forbidding nations to coin their own money. The exercise of this last prerogative has, in one case, a curious effect: it leads the Canadians to use as their currency American dollars, and thus unites Canada by a not unimportant bond of national identity with the very nation from which it is the object of all our Canadian policy, armaments, and fortifications to keep her jealously distinct.

The Duke expatiates on the rapid growth and wonderful prosperity of the Australian Colonies. He describes them as being, though infants in age, " giants in aspiration, in effort, and prosperity." But can it be shewn that this marvellous prosperity has ever depended or that it now depends on the subjection of the Colonies to the Colonial Office? Can it be shewn that it has ever depended or that it now depends on their subjection to the Colonial Office, any more than on their subjection to the Heralds' Office, which, I presume, equally embraces within its venerable jurisdiction the shepherds of Australian plains and the gold-seekers of

Australian wilds? There are certain qualities and faculties which the Englishman carries with him wherever he goes, and which, in a land that repays energy with wealth, are apt to produce great results, even when regulated by no central office and provided with no charter but that of nature. Some of the British Colonists of Van Diemen's Land wished to establish a settlement at Port Phillip. Two successive Secretaries for the Colonies positively prohibited the enterprise, declaring that no settlement could be allowed at that point, the policy of the Government being to concentrate and not to disperse the population. The Colonists disregarded the prohibition, and founded the settlement [d]. It is now Victoria, the marvel and paragon of Colonial prosperity. Is its prosperity due to its having been a part of our Colonial dominions?

" The system works, indeed," says a Colonist, speaking of what he angrily calls the Colonial Office Bureaucracy [e], " but by means of what is contrary to it: it works in spite of its un-English self, by means of the English energy which it depresses, of the self-reliance which it cannot destroy, of the fortitude which resists it; and finally by means of the national institutions and sentiments to which it is wholly antagonistic. In a word, it is worked by counteraction." These are splenetic words, perhaps, and they were written twelve years ago. But it would not be easy to shew that they were false at the time when they were written; and unless they were false the prosperity of the Australian

d See Mr. S. S. Bell on Colonial Administration, p. 101.
e Wakefield on the Art of Colonization, p. 259.

Colonies is a weak argument for the maintenance of the present connexion.

It is true, of course, that a part of the population of some of the Australian Colonies which are now flourishing was sent out by the Home Government, to whose credit the foundation of those Colonies may to that extent be placed. But the Colonies vehemently decline any further additions to their population of that kind: and by putting an end to transportation they have cut away, I believe, the last pretence for saying that our nominal dominion over them is of any use to this country.

As to the political education which the infant Colonies have received in the shape of forms of government given them by the Colonial Office, another Colonist says[1], "Each Colonial Minister has struggled with the difficulties of his time, as best he could, keeping as much power to the Crown as he could, and giving as little constitutional power to the people as he durst well refuse; trying a government here by the governor of the Crown with a council of nominees—there by a governor and a council partly of nominees and partly of elected members—here by a governor, a nominee council, and an elective assembly—there by a governor and executive council irremoveable, and an elective legislative council and assembly—here by a governor with an executive council removeable, and an elective legislative council and assembly. Here the Crown has the appropriation of the revenue, there the Colony has the appropriation. . . . Joseph's coat had not so many colours."

Is it possible to believe that any unity of design, or

[1] Colonial Administration, by Mr. S. S. Bell, p. 357.

indeed any design at all, has run through this the supposed political training of the infant Colonies by the
Central Office which we and they in imagination identify
with England? Can any act of the Central Office be
shewn to have been beneficial to the political character of the Colonies, saving those by which, under
the auspices of wise and generous Colonial Ministers,
it has parted of late years with a great part of its
power?

To ask these questions is not to disparage English
statesmanship. When we consider what the political
education of a nation is—how natural yet how complex
—how evidently it depends, like that of a man, on
self-exertion, on self-control, on self-applied experience,
on the instinctive adaptation of institutions to circumstances,—and how little any one can comprehend the
circumstances but those who actually feel their pressure,—we shall be inclined greatly to doubt whether
this process can be successfully carried on or guided
from without, and not only from without but from the
distance of the whole globe, not by a single man whose
actions might at least be uniform, but by a succession
of men, at the rate of thirteen in twenty years, each
bringing to the task notions, a temper, party connexions, and a party bias of his own. We shall be
inclined to cry that we must "let that alone for ever."
Is there anything in the experience of the world recorded by history that at all approaches to such an
undertaking, or holds out the slightest hope of its
success?

Nevertheless, though it is beyond the power even of

E

a Permanent Under-Secretary for the Colonies to carry
on at once the political training of thirty nations, the
rule of this country over the Colonies is, in a political
point of view, by no means without effect. It is lending, as I believe, a bias of the most fatal kind to the
political character of these young nations, and shooting
a deadly poison through their political frames.

The natural tendency of English settlers, endowed
as they are with shrewd intelligence and sturdy self-
reliance, is to manage their concerns as much as possible in local assemblies, which they can attend in person; and to delegate as little as possible to a central
government. Such were the institutions which nature established in the American Colonies; and, while
they lasted, American politics were pure and American
government was cheap. There were no prizes for successful demagogism, and therefore there were no dema-
gogues: there was no rich patronage to give away,
there were no lucrative jobs to be done, and therefore
there were no corrupt factions fighting for power. The
expenses of the civil establishment in Massachusetts
Bay, in those days, was only £18,000 a-year; that of
New Hampshire and Rhode Island £3,500 each; that
of Connecticut £4,000; that of New York and Penn-
sylvania £4,500 each; that of New Jersey £1,500;
that of Virginia and South Carolina £8,000 each. At
this small cost three millions of people were well governed[g]. The civil expenditure of Canada in 1860 was
upwards of six millions. The public debt was twelve
millions.

[g] Adam Smith.

But we are introducing into each of the Colonies under our rule the opposite system of central government in the shape of a parody of our Constitutional Monarchy, the Monarch being personated, as far as such personation is possible, by the Governor sent out from this country. Together with this parody of a Constitutional Monarchy, we are introducing the concomitants of that peculiar institution, party government, and Cabinet administration.

In the old country this system has hitherto not been insufferable because here we have a real monarchy with its dignity, with the chivalrous loyalty which it excites, and the tempering and refining influence which it exerts; and because we have great historical divisions of opinion, which give a meaning to parties, and render the eternal struggle between two sets of public men for the Cabinet offices in some measure a contest of principle and not a mere intrigue. Moreover, we have in this country men of large fortune and high cultivation, who devote themselves to public life from public motives, or, at all events, from an ambition superior to the emoluments of office, and who can make legislation their calling without making it their trade.

In the Colonies there are none of these things. The mock monarchy lacks all the dignity of the original; no loyalty is felt towards it; nor does it exercise as an institution any elevating or restraining influence. The parties are founded on no historical divisions of opinion; they have no real public basis; and therefore they inevitably degenerate into unmeaning factions. The Cabinet is the organ through which the dominant faction grasps an extensive patronage, and plunders the country by jobbing and corruption. There are no cultivated men of leisure; respectable farmers and traders cannot leave their callings to devote themselves to politics; and therefore political life is apt to become the trade of needy adventurers of the lowest kind. As the combinations on which Cabinets are based are personal rather than political, and as everybody is hungry, the Ministry is changed about once in six months, and thus all stability, as well as all honesty, of government is destroyed. Of course the gambling spirit of commercial speculation, and the loose commercial morality characteristic of young commercial settlements, find their way into the transactions of public life and aggravate the evil.

The Times in vindicating the "noble fabric" of our Colonial government against my crazy speculations, selected as its palmary instance of success the colony of Melbourne. The state of that community is the admiration and envy of the world. "Every French traveller breaks forth into raptures at the prosperity of Melbourne." I append to this letter, as they are too long to be quoted entire, the expressions of the rapture felt by *The Times* at the state of Melbourne in the month of October last. It will be seen that, at that date, this portion of the "noble fabric" was a sink of political roguery, demagogism, and corruption, as hopeless as it was vile; that ministries "not of high character" subsisted by appeals to "the lowest and most ignorant of the people;" that the support of the Assembly was enlisted by bribery, in the coarse shape

of payment of members; that the "balance of society
and government had been overthrown;" that the community was "in the hands of a single class, and that
class the least respectable of all;" that "the grossest
fallacies and the most mischievous delusions were the
means and the only means of reaching and retaining
power." "Each Assembly, each Government, was
worse than its predecessor, and the men who were too
bad for the uses of to-day, were found too respectable for
the purposes of the morrow." We were told, moreover,
"that there was no limit to this downward tendency,
no power in the single class which governed these communities to regenerate itself or reform them." "Safe
under the ægis of British power, the Colonists were
relieved from the responsibilities which ordinarily attend on the exercise of self-government." Their legislatures were given over to the Spirit of Protection,
and were on the very verge of Repudiation. "We
have endeavoured," concluded *The Times*, "with much
reluctance, to point out the magnitude of an evil which
it is in vain any longer to palliate or conceal. Enough
has been conceded to these elements of confusion; it is
time that the Imperial Government should assert itself
a little, and try to bring some order out of the chaos
which it has created. We are satisfied that, at the rate
at which legislation is proceeding at the Antipodes, the
veto of the Crown might be very freely and very beneficially exercised. We do not know whether it would
be the duty of the Imperial Parliament to interfere on
behalf of defrauded creditors who trusted the existing
Government and the existing Constitution, but we are

quite clear that it would be the duty of the Secretary for the Colonies to veto all laws imposing protective or discriminating duties, proscribing nations at peace with us, like the Chinese, or in any other way infringing the great principles of Imperial policy. The whole subject must before very long force itself on the attention of Parliament, for the evils which we have pointed out are not of a stationary nature, but must go on in a progressive ratio, extending and increasing their baneful influence." The present Secretary for the Colonies is too wise to listen to any wild cries of frightened capitalists for the use of the veto : but there is another way of putting an end to the progress of the evil.

Let those who are disposed, perhaps not unnaturally, to resent the attempt of a student, remote from political life, to write on a political subject, compare *The Times* of October with *The Times* of February, and note that, had the conduct of the nation and the Government been guided by the great organ of practical wisdom, we should, upon this momentous question, have acted within six months upon impulses of a directly opposite kind.

It is not manhood suffrage in itself that is the cause of the mischief. Manhood suffrage is inevitable in a country where all men are equal. The cause of the mischief is manhood suffrage, or rather the social circumstances which involve manhood suffrage, combined with central institutions which belong to a totally different state of things. Underneath, in the local parts of Colonial society and administration, where nature has her way, all is still comparatively sound in our

Colonies as it is in the United States. On the top we, by our beneficent tutelage, are creating an artificial anarchy of rogues; and of course the longer we carry this on the more deeply we shall infect the political character and the more we shall blight the political prospects of the young nation.

To put the same thing in different words, it is not democracy that is an evil. Democracy is the necessary lot of these new worlds: for no one can doubt that where society is essentially democratic, institutions, whatever their form or their names, must be essentially democratic also. The evil is demagogism, to which all public bodies, even those elected by the narrowest suffrage and those which are most aristocratic, are liable, when there are prizes for unprincipled ambition: and by the system of government which we are introducing into the Colonies we are providing that such prizes shall abound.

Washington, an English gentleman, made a natural but a fatal mistake when he gave America a republican counterpart of the English Constitution, on the central principle, with an elective President for a King, an elective Senate for a House of Lords, a Congress for a House of Commons, a Cabinet Executive, great powers vested in the Central Government, and, worst of all, with extensive patronage. The result has been American parties, American politicians, and American public life. The local institutions, the English qualities of the race, and the undying energy of the old Puritan virtue, have had a hard struggle to save from utter ruin the political character of the nation.

In these communities, where all are intelligent but few are highly cultivated, where all are well off but few have wealth and leisure to devote themselves to public life without sordid objects, the more men manage their own affairs and look to the application of their own money in person the better. The delegation of power and the functions of the central government should be confined within the narrowest bounds. Above all, there should be as little as possible of patronage vested in the central government to tempt unprincipled ambition. Such powers as the central government has, should be exercised by all the members of an open Council. There should be no Cabinet Executive, nor anything approaching to a close or secret policy, foreign or domestic. Every corner of the administration should be open to the most searching light of publicity, the guardian of political purity and virtue. All this is feasible as well as desirable in those communities which have no great standing armies, no empires, no occasion for any but the simplest and most straightforward dealings with foreign powers; where government, local or central, has no duties properly belonging to it but those of enforcing the law and laying out a very small amount of public money on objects which everybody understands. If the extent of territory is such that great responsibilities would inevitably be thrown on a single central government, federation is the natural remedy; and in that case the functions of the federal government should be limited as strictly as possible to keeping the peace in the federation and managing its relations with foreign powers.

If such a form of government as this has not the majesty of the old governments, with their costly trappings, their vast armaments, their State secrets, their dark diplomacy, and their enormous patronage, perhaps it may be found that it will have a majesty of its own, derived from its simplicity, its integrity, the reasonable loyalty which it is capable of exciting, and its fitness to secure the great objects of society and the happiness of man.

After all, government is a remedy for the bad passions of mankind. The less of it a nation requires the greater is the dignity of that nation. And the tendency of advancing Civilization probably is to diminish the functions of governments altogether, not, as we, in aspiring to found Colonial governments assume, to invest them with a more beneficent and majestic form.

Much praise is bestowed on the Government of Queensland, and no doubt with justice, so far as the present administration is concerned. But the Government of Queensland, if you look into it, is not the natural growth of the Colony, rooted and destined to flourish in its native soil. It is an imported Government of Englishmen, making administration their profession. If an equivocal term may be used in a good sense, it may be called, in fact, a bureaucracy, balancing itself with great ability and address upon the top of a community with which it does not cohere. The English administrators who are now at the head of it must in time pass away; and what will they leave behind them? What will the state of things be when their places are

filled by Colonial adventurers? Melbourne gives us
the reply.

It may be readily granted that while the present
system of government in the Colonies continues, the
personal influence of the Governor, an English gentleman, trained, if not in the school of English public
life, at least in the school of English honour, may be
the most redeeming part of the whole. His good
sense and rectitude may in some measure temper the
coarse and unscrupulous party struggles of which he is
the centre and the offices and patronage of his government are the exciting cause. But to mould the political character of a nation, if that is the work expected
of him, he must be nothing less than a great master of
political science combined with a great man of action.
Several of the Colonial Governors have been men of
mark: some of the Governors-General of Canada, the
greatest of all these proconsulates, have been first-rate
statesmen. But as to these appointments generally,
Lord Grey says[h] that " their advantages are not such
as to lead to their being often accepted by persons who
have much distinguished themselves by the ability they
have shewn ; so that the services of men who have filled
other important offices, and who would therefore be
preferred for such situations, cannot be commanded."
" Hence," he says, " the choice generally lies among
persons of less tried fitness." Surely this does not
sound like the description of men able to strike their

[h] Colonial Policy of the Administration of Lord John Russell,
vol. i. p. 41.

hand on rampant democracy and to heal it of its leprosy.

The days when Mr. O'Connell told an adherent of tainted character that he could not undertake to get him anything at home, but that he would get him something in the Colonies, are happily gone by; but those days, like transportation, have left their mark.

The Duke tells us that the Colonies are now all loyalty and affection to the Mother Country. That they are, is a proud thought for England; and it is due in a high degree to the policy of diminishing the interference and giving up the patronage of the central office, a policy virtually tending to emancipation, which the Duke has magnanimously pursued. Now, then, is the time, before any subject of dispute arises, to make this loyalty and this affection sure for ever.

Colonists may be full of loyalty and affection for the Mother Country, and yet they may quarrel with the Colonial Office. The American Colonists were as full of loyalty and affection for the Mother Country as Colonists could be when they quarrelled with the Ministers of that day. If the sky of Colonial government is bright on the whole, it is not without a cloud. There is a difference with New Zealand about the use of our troops, with Australia about the rate of the soldiers' pay, with Jamaica about the repayment of the loan, with the Canadians about their military preparations. The Colonists are rough people to deal with; and the language commonly held about them is such as to possess them with the belief that they are indispensable to us, and that they have only to stand their ground and be a little rude on any question to make us give way. Out of any one of these clouds there may suddenly burst a storm.

The Committee on Military Defences in the Colonies point out the absurd inequality of our dealings with the several Colonies in the matter of military expenditure and allowances : an inequality, be it observed, which would not be cured by adopting any uniform rule, since the application of a uniform rule to communities so diverse as well as distant from each other, and whose prosperity is so fluctuating, would in itself be the height of injustice. "It is not surprising," say the Committee, "that a state of things so anomalous and irregular should lead to disputes and confusion." "Not a year," they add, "passes without the occurrence of difficulties and discussions with regard to the respective liabilities of the Imperial and Colonial Governments in every part of the world; and it is to be observed that such questions are never settled; they are adjourned for the moment, leaving behind them often much soreness on both sides, and the Imperial Government almost invariably yielding the points at issue; but the next year, or the year after, they are raised again, there being no recognised principles of mutual relations to which appeal can be made, or upon which a permanent settlement can be founded[i]." Nor is it possible that there should be "recognised principles," since the relations themselves are in truth mere unreason and bewilderment. The scholar gave up at last with a hearty

---

[i] Report of the Committee on the Expense of Military Defences in the Colonies, p. 5. (1859.)

curse his attempt to master "the theory of irregular verbs."

In case of a quarrel, the Duke thinks he would courteously retire from that part of his dominions without a bayonet levelled or a shot fired. I do not doubt that he has formed this wise resolution, but I doubt the power of a man of his spirit to fulfil it. In the year 1826 *The Edinburgh Review*, the great organ of the Liberal party, said, "There is not a man of sense in the Empire who does not look forward to the dissolution, at no distant period, of the present connexion between Canada and England." Ten years after this a Liberal Ministry were putting down a rebellion in Canada arising from a dispute in which, though the Colonists were petulant and impatient, the Home Government, which had bestowed free institutions and then tried to check their working, was in the main to blame. Lord Brougham, in his " Life of Lord North," says of the conduct of the Liberal Ministry on this occasion, " A new and perhaps unexpected vindication of Lord North has been recently presented by the Canadian policy of Liberal Governments, as far as mistakes by inferior artists can extenuate the failures of their more eminent predecessors. When the senseless policy was stated of clinging by Colonies wholly useless and merely expensive, which all admit must sooner or later assert their independence and be severed from the mother country, none of all this was denied, nor indeed could it; but the answer was that no government whatever could give up any part of its dominions without being compelled by force, and that history afforded no example of such a surrender without an obstinate struggle. What more did Lord North and the other authors of the disgraceful contest with America, than act upon this bad principle?" Had the members of the Liberal Government been calmly deliberating beforehand on a possible contingency, or reviewing the acts of other statesmen, they would probably have seen all this as clearly and acknowledged it as fully as Lord Brougham. And had Lord Brougham been in office, charged with the honour of the Empire, and dealing with a rather rough and very irritating set of people, he would not improbably have acted like the members of the Liberal Government.

It is not unlikely that Canada itself may again prove, before long, the source of trouble to our Government, owing to a formidable question which is looming among the Canadians themselves, in addition to the dangers which, while the country remains an English dependency, will always threaten it from without. When we united the English and French provinces and gave them a common Parliament, the inhabitants of the English province being then fewer in number than those of the French, we established representation by provinces, instead of representation by population, giving each province the same number of representatives. Now, the inhabitants of the English province, finding themselves more in number than those of the French, begin to demand representation by population instead of representation by provinces. The difficulty is great: but if left to themselves the two parties will be compelled, by their responsibility for the consequences and by a sense of each other's strength, to control their tempers and to bring the question to some equitable solution. The natural solution is that in place of the incorporating union of English and French Canada should be instituted a federal union, the principle of which is in fact contained in the system of representation by provinces ; and that all the British Colonies in North America should be included in the federation. But of this we may be sure, that if we remain arbiters of the dispute, and responsible for the enforcement of legal right, the party in favour of which we pronounce will cast all compromise to the winds ; and that if the other party is contumacious (as the English party in case they lose their cause will most certainly be) we shall have to carry our sentence into effect with the strong hand.

Fancy pictures everything going quietly and happily on, till the Colony, having grown at last into a nation, becomes conscious of its maturity, and sends a respectful deputation to the Colonial Office to announce to the Secretary of State that the Colony wishes to set up for itself in life, and to sue for his consent, and beg his paternal blessing. Reason and experience suggest that if you place yourself in false relations with other people, and go blindly on, you stand a chance of finding out, in some less agreeable and dignified way, that the relations are false.— I am, &c.

GOLDWIN SMITH.

Feb. 16, 1862.

Remarks of *The Times* on the Political State of the Australian Colonies, Oct. 18 and 21, 1861 :—

"If there be something in the misfortunes of our best friends which does not displease us, there may possibly be some persons who derive considerable satisfaction from the existing state of things in the United States of America. We do not now speak of those who see in the disruption of the great Confederacy the realization of long cherished anti-democratic theories, nor yet of those who rejoice in the probable withdrawal of a powerful rival, nor yet of those who believe that they see in this contest the extinction of Slavery. We speak of the Colonies and those intimately connected with them and interested in them. In the matter of emigration the United States had fairly got the start of all other countries speaking the British language, and the emigration to our colonies was counted by hundreds, while the emigration to North America was counted by thousands. This was due partly to contiguity, partly to the wish of the friends and relations of persons who had already emigrated to be re-united in their new homes, partly to the prestige of a successful revolt from Great Britain, but, more than any of these things, to the notion that America was a land of perfect liberty, where, free from the King, the noble, the landlord, and the taxgatherer, the people ruled in all their might and majesty, and gave those laws to the rich and the instructed which in less favoured lands they received from them. The introduction of passports, the imposition of an income-tax, the suppression by main force of newspapers which do not speak the language of the Government, the prospect of a commercial collapse, and the foundations which are being laid broad and deep of an enormous national debt, must inevitably check for a time at least, and perhaps for ever, the vast emigration from England, Scotland, and Ireland to the United States. Yet people must emigrate somewhither. In a community like ours there will always be ardent and discontented spirits chafing against the existing order of things, and longing to find in a new society opportunities for which they would seek in vain in an old one. The Colonies naturally expect to secure a considerable portion of this emigration. There is, besides, another emigration of which the Colonies are no less desirous — the emigration of capital. They not unreasonably expect that a considerable portion of those vast sums which now go to redeem the wilderness in North America may be attracted to other and more favoured lands, where, under a better climate and a more orderly Government, the earth may give forth her increase, and a man of wealth receive his own with usury. Probably, by those who do not look narrowly into such things it will be thought that the conjuncture is particularly favourable, and that residence in our Colonies was never so attractive as now. Time was, and that not long ago, when our Colonies were subjected to the meddling despotism of the Colonial-office, but that system has been pulled up by the roots, and has been succeeded by the rule of responsible Ministries, holding office at the pleasure of Assemblies elected by suffrage almost universal, and under the protection of the ballot. Here, then, it may be supposed, we have found apt recipients for that superfluous capital and redundant population with which we are sometimes encumbered. But we fear the picture will not be found so fair upon closer inspection, and that in these younger communities may be already detected most of the vices which have so speedily arrived at a full-grown maturity in the strong soil of the United States.

" Let us turn to the intelligence which a single mail brings us from the Australian group of Colonies. In the wealthy and prosperous settlement of Victoria there has just been, as usual, a general election. A Ministry of no great strength and no very high character—as we learn from our local correspondent, who is entirely borne out in his views by the *Melbourne Argus*—was placed in a minority, and obtained the Governor's consent to a dissolution. Once being com-

F

mitted to this step, they bethought themselves of all the
topics which were likely to have weight with the lowest and
most ignorant of the people, in whose hands, under a franchise thoroughly democratic, the power entirely resides.
The result was a programme of opinions to which they had
never committed themselves before, and with reference to
which the dissolution did not take place. This programme
contained, among other things, protection to native industry,
payment of members (£300 a-year each), and a repeal of the
gold export duty. The Protective movement was to secure
the support of the populations of large towns. The payment
of members was to give, at least until the Bill was carried,
the persons returned an interest identical with the existence
of the Ministry. All these measures are obviously most injurious to the public interest, and the payment of members
is particularly unnecessary and prodigal in a community
which is one of the wealthiest in the world. By such means
the Administration has obtained something which may possibly turn out to be a bare majority, but in doing this they
have greatly degraded the quality of the Assembly, which,
not by any means too elevated before, it is agreed on all
hands, is now sunk far below its former level. Many of its
best members have been excluded to make way for persons
of the most indifferent character. Parties are too nearly
balanced to carry on the Government with such a body, and
what we have to expect is another dissolution,—another
scandal,—a spectacle of parties bidding against each other
for the support of an ignorant rabble, and sacrificing the
public interest for a few weeks or months of precarious and
degraded official existence. The fact is, that in Victoria and
New South Wales, that has come to pass which was foreseen
by the founders of the American Constitution. Responsible
government is rapidly reducing itself to an absurdity. No
doubt the founders of the American Republic would very
gladly have included a responsible government in their plan,
if they had not been aware that in an unbalanced democracy

responsible government is equivalent to no government at all.
As soon as one set of men are in possession of power the rest
combine against them and eject them, to be in turn ejected
by a similar combination. In their efforts to retain or to
seize upon office each party seeks to outbid the other, and to
supplant it in the good graces of those constituents on whose
votes office depends. It was the rivalry at Presidential elections which completely democratized America, and the work
would have been done much more speedily if the auction had
been always open instead of being restricted to the close of
every fourth year.

" If we turn from Victoria to New South Wales we find
that by the intervention of English soldiers the disgraceful
riots and outrages practised on the Chinese had been termi-
nated, but we are also told that an Act is sure to be passed
prohibiting, in defiance of treaties, the immigration of Chinese
into New South Wales. This movement owes its origin to
the same spirit of Protection to which the present Melbourne
Ministry owes its success. The Colonies are quarrelling about
their tariffs, and the working classes, not content with protecting themselves by laws of exclusion and high import
duties, and the emancipation of those who dig gold from
taxation, are asserting their domination in another form by
having recourse to Strikes.

" This is the intelligence brought by a single mail. Although infinitely less disastrous than that which we daily
receive from America, we can trace in it the same elements
of confusion, which only need time and occasion to develope
themselves into results equally lamentable. It is evident
that the balance of society and of government in these communities has been overthrown, and that they are now governed by a single class, and that class the most ignorant
and the least respectable of all. The grossest fallacies, the
most mischievous delusions, are the means, and, as it would
seem, the only means, of reaching and retaining power. The
Colonies have gone a great way in a few years, but they have

further yet to go. Each Assembly, each Government, is worse than its predecessor, and the men who are too bad for the uses of to-day are found too respectable for the purposes of to-morrow. There is no limit to this downward tendency; there is no power in the single class which governs these communities to regenerate itself or reform them. We see in Australia the image of what we have escaped in England, and may well profit by the spectacle. But such things are not calculated to allure colonists or to attract capital seeking investment, and the misfortune of America would have been much more the opportunity of the Colonies if the Colonies had not begun to resemble her a little too closely. What effect these things have on the prospects of the Empire, and what duties they impose on the Home Government, it may be worth while to consider heareafter."

"Whatever good effects the establishment of local self-government throughout the Colonies inhabited by the British race has produced, no one can doubt, who looks impartially at the subject, that for those good effects we have had to pay a very heavy price in the destruction of the unity of the Government of the Empire. We do not regret the old system that prevailed in former times. It was unjust to the Colonies, and burdensome, without being beneficial, to the mother country. The one lost what the other never gained. It was, no doubt, exceedingly acceptable to the whole tribe of placehunters, and opened a resource to many a brokendown outcast from society. But in taking from the Colonies the power of self-government we took from them a power which we were unable to use, and rendered ourselves odious by meddling with what we did not understand. Still, our thorough consciousness of the evils of the old system ought not to make us utterly blind to the less, but by no means inconsiderable, evils of the new. When we give a Colony responsible Government, we constitute it for all purposes of internal legislation and administration—that is, for almost all purposes, foreign relations alone excepted—a separate and independent territory. We thus expose ourselves to many inconveniences. The internal legislation of the Colony may involve principles hostile to Imperial interests; the Colonies may impose protective or discriminating duties; they may get up a war of tariffs with each other, or they may pass laws inconsistent with the treaty engagements of the Empire, or contrary to our notions of justice. The Ministry, acting in the name of the Queen, may do numberless things which the Queen's Ministry in London may entirely disapprove. For the conflict that arises in the case of improper legislation a species of remedy is provided by the veto of the Crown : for conduct in the Colonial Administration hostile to Imperial interests there is no remedy whatever so long as it meets the approbation of the Colonial Parliament. These are theo-retical difficulties incident to the notion of self-government. What practical weight they may have must depend on the difference or identity of sentiment between the Colonial Legislature and the Imperial Parliament.

" Unfortunately, we have taken care that this difference shall be as great as possible. At the time when the Con-stitutions of our Colonies were granted the favourite theory of English Liberals was that all the merits of Government were increased in proportion as the franchise was diminished. In an evil hour the Colonial Assemblies were intrusted with the power of reducing at their will the qualification of electors. This one fatal gift neutralized all the good of a liberal and decentralizing policy. Very speedily the rivalry of contending parties reduced the franchise to universal suffrage. The wealthier and more intelligent classes were virtually disfranchised; Government succeeded Government in a rapid course of deterioration; dissolution succeeded dis-solution, each creating a Parliament greatly inferior to its predecessor. At last the work is effectually done, and we have a system of Colonial Government in which the American type predominates decidedly over the English. It is quite impossible for Legislatures elected by a single class, and that the lowest and most ignorant in the community, to work responsible government as it is worked in England. It is equally impossible for such Legislatures to pass laws in accordance with the spirit of the British House of Commons, elected by constituencies in which the democratic element is tempered by a large admixture of property and intelligence. That which might have been predicted has come to pass. The Government is not always such as does honour to the name of Her Majesty, in which it is carried on ; the legislation is often opposed to the notions of policy, and even of justice, entertained by the Imperial Parliament. The evil is great, but has a capacity of infinitely magnifying itself. The twig of to-day is the tree of to-morrow. These Colonial communities are rapidly increasing, and as their interests become larger the divergence between them and the Home Government will become more striking. We ought never to have given them universal suffrage, unless we intended to adopt universal suffrage ourselves. It is not that they have more liberty than we, but that they have a different form of Government. Each form of Government has its own symptoms as well as each form of disease. The political economy of democracy is protection. We see it in our own working classes, which never could be got to agitate in earnest for Free Trade, and try to erect every handicraft into a guild from which competition is excluded. We see it in the protective tariff of the North American States, of Canada, of New South Wales, and of Victoria. Another symptom is a discouragement of immigration, which we see in the persecution of the Chinese in New South Wales, and in the wish plainly shewn by the dominant working class in the Australian Colonies to discourage the arrival of fresh immigrants.

"Meanwhile the Colonial-office, once so active and meddling, has been cowed into inertness, and become an impassible spectator of the ruin it has made. The one remedy which it possesses is the power of the veto, and that seems to have fallen almost as much into disuse in the case of Colonial as of Imperial Acts. A complete system of protection has, in defiance of the policy of the mother country, been framed in several Colonies, and the Colonial-office has offered no resistance. In the meanwhile things go on from bad to worse, and the day is not far distant when the English practice of responsible Government must give way to some change better suited to the present quality of Colonial Assemblies. We have not given the Colonies self-government so much as given one class in each Colony the power of exercising what tyranny it pleases over the rest. The question raised is a momentous one. Is Parliament, with whom the ultimate power resides, to allow the state of things we have described to go on until no resource is left us but to submit to have our Imperial policy dragged through the dirt, or to break off communication with communities when they become unworthy of the British name? Our Melbourne correspondent, though evidently seriously alarmed, does not, as he assures us, consider the case hopeless; and he founds his hopes on that of which we also have heard so much—the intelligence of the working classes. It has come to this,—that he thinks it necessary to argue that in Victoria, the land of gold, there is no serious danger of repudiation. Were it to be attempted, he thinks Parliament would be justified in abrogating the Constitution and seizing upon the Land Fund for the benefit of the creditors. We are ashamed even to discuss such a question as repudiation by a Government carried on in the name of the Queen, but the word has been uttered in Canada as well as in Australia, and, with the utmost confidence in the upper classes of society in our Colonies, no one can say what the mob, into whose hands the power of Government has fallen, may choose to do with regard to keeping faith with the public creditor. There is no federal machinery to check the downward course of these Colonial democracies. There is no fear of danger from each other or from foreign enemies to force them to entrust the reins of Government to the worthiest and ablest of their citizens. Safe under the ægis of British power, they are relieved from the responsibilities which ordinarily attend on the exercise of self-government. We have endeavoured, though with much reluctance, to point out the magnitude of an evil which it is in vain any longer to palliate or conceal. Enough has been conceded to these elements of confusion; it is time that the Imperial Government should assert itself a little, and try to bring some order out of the chaos which it has created. We are satisfied that, at the rate at which legislation is proceeding at the Antipodes, the veto of the Crown might be very freely and very beneficially exercised. We do not know whether it would be the duty of the Imperial Parliament to interfere on behalf of defrauded creditors who trusted the existing Government and the existing Constitution, but we are quite clear that it would be the duty of the Secretary for the Colonies to veto all laws imposing protective or discriminating duties, proscribing nations at peace with us, like the Chinese, or in any other way infringing the great principles of Imperial policy. The whole subject must before very long force itself on the attention of Parliament, for the evils which we have pointed out are not of a stationary nature, but must go on in a progressive ratio, extending and increasing their baneful influence."

IV.
COLONIAL EXPENDITURE.

TO THE EDITOR OF THE "DAILY NEWS."

SIR,—The burden of defending Canada begins to be felt, and it is urgently demanded that the Colonists shall pay a share of their own military expenses.

Why should not these free communities pay the whole of their own military expenses? They have received the full powers of self-government, why should they not undertake the full duty of self-defence? They enjoy all the substantial attributes of nationality, why should they not bear the same burdens as other nations? If this is the reason of the matter, our people will see in course of time that it is, and at length they will require that it shall be done.

There are no Marquises of Westminster in the Colonies, but the Colonists, on the whole, are far better off than the mass of the people in this country, and they have no national debt on their shoulders. To tax our people for their defence is injustice. Once grasp this solid fact, and chimeras pass away. If rulers could but see it, plain justice comes first, doubtful objects of sentiment must come after. When Government is made to shew a case not of sentiment but of necessity for every tax, there will be some chance of a sound fiscal system.

Not that it is to be allowed that there is no sentiment connected with taxation. When privation enters
the cottage, degradation enters with it. Our labouring
population were brutalized as well as impoverished by
the twenty years' crusade against the French Revolution, the burden of which really fell on them.

Let us be taxed by all means for honour and duty as
well as for interest. But real honour and real duty
escape, while we run after these shadows of " prestige"
and " apparent power." We are now in the midst of
a European crisis on which the destiny of Europe for
centuries may turn, and in which the influence of England ought to be, and, if her power were concentrated,
might be, decisive. But our power is scattered over
the world; we tremble for our own unprotected coasts;
and therefore we proclaim, and affect to exult in pro-
claiming, total non-intervention—we who are so much
afraid, if we emancipate the Colonies, of sinking into
an island.

People may be oppressed by figments as well as by
tyranny. And our people are oppressed by a figment
when some four millions are taken from them in one
year, to keep up the shadow of a rule over Colonies,
which we are so far from really ruling, that we cannot
prevent them from contumeliously levying protective
duties on our own goods.

If the advantages of the Colonial Empire were real,
all the people would share them, though they might not
understand them, as they share the light and warmth of
scientific discoveries of which they have never heard.
But the mere pride of empire, and the pleasure of in-

dulging it, belong only to the imperial class. Can any one suppose that the scanty food of the peasant is sweetened, that the workhouse. in which he too often ends his days is made more cheerful, or that any sort of dignity or comfort is added to his life, because a class to which he does not belong, and the political privileges of which he does not share, exercise a nominal dominion over places of which he has never heard ?

The military expenditure on the whole of the dependencies for the year ending March, 1858, was £3,590,000. The expenditure on the North American Colonies was £473,000; on the West Indies, £384,000; on the Australian Colonies, £340,000. At the Cape we had an army of 10,759 regular troops, and the military expenditure alone was £830,687 [a].

But the year 1857-58 was, as the Committee say, "one of exceptional tranquillity." The military expenses of the Colonies are to be measured not by the force which it is necessary to keep in them in such years, but by Canadian rebellions, by quarrels with America, by difficulties with West India and Cape Colonists, by Kafir and Maori wars. The expenses of the Empire are to be measured by wars and quarrels in every quarter of the globe, from Tahiti to the Baltic, and from St. Juan to Hong Kong.

The military expenses are set down against our dependencies; the naval expenses are overlooked. We have at present on the different American stations alone 32 ships with 650 guns. The total number of ships on

* Report of Committee on Expense of Military Defences in the Colonies, (1860,) pp. 4, 5.

foreign stations is no less than 130. We keep up an immense fleet at an enormous cost; yet we lose the command of the narrow sea which guards our own island, and we live in ignominious fear of seeing the invader borne over our own waters to the invasion of our own shores.

We are told by some that it is not just to charge the Colonial dependencies with the naval expenditure, since if they were made independent " the demands upon our naval force would be rather increased than diminished, from the necessity of protecting our commerce [b]." But why is the commerce to be regarded as ours alone, and not also as that of the countries with which we carry it on? And if it is theirs as well as ours, why should not both parties be equally called upon to protect that which equally concerns the interests of both? That the advantages of trade are reciprocal, and that the duty of defending it is mutual, is surely a very plain and obvious fact; yet it seems to be hidden from the eyes of statesmen, as we see from their arguments and feel by the taxes which they impose on us.

In case of war, be it remembered, the whole of this vast range of unprotected territories must be defended by our arms, and an enemy may draw our forces to any point of it which he thinks fit to threaten. If a petty Colonial garrison in a third-rate fortress is in danger, it must be supported by the forces of the Empire, unless we choose to allow it to surrender, and to suffer a loss of " prestige" indeed.

The money spent on Colonial fortifications and works

[b] Earl Grey, vol. i. p. 43.

must also be included in the account. The sum of £400,000 was spent on fortifications at Corfu, which after all are too extensive to be manned in case of war. Parliament voted large sums for the making of the Rideau Canal in Canada, on the ground that it was a work of Imperial defence. A heavy guarantee for a Canadian railroad is now solicited on the same ground. Even the waste of money in these attempts to stop two or three holes in a sieve is not so bad as the jobbing and roguery which they engender, and the meanness of spirit which they leave behind in the almsmen of the Empire.

The heaviest burden of all, however, is the general character of ostentation and wastefulness which the Empire gives to our Government, and the temptation which it holds out to ambitious Ministers when they cannot win the heart of the nation by good measures at home, to win it by swaggering abroad.

The expedients of a government which thus maintains itself, in default of domestic measures of improvement, by pandering to the lust of imperial aggrandizement and to a passion for bluster usurping the name of glory, are certainly far less coarse, and may by some be thought far less degrading, than those of a government which maintains itself by the vulgar instruments of corruption ; but they cost the people far more money, to say nothing of the blood. Sir Robert Walpole has been called the father of Parliamentary corruption. Yet it would probably be taking a very severe estimate to say that Sir Robert Walpole, in the whole course of

his administration, spent a hundred thousand pounds
in bribes to his supporters; while the unambitious
policy which he pursued, till faction, playing on the
evil passions of the nation, drove him into war, reduced
the National Debt. The reckless invasion of Afghanistan, undertaken by a ministry bankrupt in reputation
at home, in the hope of gaining glory abroad, cost
twenty millions of money, besides the carnage and
the dishonour.

The weight of Canada alone, if we persist in undertaking her defence, is almost enough to drag us down
from our high place among European nations. We
have an army now in that country of 18,000 men, at
a cost of not much less than two millions. Large and
costly as this force is, it is quite incapable of defending
an open frontier of 1,500 miles, and it must be greatly
increased in case war should become imminent. The
whole force required must be kept always on the spot,
since reinforcements cannot be thrown in during a great
part of the year. It must be recruited from a nation
where soldiers are always becoming dearer; supplied
from a great distance with all the munitions of war;
and held together in a country offering high wages to
labourers, and therefore great temptations to desertion.
Besides the land force, a great fleet must be kept
always on the station. Not only so, but flotillas must
be maintained on the chain of frontier lakes sufficient
to keep the command of those lakes against the wealthy,
energetic, and, as we now see, warlike population which
swarms upon the Southern shore. All this must be

done whether we are at peace or at war with the European powers. And we are "the happy nation which has no frontiers!"

Is it possible that with this on our hands we should be able to shew a bold front in European questions, and do our duty as protectors of liberty and right towards the community of nations in which nature has placed us, and to which we belong?

Reason tells us, and experience—long, costly, and decisive experience—proves, that so long as the Mother Country undertakes the defence of the Colonies, the Colonies will not be at the pains and expense of defending themselves. The duty, the necessity, the immense moral advantage of self-defence is inculcated on the Colonists by Colonial Ministers, and Colonial Committees, without end. And the Colonists themselves acknowledge in the most satisfactory terms the truth of the doctrine which is preached to them. So the Church of England each Ash-Wednesday renews the expression of her solemn desire that the wholesome discipline of the primitive Church may be restored. Nevertheless Churchmen do not return to the godly practice of doing open penance, nor do the shrewd and hard-fisted Colonists adopt the laudable course of paying for themselves, when they can get others to pay for them.

The withdrawal of the troops is constantly threatened. Not only so, but the troops are actually withdrawn. The Colonists are not alarmed by this. They know very well that on the first war or rumour of war the red-coats will re-appear. New Zealand was to be left to her own resources: she has now 6,000 British troops engaged in fighting natives or in making roads for her at an expense to the British tax-payer of more than half a million a-year. Good authorities have suggested that this farce had better end, and that the troops had better be established once for all in the Colonies and left there, instead of aggravating the expense by taking up ships, sometimes in a great hurry and at a high rate, to ferry them to and fro between places three months' sail from each other. There would be some moral and political advantages as well as a saving of money in the more open course. The homage paid by the present system to the grand principle of Colonial self-defence is debasing as well as dear.

The Committee on Colonial Defences, while they preach the duty of self-defence to the Colonists, "recognise to the full extent the obligation which devolves upon Great Britain of assisting her Colonies to defend themselves against foreign enemies." The Colonists have the sense to know that so long as they are defended by England against foreign enemies, the maintenance of armaments against other enemies is a work of supererogation. They would shew a want of English sense if they wasted their money during peace in paying an idle tribute to the mere principle of military expenditure, knowing all the time that the armies of England would be at their service in case of war.

It is not in human nature, much less in the nature of very mercantile communities, to undertake the trouble and cost of defending themselves till they know that no one else will defend them. And this the Colonists will not know, or rather they will know the contrary, till the present political connection is dissolved.

The Committee on Colonial Defences[c] discard the argument that "England is bound to contribute towards the defence of her Colonies merely because she is interested in their safety." "It might fairly be argued," they say, "that the obligation is reciprocal, and that the Colonies being deeply interested in the safety of England, ought to contribute systematically and habitually towards the defence of London and Portsmouth." The ground on which they hold that England is bound to contribute towards the defence of her Colonies is "that the Imperial Government has the control of peace and war, and is therefore in honour and duty called upon to assist the Colonists in providing against the consequences of its policy."

It is not altogether true that the Imperial Government has the control of peace and war. The Colonists of New Zealand or of the Cape can get us into a war with the Kafirs or Maoris whenever they see fit. The outsettlers of those Colonies, if they choose to be encroaching and imprudent, can get us into a war. The Canadians can get us into a war by making pic-nic parties over the American frontier to sing 'Dixie' in the face of an agonized and frenzied nation. And the feeling that they have the forces of a great Empire behind them stimulates these young communities, full of hot

[c] Report, p. 8.

G

blood and ignorant of disaster, to indulge in acts of insolence and violence from which, if they were left to their own resources, prudence would soon teach them to abstain : not to mention that war is popular among them, because it makes the money of England fly. "Whoever created the New Zealand difficulty," says Mr. Lowe[d], "we having troops in the Colony, and having undertaken its defence, without reference to the ground upon which the quarrel arose, are bound to do that for which we placed the troops there. That is one evil of placing troops in a Colony under a responsible Government. You are placing the troops at the disposal of the Minister of the day; that is a thunder-bolt in the hand of a child. A large military expenditure is a popular thing in a Colony. Even a war in a remote part of the Colony will be popular in parts where it is not carried on, on account of the money which is made out of it. The country may suffer, but the towns often get a great advantage. I think it is a great want of prudence on the part of the Imperial Government to place the power of commencing wars, in which it will be obliged to take a part, in the hands of persons over whom it not only has no control, but who are often directly interested in getting up a war. And I would also say, that the small Colonies struggling into existence ought not to expect to be able to take things with so high a hand, and to resent every injury as boldly and rapidly as a country like England. If the New Zealand settlers have a quarrel with the

[d] Evidence on Colonial Military Expenditure, May, 27, 1861.

natives, in which the natives are doing anything which
they ought not to do, it may be a perfect *casus belli;*
but I think it much better that war should not necessarily ensue; much better that these young communities should learn that there are many things which
they must endure, and that it is better to put up with
a great deal of injury than rush immediately to arms.
If the Colony had to bear the weight of those conflicts,
it would learn to endure, to procrastinate, to intrigue,
to sow differences among the native chiefs, and practise
all the arts which the weak must exercise when they
deal with the strong; but so long as the wars they
commence must be fought out at the expense of the
Mother Country, there will always be war where there
is a pretext which will hold water. It is neither wise
nor natural that young communities should be armed
with the strength and power of old ones; the tendency
is to make them reckless and overbearing."

It is true, however, that legally in all cases, and
really in most cases, this country has the sole control
of peace and war. And so long as this is the case the
Colonists may not unjustly call upon us to pay for the
military and naval establishments. Are the Colonies
dependencies, or are they free? If they are dependencies they have a right to be protected by the Imperial
nation on which they depend, and which, it must be
taken for granted, finds it her interest to keep them
in a state of dependence. Are they free? Freemen
cannot be required to go to war without their own
consent. We have renounced the power of taxing the
Colonists directly, but we should tax them indirectly if

we compelled them to maintain armaments for the purposes of our policy, and on a scale dictated by our views and pretensions, without giving them a voice in questions of peace and war.

And yet how are we to give the Colonies a voice in questions of peace and war ? How are we to incorporate into our government and "associate with us in universal empire," to use the phrase of an eminent writer, nations separated not only from the seat of our legislature by the ocean, but from our social and political organization by the whole distance which lies between the aristocracy of the Old and the democracy of the New World ?

Some propose to solve this among other problems by reverting to the good old times, and to renew the original relations between the Government of the Mother Country and the Colonies. I fear this is a mere Utopia, having, like many Utopias, its visionary seat in the past. The original relation between the Government of the Mother Country and the New England Colonists was that of tyrant and refugee. The ancient "Art of Colonization," which it is supposed we have lost and may recover, consisted in persecuting the Puritans till they fled to the New World. In what the "Art of Colonization" consisted in the case of the first Australian Colonists we will forbear to say.

That which James I. gave the founders of New England, under the name of a charter, was the inestimable boon of his neglect. It made them the fathers of a great nation. Later governments were more beneficent. They forcibly endowed the Southern

States with the slave trade, the root of the present war. Let us bless Lord North and Mr. Grenville that the war is not on *our* hands.

The scheme of giving the Colonies representatives in our Parliament may be said to have been generally abandoned. Independently of the obstacles arising from distance, from the difference of the franchise in the different countries, and from the hopeless difficulty of settling the proportion between the numbers of the English and the Colonial Members, there is a decisive objection arising from the fact that the Colonies have now Parliaments of their own. Such a piece of political machinery as a set of Parliaments, one of which should be at once national and federal, while all the rest were national only, would scarcely find an advocate even among the defenders of Imperial Unity at all costs.

The other scheme is a vast federation. It is almost enough to say that if there is a federation, there must be a federal Government, and that this federal Government must be made, in the matters belonging to its jurisdiction, supreme over all the national Governments, including the British Crown. We need scarcely discuss in detail the possibility or expediency of summoning from the ends of the earth people who could not be convoked in less than six months, to decide whether England should go to war upon some question solely affecting herself, and not admitting perhaps of an hour's delay. The German Confederation has been cited as an example of the federal union proposed. In the German Confederation the Diet, in the matters belonging to it, is supreme over all the national Governments;

and the Germans on the Danube are not three months'
sail from the Germans on the Rhine.

Do not these schemes of "universal empire" and a
universal state, of which we and our antipodes are to be
citizens, spring, in part, from an exaggerated estimate of
the moral grandeur to be derived from enormous political
combinations? A political unity is not a moral unity,
nor will moral grandeur be gained by stretching it till
it bursts. If people want a grand moral unity, they
must seek it in the moral and intellectual sphere. Religion knows no impediment of distance. The dominions
of science are divided by no sea. To restore, or to pave
the way for restoring, the unity of long-divided Christendom, may seem the most chimerical of all aspirations,
yet perhaps it may be less chimerical than the project
of founding a world-wide state.

To cast the Colonies off suddenly, rudely, and without
regard for their safety, is what no one has proposed.
In emancipating those among them which are adult
and fit to be nations, we might guarantee their independence against unprovoked aggression for a certain
term of years. By the end of that term they would be,
or ought to be, ready to defend themselves.

At all events "kill us in the light." Let us know
on what principle we are proceeding. *The Times* per-
mits us to believe that there will come a period when
it will be better for both parties that the Colonies
should set up for themselves, and it only forbids us to
foresee that period and provide for its coming. The
Colonial Minister, on the contrary, seems to regard the
present connexion as perpetual, or at least as indefinite.

This is a question on which the greatest " statesman," and the most averse from " thinking," need not be ashamed to have made up his mind, especially as it seems we are still sinking money in Colonial fortifications. But our statesmen, peerless in integrity, in dignity of character, in administrative capacity, have also been almost peerless in their want, or rather their contempt, of foresight. In this matter, as in others, they will " drift." They will hold every Colony, however completely it may have outgrown dependence, till they lose it, as they lost the United States, by a rupture or some other calamity; and they will hold every point, however useless and untenable, in the vast strategical position constituted by our military dependencies, till they lose it in disastrous war.

I am, &c.,

GOLDWIN SMITH.

March 7, 1862.

V.

COLONIAL TRADE.

Sir,—Allow me to call your attention to the following paragraph of an article in *The Times* of Tuesday last on the subject of our trade. Its reference to the present controversy and its purpose are sufficiently obvious.

"Our best customers, beyond all comparison, are our own Colonies. One-third and upwards of our entire business is done with them. They took from us last year goods to the value of £42,000,000, our whole exports being computed at £125,000,000. India stands for £16,000,000, Australia for £10,000,000, and British North America for £3,000,000. Together, these three customers represent £30,000,000, out of the £42,000,000, and their purchases have been but slightly affected by the disturbances of the year. In fact, the Australian trade shews an actual increase of a million. From this beginning we go through a long catalogue of more than twenty names till we come to Heligoland, which expends in our markets about £300 a-year. Without this list our trade would dwindle to comparatively small proportions, and the fact may be held to count for something in our political estimate of these dependencies. It will be replied, however, that all these countries would deal with us still, even if they were not our Colonies; and we do not deny that evidence to that effect might be gathered from the tables before us. Foreign West Indies, for instance, deal with us still more largely than British West Indies. Java is an excellent customer—better, in fact, than Austria; and the Colonies of Portugal buy of us freely. But it is not too much to say that the custom of our Colonists is rather more secure than the custom of foreigners, and that the trade, for example, of India or Australia is not likely to be reduced by 50 per cent. in the course of a few months, as that of the United States has been. Our Colonial traffic forms a solid nucleus of business, round which the proportion of foreign trade may either shrink or expand."

I beg leave to point to this paragraph as a specimen of the manner in which dust may be thrown in the eyes of the public by the advocates of an enormous and unproductive expenditure, and as a justification of the attempt to rouse the nation from apathetic acquiescence to active reflection on the subject.

" Our best customers, beyond all comparison, are our own Colonies." The proof given of this is that *one*-third of our entire business is done with them. They, it seems, are better customers than those with whom we do the *two*-thirds.

Of the one-third set down to the credit of the Colonies, two-fifths belong to India, which is not a Colony, but only a dependency, differing from a Colony in this among other essential respects, that it pays, or is meant to pay, its own expenses.

We are told that the export trade to Australia has increased, but we are not told that the export trade to the North American Colonies is declining, as I have shewn in a former letter that it is.

The obvious cause of the increase of exports to the Australian Colonies is, that the group of markets in Australia has been actually undergoing numerical extension, not to mention the discoveries of gold: while, as new communities, those Colonies have necessarily for the time to import every description of manufacture. The case of North America shews that a long settled Colony beginning to manufacture for itself is not necessarily a good customer at all.

Are we altogether far-sighted in rejoicing with unmixed joy over the sudden and almost fabulous growth of a special trade, which gives our industry an abnormal development in a particular direction, and which, arising to a great extent out of the temporary wants of our customers, may hereafter fail or decline, and leave our merchants and manufacturers in the lurch?

It is to be observed, too, that the Colonists have a strong propensity to the commercial vice of Protection. They have shewn this evil tendency not only in Canada, but, *The Times* itself being witness, in Australia also. There are two reasons for this. In the first place, Protection is the natural resort of ignorant cupidity, and ignorant cupidity is the besetting sin of communities intensely commercial and wanting in education. In the second place, these communities are excessively impatient of direct taxation, and therefore

if their taxes are high, heavy import duties are the
inevitable result. Their taxes must be high while
their public expenditure is extravagant; and the extravagance of their public expenditure arises in part,
as has been shewn before, from their being inoculated
by us with the system of central Government, and the
abuses which, under their social circumstances, central
Government entails.

We will say nothing of the mercantile morality characteristic of commercial Colonies in the wild heyday
of their gambling youth, or of the danger of repudiation looming in Australia, which a short time ago
caused frightened capital to sound its note of alarm
in *The Times.*

To save the remnant of a plea for keeping up the
present Colonial system on commercial grounds, it is
suggested that " the custom of our Colonists is rather
more secure than the custom of foreigners, and that
the trade, for example, of India or Australia, is not
likely to be reduced by fifty per cent. in the course of
a few months, as that of the United States has been."
The export trade to the North American Colonies fell
from £5,980,000 in 1854 to £2,885,000 in 1855, or
rather more than fifty per cent.

We do not by keeping the Colonies in a state of
dependence guarantee them against disasters affecting their trade. We have not been able to guarantee
Canada itself against the disaster of civil war. It can
scarcely be supposed that if the old American Colonies
were now under our nominal dominion we should be
able to prevent the conflict between the free North

and the slave-owning South which causes the sudden fall of our export trade to that country. On the other hand, we artificially expose all these communities to disasters affecting their trade by gratuitously involving them in our wars. If they were independent, their trade with us would still be respected as that of neutrals though this country were at war.

In face of the sudden fall in the export trade to North America in 1855, and in face of the general decline of that trade, notwithstanding the rapid and steady increase of the population of those countries, it is idle to say that the "solidity" of a trade depends on anything but its reciprocal advantages. The Colonist does not trade with us because he is a Colonist, but because at present he can get what he wants better and cheaper from us than from other merchants. If he is conveniently content at present, as *The Times* boasts, to take from us "English. eatables and drinkables though sometimes far from delicate or wholesome," we may be sure that his necessity, and not his patriotism, is the cause. And we may be sure that an export trade in unwholesome eatables, or any other kind of trash, though it may go on merrily for a time, and make the merchants who ply it much in love with the "noble fabric" of the Colonial system, will prove a treacherous and failing trade.

If the Colonists are Englishmen in character and habits, they are rather more likely, other things being equal, to take to English departments of industry; and if they take to English departments of industry, they are less likely to want English products. Dissimilarity

of character is, to a certain extent, a promoter of trade
as well as of love. If France were inhabited by Englishmen, the climate and the soil remaining as they are,
the trade between the two countries would probably be
less brisk than it is.

The best of all trades is the home trade with the
butcher and baker, which cheap Governments foster,
and Governments of Imperial aspirations bring to decay. The next best trade is that with neighbouring
countries, because in that trade the expense of carriage
is not great, and the state of supply and demand are
certainly known. The worst is that with distant countries like Australia, because the carriage is expensive
and the speculations are hazardous. But the distant
and hazardous trade employs great merchants, and
therefore it is more considered and has more power
in the State.

In ancient times Empire was Empire. The Roman
extorted from his dependencies both military force and
revenue. Spain extorted revenue. We are too moral
to extort either force or revenue from our dependencies
even if we had the power. While we monopolised their
trade in a general reign of monopoly, they brought us
a real advantage, though of a narrow and selfish kind.
Now they bring us no advantage at all. But the system
has been established, many prejudices and some interests are bound up with it, and reasons must be found
or invented for maintaining it. The reasons found or
invented are, as might be expected, various and discordant enough. Now it is the amount of the Colonial
trade; now it is the security of the Colonial trade;

now it is the preference of our people for the Colonies as places of emigration. When facts overturn all these arguments, it is glory, national spirit, *prestige*. I give an agent an immense sum of money to invest for me. He tells me that he has bought me an estate. I ask to see the estate: he tells me that the money is laid out not in an estate but in houses. I ask to see the houses: he tells me that it is laid out not in houses but in railway shares. I ask for my scrip: he tells me that it is not laid out in railway shares but invested in the Funds. I ask for the transfer receipt; and he tells me that it is not invested in the Funds but in something much better and nobler, in *prestige*. I look in the French dictionary for *prestige*, and find that it is " an illusion, a juggling trick, an imposture."

I am, &c.,

Goldwin Smith.

March 14, 1862.

VI.
CANADA.

TO THE EDITOR OF THE "DAILY NEWS."

SIR,—If any Canadians have been offended, as it appears some have been, by my first letter to you on the subject of Colonial Emancipation, it is the fault of *The Times*, not mine. I send to you, whose motto is open councils, a letter obviously intended as a contribution to English discussion, but which, when read entire, could not be thought disparaging to the Colonists. *The Times*, being apprehensive lest my remarks should do mischief at "Quebec and Montreal," "draws the letter from its obscurity," and calls the particular attention of the people of Quebec and Montreal to the passages which it thinks likely to offend them. I confess once more that I do not wish to flatter the Canadians. I have no wish to cajole them into a military expenditure beyond their means and against their interests. It would gratify no antipathies of mine.

My first thought, I allow, was justice to the English people, who maintain, by the sweat of their brow, that "noble fabric," as *The Times* calls it, of reckless and useless expenditure, which the ambition of former days reared, and the blindness of these days upholds. A Quebec journal tells me that "my God is Mammon." My neighbour tells me that my God is Mammon, because, when he is better off than I am, I do not wish to pay his rates. Our statesmen need not fear to encounter the reproach of Mammon-worship from the Colonists or anyone else when public money is to be saved. A wealthy Italian, long noted for his splendid liberality, all at once turned miser, and became by his sordid parsimony the object of general wonder and of general scorn ; but at last, with the savings of that parsimony, he paid the public debt of his city, and with her solvency restored her greatness. The reproach of Mammon-worship did not attend his name.

Even the reproach of being unwarlike would not attach to the policy of a minister who should take the side of economy and reason. This extravagance, spirited and vigorous as it may seem, not only diminishes the comforts of our people in peace, but cuts beforehand the sinews of just war.

To do justice to the English people is the first duty not only of English writers but of English statesmen, whose sense of "responsibility" in this matter seems sometimes to range a little too far from home.

But my argument is that timely separation, while it is good for both parties, is especially good for the Colonists. They have a fresh start in the world, with a heritage of modern liberty and civilization, unencumbered by the feudalism which still presses, and will long continue to press, on the energies of the Mother Country. Their destiny, as it is the last gift of Providence, is probably higher than ours, if they will only go forward like men to meet it, instead of clinging, like frightened children, to the skirts of the Old World.

What is it that the Canadians hope to gain by remaining a province? What is it that they fear to lose by becoming a nation?

We have given them all that we really have to give —our national character, our commercial energy, our aptitude for law and government, our language, with all the stores of wisdom and beauty which it contains, the memory of an illustrious origin, and a bond of affection which will not lose its force when the Governor General ceases to exercise his nominal rule. We have given them the essence of our constitution—free legislation, self-taxation, ministerial responsibility, personal liberty, trial by jury. The accidents of that constitution—the relics of the feudal mould in which it was wrought—we can no more give them than we can give them our history or our skies. Do they, or any of them, desire an hereditary aristocracy? Then they must be prepared to accept the necessary basis of an hereditary aristocracy—primogeniture and great settled estates, with waste, neglect, absenteeism, and pauperism in their train. An aristocracy without acres would soon prove anything but an august institution or an element of political stability. I find it difficult to soar to the poetic conception of a fire-new Canadian monarchy, with Colonial lords of the bedchamber and ladies in waiting; but I find it still more difficult to soar to the conception of a Canadian peerage, with the Duke of Montreal, the third perhaps from the creation of the title, begging like Belisarius for an obolus, or whistling on a costermonger's cart.

Again, the Canadians possess what is essential in

H

our religion. Do they or any of them wish to import our ecclesiastical institutions, with Bishops sitting in Parliament, and with Ecclesiastical Courts to enforce Church authority in matters of opinion, and to bring men to trial for writing what they believe to be the truth? Does not the very mention of these things at once remind us that ages as well as oceans lie between the feudal civilization in Church and State, and that of which the Colonies are born the heirs?

Or, to descend from these refined and airy speculations to those which are more vulgar and substantial, do the Canadians hope that this country will always go on paying for their army and navy? If they do, I believe they hope too much from the sufferance even of the English people. And when the inevitable hour arrives, and England looks to herself, the withdrawal of her protection will leave the Canadians defenceless indeed, since they will never have learnt self-defence. The Committee on the Expenses of Military Defences in the Colonies regard it as a great objection to the present system that it "throws an enormous burden on the people of England, not only by the addition which it makes to their taxes, but by calling off to remote stations a large proportion of their troops and ships, and thereby weakening their means of defence at home." But they regard it as a still greater objection that the system "prevents the development of a proper spirit of self-reliance amongst the Colonists and enfeebles their national character." "By the gift of political self-government," proceed the Committee, "we have bestowed on our Colonies a most important element of national education; but the habit of self-defence constitutes a part hardly less important of the training of a free people, and it will never be acquired by our Colonists if we assume exclusively the task of defending them *." If this is the truth, surely it is truth of a practical kind.

If, then, the Canadians have nothing to hope from continuing a dependency, have they anything to fear from becoming a nation?

That their trade with us would not suffer they know, not only from the reason of the case, but from the decisive example of the Independent States, whose trade with this country has rapidly increased from the first hour of their independence.

They dread annexation to the United States. But I submit that their greatest, and in fact their only, danger of being annexed arises from their position as a dependency of England. That England will some day get into a war with the Americans is only too probable, were it only from the antipathy which our aristocracy naturally feel to the model republic, and which has so signally broken forth since the commencement of the civil war. And in case of a war between England and the Americans, Canada, as an outlying dependency of England, would no doubt be placed in jeopardy. But is there any reasonable ground for presuming that the American people are so extravagantly ambitious and so outrageously profligate as, without provocation, to invade and annex an independent nation?

* Report, p. 4.

The slave-owning republican of the United States was domineering and aggressive; like those slave-owning republicans of ancient times whose example, though quite irrelevant (since they were in fact aristocrats of the most exclusive kind), has brought the reproach of rapacity upon freedom. All such communities are sure to be domineering and aggressive, because in them the homes of the ruling class are a school of tyrannical passion, and the idle population is always ready for war or piracy, scorning honest labour, which is the badge of the slave. But whatever may be the issue of the civil war, it can scarcely end in restoring the ascendency of the slave-owner and his propensities over the politics of the North. The Northern people are brave, full of power, and formidable if provoked. But, to say nothing of the restraints imposed on their passions by their morality or their religion, they are an industrious race, among whom labour is had in honour, who cannot afford themselves to leave their callings for war, and are too frugal to bear the expense of standing armies to fight for them. Such people may of course be goaded into war, and even into conquest, by insulting them and making military demonstrations on their frontier: but it is not likely that, if they are left to themselves, their military ambition will ever disturb the world.

Even in the days of the Union the influence of the free North, though it was excluded from the Government, was strong enough in the nation to curb the buccaneering propensities which the South shewed in its piratical attacks on Cuba and on other occasions.

And supposing the Americans to be bent on the annexation, could England undertake ultimately to prevent it? We are now able to spare a large force for Canada, because we have no other enemy on our hands. But the day may come when we shall be engaged in a death struggle with some European nation. And shall we then be able to keep a great army in Canada, a flotilla on her lakes, and a fleet upon her coast? Are not the Canadians leaning on a bruised reed if they rest their national existence on the support of a Power divided from them by the Atlantic, and with many enemies of its own?

I rather doubt the judgment of the Canadians in these matters, because I see that some of them are animated by a childish antipathy to the Americans. Their reliance on the protection of England encourages them to give vent to this antipathy, which may some day lead them into acts of folly, and consequently into disaster.

The fear generally expressed is that of American aggression. But, on the other hand, Canadians sometimes speak as though, from moral or geographical attraction, they were themselves gravitating towards the adjoining confederacy with a centripetal force beyond their own control; and as though they were looking to us to arrest their course. In that case it can only be said, Are we gods that we should be able to arrest for ever the force of gravitation?

Do the Canadians renounce the hope of ever being a nation? Have they written on the opening page of their history the sentence of perpetual dependence?

If they have not, when will the day of independence
arrive? what will be the signs of its coming? If
population is the test, the population of the British
Colonies in North America, which are plainly destined
to form a united confederation, already exceeds that
of Switzerland, and equals that of Holland, countries
whose independence is not doubtful, and whose names
are not unknown to fame. If wealth is the test, we
are assured by the Canadians that their wealth is such
as to afford us a complete security in backing their
undertakings with the heaviest guarantees. If the
gifts and qualities of the people are the test, let
the Colonists look on the work of their own hands in
the country which they inhabit, and assure themselves
that the gifts and qualities of the English race are in
full measure theirs.

That the Canadians should be a separate nation from
the Americans seems a thing manifestly to be desired,
not only for their own sake but for that of the Americans themselves, who have shewn only too plainly that
they stand in need of the lessons which nations, like
men, derive from the society of their equals. This
seems so; though I am aware that we may be too hasty
in reasoning from that which has been in the Old to
that which is destined to be in the New World. But
it is idle to think that Canada can be made a part of
Europe. Let us see a Canadian dollar. Whose image
and superscription has it? Those of England or those
of America? And ask the holder of Grand Trunk
shares, or of Hamilton bonds, whether the people of
the country in which that dollar circulates are so very

different in point of commercial morality as they imagine from their neighbours of New York.

Not that the character either of the Canadians or of the Americans ought to be judged exclusively by their commercial morality. A lax commercial morality is, in effect, the barbarism of a young commercial nation. The progress of civilization will introduce nobler objects of pursuit than money, which at first it is every Colonist's natural business to make, and assuage that craving desire to grow suddenly rich, from which wild speculation and profligate repudiation spring.

If the interest of the Canadians, as well as ours, is on the side of separate government, and if they are fit for independence, they would be no more "discarded" by being made a nation than the heir is discarded when he comes of age and assumes the liberty and responsibility of a man. And, if I am told that it is strange and ungracious to propose separation at a moment when the Canadians are so loyal, my answer is, that I believe no greater or nobler boon can be given them than independence, and that no time can be better for bestowing that boon than one of perfect mutual confidence and affection.

I am, &c.
GOLDWIN SMITH.
March 21, 1862.

VII.
THE CANADIAN MILITIA BILL.

TO THE EDITOR OF THE "DAILY NEWS."

SIR,—No doubt you are right in saying that *The Times* has put an exaggerated construction on the act of the Canadian Legislature in throwing out the Militia Bill. No doubt those who voted against the Bill intended to condemn the particular measure and beat the Government, not to renounce the duty of self-defence. Still, this event proves that the Canadians are in no hurry to arm. It proves that they do not respond to the desire of certain classes in this country who wish to take up an aititude of hostility towards the United States. It proves, I venture to think, that Canadian enthusiasm, however strong its manifestations may have been, would be but a frail support to lean upon in case of an American war. England is an European aristocracy, Canada is an American democracy; it is vain to hope that they will be one in love and hatred, and always act perfectly together.

The Times rates the Canadians as if they were fractious and ignorant children. But the truth is, they see through fictions, and act on the real facts of the case. As a nation they are in no danger. As a dependency, they have a right to be protected by the country on which they are dependent.

It is idle to tell them, as *The Times* does, that if we get them into a war with America, we shall not be able, with our limited population and burdened resources, to send them troops enough to carry the war on. They know very well, and they act upon the knowledge, that we must, at whatever cost, save our troops in the Colony from defeat, and that the presence of a single red-coat pledges the forces of the Empire.

The Times has at last opened its own eyes, though I fear it has hopelessly closed those of the nation, to the fact that the American Republic, though it may miscarry with untrained soldiers (as the English aristocracy has repeatedly miscarried with trained soldiers) at the beginning of a war, is, when fairly roused to arms, a powerful antagonist; and that we have reason to fear lest the surge of the great tempest now raging in the States should strike the neighbouring British possessions with formidable force. The truth is, if we are to indulge our aristocratic antipathies to the Americans, and to hold the enormous extent of Canadian frontier against their armies and flotillas, we shall need not only the 18,000 men already on the spot, but three times that number at their back. We shall have, in short, to devote our available force to that object alone, and to give up our vote in the councils of the European powers.

The English aristocracy have been led to repose in the belief that, by the great qualities inherent in aristocracies, they would certainly beat the American Republic. Their minds are filled with the glorious memory of their twenty years' struggle against Revolutionary France. But they, and those who rely on their support, ought to recollect that, in those days, an unreformed Parliament gave them an absolute control over the resources of the country, which they, in truth, expended with unwavering constancy and indomitable courage. Their own taxes, and those of their tenants, and of the clergy who were their allies, were mainly paid back in the high rents and high tithes which arose from the strict "protection" given by the war. The constancy of an aristocracy would be put to a severer trial at the present day. I doubt whether it would even get over such reverses as were encountered during the early part of the Revolutionary war, before the enthusiastic energy of the French Republic had been quenched by the selfish despotism of the Empire. And, be it remembered, an unsuccessful war against the great Republic of the New World might quicken the march of events in the Old. Even the disasters of the Crimean war caused a movement of opinion which must have given a warning to all minds not incapable of admitting unwelcome truth.

The Times has found an ally (and may find an example of courtesy towards opponents) in Mr. Rose, an eminent member of the Canadian legislature, who has made an able speech in favour of the present connexion. But what says Mr. Rose? "We know," he says, "that be the cause of rupture with America what it may, the horrors of war will be at our doors; that whatever the issue be, we must be the sufferers, and can by no possibility be the gainers. We know also by experience that Canada may have no concern or interest in the quarrel, except as an integral portion of the Empire. What was the question of the right of search to us? What interest had we in Ruatan? What in the Oregon boundary? What in the enlistment question? What in the Island of St. Juan? What in European interference in Mexico? What, save indeed as British subjects interested in the honour of our flag, in the 'Trent' affair?" On the other hand, *The Times*, moralizing on recent events, said, "If Canada had not been a British possession, there would have been no reviling of England, no warlike demonstrations against England, and no outrages committed on the English flag." So that, according to the advocates of dependency both in Canada and England, the system which they maintain is fraught with the danger, to each party, of gratuitous and desperate war.

Surely, then, it was not fatuous, nor, in the present state of what *The Times* calls "the great American volcano," premature, to propound for serious consideration the question whether this danger to both parties is countervailed by any advantages to either.

As to England, I have more than once before quoted the avowal of *The Times*, that "we derive no single advantage from Canada which we do not equally derive in time of peace from the United States." In its article on the Canadian Militia Bill *The Times* says:—"Opinion in England is perfectly decided that in the connexion between the Mother Country and the Colony the advantage is infinitely more on the side of the child than of the parent. We no longer monopolise the trade of the Colonies; we no longer job their patronage; we

cannot hope from them any assistance for defending
our own shores, while we are bound to assist in protecting theirs. We cannot even obtain from this very
Colony of Canada reasonably fair treatment for our
manufactures, which are taxed 25 per cent. on their
value, to increase a revenue which the Colonies will
not apply to our, or even to their own defence. There
is little reciprocity in such a relation."

As to Canada, *The Times* in its present article says:—
"The finances of the Province are in an exceedingly
embarrassed and discouraging state. The revenue is
diminished, partly no doubt by the calamity of the
American war, but partly by an injudicious Protection
policy, which has straitened the income without de-
veloping the resources of the Colony. The expenditure
is enormous, inflated by a succession of jobs, by which
Parliamentary support has been purchased for embarrassed Ministries. At the time when the Colony is
called upon to incur heavy expenses for the support of
its militia, the revenue is estimated in round numbers
at 7,000,000 dollars, and the expenditure at 12,000,000
dollars, leaving a deficit of 5,000,000 dollars to be
supplied by fresh taxation or by loans." Such are the
political fruits of the present system. It would seem
that if Canadian monarchy differs from American democracy, as painted by its worst enemies, it is only as
the Irishman's ride in a sedan chair with the bottom
out differed from common walking. The truth is, as
I have before endeavoured to shew, that the nominal
tutelage of the British Crown aggravates the improvi-
dence of these young communities, by masking from

them the necessity of self-control : while their connexion
with the Imperial exchequer, lending them false credit
and facilitating their extravagant undertakings, does
them all the mischief which the presumed intentions
of a wealthy relative do to a spendthrift boy. The
evil is increasing, as the figures given by *The Times*
prove. But "practical wisdom" naturally hopes that,
provided we only avoid "thinking," we shall "drift"
through the indefinite continuance of evil into good.

Leave the Canadians to themselves, and experience
will soon teach them to struggle against their own
political infirmities, to take care of their own money,
to provide for their own defence, and to avoid giving
unnecessary provocation to a powerful neighbour when
she is (not unnaturally) in a rather irritable mood.
But, as Mr. Adderley says, "England was not herself
nursed or dandled into her present vigour." Neither
into her present vigour, nor into her present sense.

It seems a question whether, in their present financial condition, the Canadians may not, in answer to
the objurgations of *The Times*, plead simple inability
to contribute effectively to their own defence. Evidently
they are not capable of sustaining the expense of a
long war.

Mr. Rose, in his speech, does me the honour to combat my arguments in favour of timely separation. He
meets them mainly by an appeal to higher considerations than those of expediency, to which he thinks I
am too much bound. " Are great national questions,"
he exclaims, " to be tried by the mere test of the
balance-sheet ?" And he proceeds to ask me " whether

I care nothing for the power and greatness of England—nothing for the dishonour which would attach to the Throne by throwing off loyal and grateful subjects, or, what is the same thing, leaving them unprotected, because the responsibility incident to the acquisition of dominion cannot be borne without expense?"

I answer that I have not based my arguments on the mere "balance-sheet," but on the highest interests of both nations; and that in matters political, as distinguished from those which are moral or religious, I apprehend that interest must be considered, and that sentiment divorced from expediency will not be long-lived. The power and greatness of England, I trust, are not to me matters of indifference; and my reason for objecting to this sham "Empire," with its Canadian frontiers and its islands of St. Juan, is that it is eating out the heart of our real greatness.

As to the claims of "loyal and grateful subjects," let us, at whatever risk of dissipating agreeable fictions, look facts in the face. The loyal and grateful subjects of Her Majesty in Canada lay heavy protective duties on the subjects of Her Majesty in England. I do not blame the Canadians for regulating, as they think fit, their separate interests. But that they have interests separate from ours, is a proof that they are not a part of the same nation. The Colonial Minister of Her Majesty remonstrates against a policy so hostile to the interests and opposed to the general system of the Empire. The Canadians not only make him strike his flag, but warn him not to interpose again, on pain of future complications. Is this—let me ask the Eng-

lish advocates of "empire"—is this empire or humiliation?

As to our leaving the Canadians "unprotected," the
answer is that which I have given before—their artificial connexion with us is the sole source of their danger.
The Times says :—" It is not in our power to send forth
from this little island a military force sufficient to
defend the frontiers of Canada against the numerous
armies which have learnt arms and discipline in the
great school of the present civil war. Our resources
are unequal to so large a concentration of force on
a single point ; our empire is too vast, our population
too small, *our antagonist is too powerful.*"

" The generous sympathies of kindred communities,"
on which Mr. Rose afterwards dwells, will live, I trust,
as long as the communities are kindred; and the communities will not cease to be kindred when the Governor
General is withdrawn. But is not "sympathy" in some
danger when an ostensible identity of interest is accompanied by a real divergence, and when the different
policy which follows a diverging interest calls down
such ratings as that which the Canadians have just received from *The Times?*

With "the vague but generous desire to spread our
religion and civilization over the world," which Mr.
Rose, quoting with applause the words of Mr. Herman
Merivale, puts forward as a reason for continuing the
union, I have endeavoured before to deal. We have
spread already that part of our religion and civilization
which is capable of being spread. The Colonists have
our freedom and our Christianity; our feudalism and

our State Church they cannot have. The English
Colonies in the New World are simply the last of that
long series of migrations through which, in the course
of Providence, not only has the human race been spread
over the earth, but the drama of history has been unfolded. In that drama Providence does not repeat the
scenes. The migrations of the Puritans to New England
were the final exodus of humanity from feudalism in
the State and "authority" in the Church. That the
privileged classes and the clergy of the old feudal
nations should be slow in recognising this fact is not
wonderful. Nevertheless, so it is, and so it must be.
We must leave this new plant to grow as nature has
planted it, and bring forth fruits to the world after
its kind. Mr. Rose and *The Times* call my views "anti-
Colonial." If the writers in *The Times*, and the class
whom those writers represent, appreciated the value
of the Colonies as deeply as I do, perhaps they would
love them less.

Mr. Rose quotes with admiration the opinions of
aristocratic statesmen, who dolefully portend that upon
the removal of their nominal tutelage from the Colonies, "anarchy" will ensue. He complains of my
"taunting" the Canadians. I have used no "taunt"
so bitter as this. I must own, however, that Mr. Rose
takes up an impregnable position when, in a question
of political philosophy and economy, he appeals from
"the theories of philosophers and political economists"
to the "political views expressed by those who are responsible for their opinions as directing the national
policy." He may well place unlimited confidence in

the practical wisdom of English statesmen to which he here appeals. At the outset of their disastrous war with the American Colonies Adam Smith pointed out to them the absurdity of the system for which they were fighting, in language which it is startling now to read. But Adam Smith was a "philosopher," and a "political economist." "Practical wisdom" is that wisdom which will learn of nothing but practical disaster, and destiny seems now to be preparing for it a lesson of no ordinary kind.

I am, &c.,

GOLDWIN SMITH.

June 9, 1862.

VIII.

THE DEBATES ON THE CANADIAN MILITIA BILL.

TO THE EDITOR OF THE "DAILY NEWS."

SIR,—In my second letter to you on Colonial Emancipation, a fear was expressed that unless the question was dealt with promptly and in the right way, we should have a quarrel with our great Colony; and that England would forfeit the glory of being the first to confer independent existence on a daughter nation. That fear seems likely to prove true.

What right, I would ask, has the Prime Minister of this country to call the Opposition in the Canadian Parliament "factious" because they throw out the Government, or to style the conflict of parties there "a factious conflict"? Has he never, as a leader of Opposition in the English Parliament, been guilty of the same kind of "faction"? Did he never, for instance, take advantage of a question about a Militia Bill to overthrow a Government which had ousted him from place? Why should not the Canadian Parliament have its parties, its party objects, and its party struggles as well as ours?

We profess to have given the Canadians independence. We claim their gratitude for the gift.

They exercise that independence in determining what is and what is not necessary for the defence of their own frontiers. They apprehend no danger at present, and therefore they refuse to waste their money in armaments and throw out the Militia Bill. They use the same opportunity to get rid of an unpopular and, as they declare, very corrupt Government. If they are not to be permitted to do this, in what do their Parliamentary liberties consist?

Our ministers, no doubt, are left in an embarrassing position. When they despatched their forces to Canada they expected, it seems, to produce a great moral effect by a grand military demonstration against the Americans. But they had no assurance beyond vague expressions of loyal enthusiasm that the Canadian Parliament would join them in that demonstration. On the contrary, they knew that the Canadian finances were in a desperate condition, and that the Colony could not bear the expense of an armament. The dilemma in which they are placed is an awkward one. Their vexation is natural. But the simple and rational course is, as the Canadians decline to contribute their contingent to the proposed armament, to withdraw ours. Nothing but mischief, perhaps most serious mischief, will be done by bullying the Canadian Parliament, and attempting to coerce them in the exercise of their independent functions.

As has been before pointed out, the Canadians would be virtually deprived to a great extent of the right of self-taxation if they were compelled to find forces as often as we might think fit, in the course of our diplo-

macy, to create the danger and the need. With our
past experience, we shall not commit the same blunder
over again in the same form, but may we not commit
the same blunder over again in a somewhat different
form? We shall not bring on a rupture with the
Canadians, as we did with the American Colonies, by
attempting to tax them; but may we not bring on
a rupture with them by attempting to force them to
tax themselves?

We have solemnly renounced the right of taxing
the Colonists. But people are in effect taxed whenever the money is taken out of their pockets without
their own consent, no matter by how indirect or subtle
a process. Chatham drew what he fancied to be an
important distinction between the right of taxation
and that of legislation: and he included under the
right of legislation restrictions laid in the interest of
the Mother Country on the Colonial manufactures and
trade. He declared that you could not levy a Stamp-tax
without violating the indefeasible rights of Englishmen, and justifying a rebellion. But he held that you
were warranted in forbidding the Colonists to make
a nail for a horseshoe, in order that you might sell
them nails at a rate above the fair price: as though
this were not a tax on nails [a].

We can smile at this; but would not the practice
of making the Canadians pay a tribute in the shape of
armaments to the antipathies of our aristocracy, be as

[a] See the remarks of Mr. S. S. Bell, On the Administration of the
Colonies, pp. 60, 61.

great a breach of their privileges as the practice of making them pay tribute in the shape of dear horse-nails to the cupidity of our merchants?

We see from this debate in what a wood we are wandering when we attempt to carry on a system which is neither that of acknowledged independence nor of real subjection, a system under which the Colonists are bidden to think and act for themselves, but expected always to think and act with us.

The Canadian rebellion sprang, in a great degree, from the same unwillingness of our statesmen to face the fact that in giving free Parliaments to Colonies they had given Parliamentary freedom.

The want of clear views and of a clear principle of action on this subject may be traced in the language even of our most enlightened and liberal statesmen. Lord Grey, for instance [b], says that "it seems to have been overlooked by those who would adopt without any qualification the rule that the Colonies should be left to govern themselves, that this would in some cases imply leaving a dominant minority to govern the rest of the community without check or control." What does Lord Grey think of the unchecked and un-controlled freedom of the English Parliament? Does not a dominant party here govern the rest of the com-munity? And may not that dominant party be, under the present conditions of the franchise and with the present distribution of seats, not only a minority, but a small minority of the whole nation?

[b] Vol. i. p. 22.

The political tie between the two nations is, as
"Hochelaga" says, "as weak as a silken thread for good,
and as strong as adamant for evil." This tie has now
been strained almost to snapping. Drawn different
ways by our divergent interests, and by divergent
feelings, we have quarrelled about taxes, and we have
quarrelled about armaments. Unless wisdom step in,
in the shape of some statesmen who will look facts in
the face, we shall part in anger, and there will be
another disastrous schism in the Anglo-Saxon race.
The existence of two independent legislatures under
one crown was found intolerable in the case of England and Ireland, and the most extreme measures were
taken by Mr. Pitt to put an end to that state of things.
Yet Ireland was not divided from England by an
ocean, nor was the society which the Irish Parliament
represented radically different in its character and tendencies from ours. In the case of Ireland the obvious
remedy for the evil of discordant Parliaments was an
incorporating union. In the case of Canada, an incorporating union being impossible, the obvious and only
remedy is complete political separation. Political separation will preserve, and it alone will preserve, the tie
of nature and affection.

Sir G. C. Lewis, who has thought deeply and written
well on these subjects, looks forward to separation without regret, though, like most of our statesmen, he seems
inclined rather to drift to that issue than to prepare for
it. Lord Palmerston tells us that separation will be
a calamity both to the Mother Country and to the
Colony; but he gives us no reasons for his opinion.

The questions touching the relation between the Mother Country and the Colonies are becoming numerous and urgent. By which of the two opposite principles thus enunciated by our statesmen at the same time is our policy to be governed?

I am, &c.,

GOLDWIN SMITH.

July 26, 1862.

IX.

ENGLAND AND CANADA.

TO THE EDITOR OF THE "DAILY NEWS."

SIR,—Now is the crisis of this question. It must now be determined whether English statesmen will control events, or, as in a case fresh in terrible memory, " drift" upon their current to some disastrous issue. I ask your permission, then, to speak once more ; and I ask it with more confidence, since my views have been supported in your columns by " Hochelaga [a]," who, looking from the side of Canada, while I look from the side of England, declares the present bond of political connexion between the two countries to be weak for good, and strong only for evil.

It is most true, of course, that my opinions are those of a student, not of a statesman. Compared with the opinions of a real statesman, the opinions of a student could have little value. They may have some value compared with those of political tacticians living from hand to mouth, or of journalists deserting their high task of guiding the public mind to traffic, like stock-jobbers, in the passion of the hour. Mr. Rose, who speaks against my views in the Canadian Parliament, tells us that he turns gladly from the theories of philosophers and political economists to the responsible judgment of statesmen. How gladly would he have turned

[a] See his letter in the Appendix.

from the Colonial theories of Adam Smith, that "ingenious but dangerous speculator," as he was called by the
statesmen of his day, to the responsible judgments of
Mr. Grenville and Lord North. Pitt, a student at
Cambridge, read Adam Smith with the fresh mind of
youth, and among those applications of his teacher's
principles which placed veteran tacticians under the
boy-statesman's feet, he took, as I have said before, the
first and greatest step towards making Canada an independent nation, by giving her a Parliament of her own.

Grant that we who take this side are theorists, philosophers, thinkers, professors. Now answer the arguments, or cease wantonly to squander the public money
and imperil the safety of the nation.

We might listen in mute reverence to the oracles of
practical wisdom if the voice of those oracles were one.
But, unluckily, it is a Babel of contradiction. In Parliament, one Minister, who has thought and written on
the subject, tells us that he looks forward without regret to the day when Canada shall be separated from
England. The Head of the Government, rising immediately afterwards, declares that the day when any
Colony shall be separated from the Mother Country
will be an evil day for both Colony and Mother Country, though he gives us no reasons for his opinion.
In the press, one great advocate of the present system
admits that the time must come when it will be better
for both parties that the Colonies should set up for
themselves, and allows us to look forward to that time,
provided only that we use no forethought to provide
against its coming. But another great journal on the

same side denounces the rash admission as manifestly
fatal to the common cause. *The Times*, the great organ
of that political sagacity whose seat is in the Clubs, has,
in the course of this discussion, veered to all points of
the compass. It first said that Canada was a useless
and perilous possession. Then it reviled me for saying
the same thing in milder words. Then it said the same
thing itself again. It is true that these changes, if
they were without a reason, were not without a motive.
The first was produced by the apparent enthusiasm of
the Canadians for the cause of the Slave-owners ; the
second by their unexpected refusal to take part in
a great military demonstration against the Northern
States. Practical men have their theories—the Norths
and Grenvilles had their theories—as fine-spun as any
that ever came from the brain of a German professor.
What redeems their theories from the charge of " thinking" and makes them practical is, that they are framed
at the time to suit passion, not beforehand to control it.

Nor are practical men without sentiment. They
nobly refuse to " try great national questions by the
test of the balance-sheet." They are above caring for
the waste of public money or for the constant peril of
war into which the present connexion brings both
nations. Their thoughts soar to higher objects, Government guarantees for Colonial railroads, armaments at
the expense of the Mother Country, and the red-coats
whose profitable presence fills with thankfulness the
heart of the Mayor of Montreal [b]. Hitherto, perhaps,

---

[b] " Canada might esteem herself a most fortunate community in being
protected by one of the most powerful nations of the world, which sent

they have had reason to think that they could make no
demand, however unreasonable, upon the English tax-
payer which the liberality of our Government and the
patriotism of our Parliament would not grant. Hitherto, in the sunshine of commercial prosperity, we have
been going merrily down hill under the guidance of
light-hearted politicians, who have scattered the public
money with aristocratic generosity and amidst general
glee. Adversity, whose shadow begins to fall upon
the scene, will call up more serious thoughts and
greater men.

Mr. Rose calls my views " anti-colonial," fancying
that I am against Colonies ; though he is not capable
of committing such a platitude as that of the writer in
The Times who vehemently defended against me the
useful practice of " occupying the waste places of the
earth." I am no more against Colonies than I am
against the solar system. I am against dependencies,
when nations are fit to be independent. If Canada
were made an independent nation she would still be
a Colony of England, and England would still be her
Mother Country in the full sense in which those names
have been given to the most famous examples of Colonization in history. Our race and language, our laws
and liberties, will be hers. Our God will be her God.
Our great writers, the ministers of our moral empire,

her as many soldiers as might be required without rendering them
liable in purse or person. No matter how many red-coats might be
required, the more there might be, the better pleased they would be to
see them. It would not take one single sous out of their pockets."—
*Speech of the Mayor of Montreal at a public dinner given to the Go-
vernor General.*

will still sway her mind ; and when she turns from re-
claiming the wilderness—her first duty—to intellectual
pursuits, her great writers will sway the mind of England in their turn. Queen Victoria may still reign over
her as she reigned over the free States of America till
The Times and its confederates " dismembered " her
" dominion." The Prince of Wales was received in
the United States with an enthusiasm quite as intense
as in Canada, and more unanimous, since there it was
not broken by a Colonial offset of our Orange faction.
The correspondent of *The Times* on that occasion told
us that the one sentiment in which the Americans
were united was that of loyalty to Queen Victoria. He
moreover told us that if there was a place on the earth
where Englishmen were more heartily welcomed than
in Australia it was New York [c].

[c] "The whole of the enthusiasm in favour of the Prince might be
traced to three causes. The first was the admiration in which the
Queen's name is held throughout America. Loyalty does not of course
enter into this feeling : it is a pure love of her character as a great
Sovereign and a good mother. It is a feeling which has been growing
up for years in America; no matter where you may be in the Union,
North or South, East or West, there is one great topic on which all
men agree, one subject on which they seem never tired of expatiating,
and that is Queen Victoria. The simple fact of being her subject and
her admirer is a passport to the friendship of all Americans, and an
Englishman feels a double pride in going among Republicans with such
a lady at the head of his country. The second cause was the Prince's
own kind and genial behaviour throughout the tour. The last, though
not perhaps the least cause of all, was the feeling of hospitality which
always pervades New York, and which, as an almost invariable rule,
makes its inhabitants think nothing can be done too much in the way
of cordiality and welcome for the visitor. As a city, New York is to
Englishmen the most hospitable under the sun. Foreigners are always
welcomed there; but for the traveller from the Mother Country there

In the first ages of the world emigrants, wandering forth in quest of fresh pastures or new hunting-grounds, care no more for the tribe which they have left, nor the tribe which they have left for them, than a weaned foal and its dam care for each other. But in civilized times the bond of sympathy remains. It is the bond of nature, and needs no artificial tie to make it sure.

When we talk of founding Colonies after the model of the heroic times, we mean not the Roman Colonies, which were military outposts of the Empire and seminaries of Roman manners and vices in conquered lands, but the Greek Colonies, which took nothing from the Mother Country but the sacred fire and freedom.

What is proposed is, not that Canada shall cease to be a Colony of England, but that she shall cease to be a dependency: that she shall elect her own chief magistrate, coin her own money, decide her own causes finally in her own law-courts, and have the power of making peace and war.

Is there any reason why, after the separation of the Governments, natives of Canada should not still be allowed, on coming to reside within the pale of English law, to become British citizens, to acquire all kinds of property, and to exercise, if otherwise duly qualified, all political rights? Is there any reason why wealthy and aristocratic Canadians should not still look to this·

is a kindness and courtesy shewn, such as he can meet with in no other part of the world."—*The Prince of Wales in Canada and the United States, by N. A. Wood*, pp. 370, 371.

It is curious to contrast the language of Mr. Wood with the subsequent conduct of *The Times* towards the Americans.

country for the honours and rewards of life, if their own country, unhappily for her and for them, fails to win the allegiance of their hearts? Is this any reason why Canada should not keep the old flag, with such difference as the Heralds' College may require? There would, let me say once more, be no "casting off" in such an emancipation, except the casting off of the child, who, grown to manhood, leaves his father's house to win wealth and honours of his own.

At present there are two independent Parliaments under the same Crown, as there were in the case of England and Ireland before the Union. The supreme legislative power of the English Parliament has been tacitly abandoned in the case of Canada, as it was renounced in the case of Ireland. But the English Government manages the Canadian Parliament through the Governor General, as it managed Ireland through the Viceroy. In the case of England and Ireland the jarring of the two independent Parliaments was such, and the whole system was found so intolerable, that, to abolish it, Pitt himself waded knee-deep in pollution. Irish repealers have since demanded it back again; and English statesmen have answered that they would yield to the demand only after a struggle "which should convulse the four quarters of the globe." Yet England and Ireland lay close together; and the sympathy was only too strong between the Protestant aristocracy of England and its Irish ally. Can we expect two Parliaments, on opposite sides of the Atlantic, representing different interests and different states of society, to think, feel, and move together as one?

There has already been a quarrel about tariffs and commercial policy. We are free-traders; the Canadians are not. The Canadians have laid protective duties (as our traders aver) on our goods, which, on the poetical supposition of our national identity, are also their own. This question may perhaps be further embroiled in consequence of the recent commercial measures of the Northern States, with which the Canadians are commercially one nation.

There is now a quarrel about armaments. We have sent out our contingent of a great army, and the Canadians refuse to raise theirs. Their interests and feelings in the matter are different from ours. As a democracy, they have no political antipathy to the Americans; they have no ancient hate to wreak on them; they are commercially bound up with the rest of the continent in which they live, and war, if it breaks out, will be at their doors with havoc and ruin in its train. Upon their refusal, there whistles out to them a shrill blast of objurgation from our Parliament and press—a warning to the wise that we should part in good time if we wish to part friends. A correspondent of *The Times* has gone so far as to tell the contumacious Colonists in plain terms that, in case of a war, we should not care for the fate of a particular province which does not choose to raise soldiers when we bid it, but let it be ravaged as it may, and look to the general result. Perhaps the same writer would propose, in case the general result should be unfortunate, to purchase peace by ceding our North American dependencies to the States, as we have an undoubted right to do.

Besides its separate interests, the Parliament of Canada has parties and party objects of its own, which, like ours, often cross the interests of the Empire. The Militia Bill is thrown out by the Canadian Opposition to beat the Government. The Prime Minister of this country is full of indignation. Suppose when he, having lost his place in the Cabinet, took his revenge by throwing out the Government on a Militia Bill, the Canadian Prime Minister had read him a sharp lecture on "factious conflicts" which interfered with the defence of the Empire. It seems that our statesmen in giving the Colonies Parliaments, did not know what they were giving. They have bestowed liberty, and start at seeing that it is free.

In this case of the armament, the Governor General is set to work after the old fashion of the "Castle" in Ireland, to wheedle and rebuke. Whereupon he is accused by the Canadians of overstepping his bounds; and with justice, if he represents a constitutional sovereign, whose duty it is to reign, and not to interfere with the Government, but let it be carried on by his constitutional advisers. In the case of the tariff, the Colonial Minister ventured to interfere, and received a smart rebuff as a tribute to his imperial sway. A Norman rover who had received a fief from a King of France was told that he must kneel and kiss the foot of his liege lord; he knelt, and seizing hold of the foot threw his liege lord head over heels. Some time ago we put down a rebellion in Canada with the aid of the loyal party. Then we assented to an Act of the Canadian Parliament indemnifying the rebels for the losses which the loyal party had inflicted on them in the course of the war, by our command. Men on whose head a price had been set were forced into the councils of the Crown. This is that "Empire," at the thought of which the heart of every Englishman must swell within him; which, and not England, is the true source of English greatness; and without which the high spirit of the nation would at once decline. It would decline, perhaps, to what it was in the days before this unwieldy growth of dominion existed. In those days our cannon were heard in the Vatican. Now our remonstrances are heard in the Vatican : our cannon are heard at Canton, telling our greatness to the extremities of the earth. We still vindicate the rights of nations with imposing vigour when they are ignorantly and casually violated by the weak. But when they are wilfully and contumaciously violated by the strong, there is no help, as our statesmen confess, but prayers : prayers which, if they have anything of the majesty of England in their hearts, they will not too often use.

When people talk of the dependencies as the very soul of England, they forget that the oak flourished broad and deep before these parasites began to cling round its trunk and feed upon its life.

Mr. Rose triumphantly challenges the party of sordid economy to shew him an instance in history of a great "dominion" without expense. We must ask him to shew us an instance of a great dominion without revenue, without military force, and without power.

We are told that the Emperor of the French—that

K

divinity of practical wisdom—envies our Colonial empire, and desires a Colonial empire of his own. Let us
pray that he may obtain it. Nothing else can prevent
him from being quite, as he is now almost, master of
the destinies of Europe. We, with our forces scattered
over the world, and our fleets guarding all the globe
except our own coasts, have nothing left to check the
oppressor of Italy but moral influence, on the superior
efficacy of which we are beginning rather ominously to
descant. No doubt the lust of aggrandisement kindled
by the conquests of the First Empire still burns in the
veins of the French nation. But we may be permitted
to doubt whether its dictates are those of a wisdom
which we should follow. I have heard it said that
Algeria was a blessing to Europe, but I never heard it
said that it was a blessing to France. Does Cochin
China seem likely to prove an addition to French
power, and enable the French to "impose more majestically" on other European nations?

Not only are we Emperors without revenue or power,
we are Emperors on sufferance. The Colonial Minister
tells the Colonies in plain terms, that they may break
from us when they please, and not a shot shall be fired
or a bayonet levelled to prevent them. The "dominion" of Queen Victoria over the Colonists, which it is
treason to "dismember," consists in being their Queen,
provided she does not govern them, for so long a time
as they think fit.

For this we are keeping an army of 18,000 men in
Canada, and, be it always remembered, a great fleet on
the American stations besides. We are doing this with

the war income-tax upon us, and while we are trembling for our own shores. Gather the forces of England, gather even those on the American stations, round
her heart, and the degrading fear of invasion will
vanish like a dream.

But the expense of this connexion is swallowed up
in its danger. For Canada, and for Canada alone, we
stand always on the brink of a war with the great
Anglo-Saxon Republic, our best mart, and, if we were
not compelled to stand in the path of her advancing
greatness, our closest and surest ally. Suppose the
Americans crossed us in our hemisphere as we cross
them in theirs. Their possessions here might be held
by a flawless title, but would they not be held with
some peril?

As to Canada, Mr. Rose tells us that, be the cause of
war with America what it will, the Canadians cannot
gain and must be terrible sufferers; and that, as they
know from experience, they may have "no concern or
interest" in the quarrel, "except as British subjects
interested in the honour of the flag." To the honour
of the flag he says they are ready to offer themselves
"a generous sacrifice." But the sacrifice which their
generosity prompts them to make, our generosity forbids us to accept. The flag of England has never
waved over those whom it could not protect. Its glory
asks for no wanton tribute of devoted blood.

Among the causes of war in which Canada has no
interest or concern, Mr. Rose mentions the Oregon
question. What would he say to the question of Bel-
grade? Such is the temper of the people on whose

zeal and endurance we are to rely in undertaking a
war with the American Republic on its own soil, and
along an open frontier of fifteen hundred miles, which
can no more be defended by our 18,000 men than
Niagara can be stopped with a sieve!

For this outlay and danger what is the return? Will
any one seriously undertake to say that there is any
return at all? As to our trade with the Colonies, we
know not only by reason but by experience that it
would in no way suffer if they were made independent.
Rather it would increase, and they would become more
active producers and customers, since independence
sends life through all the veins of a nation. The
rivulet of trade which ran between England and her
American Colonies before they became independent
swelled, from the moment when they became independent, to a current as mighty as the Gulf Stream
flowing between shore and shore.

Mr. Rose vaunts the prosperous energy of the Canadians. No doubt his vaunt is just; and it proves that
Canada is fit to stand alone. Yet the traveller who
passes from the British Colonies into the States feels
that he has passed from the smaller to the greater, from
the less prosperous to the more prosperous. He has
passed from a province into a nation.

Moreover, if Canada were a separate nation, we
might negotiate a free trade with her. It has been
proposed by some advocates of the present state of
things that questions about which the two countries
are likely to differ, such as tariffs and armaments, shall
be settled by treaty. Queen Victoria will sign the

treaty on the one part—who will sign it on the other? If we could but treat with the Colonists as equals we might get justice. Commanding them as superiors, we put up with wrong at their hands for fear of disaffection. Jamaica refuses to pay us a just debt, and we are told that "it would not be safe" to attempt to exact it [d].

As to emigration, for one emigrant that goes to our American dependencies seven go, in common times, to the land of perfect independence and of unbounded enterprise and hope, in the United States. Even of those who go to Canada, many afterwards straggle across the frontier. We are naturally apt to flatter ourselves that the emigrant desires always to find him-

[d] The object of the Jamaica Loan Settlement Bill, 1862, was to settle by compromise a debt of £200,000 due from the island, which the Government had never been able to recover. The money was lent in 1831, the interest was paid until 1847, and then dropped. The terms of the compromise under the act seem to be that we give up the whole of our money and obtain in return for it an annuity of £6,400, every sixpence of which is to be spent on local government and improvement, without yielding the slightest advantage to this country. So that in fact the alleged compromise is a mere illusion. *The Times,* in an article July 16, 1862, says, "To put a premium on repudiation is the direct effect of the measure, and we know not who is to ensure us against a repetition of the same policy on the part of the Colonists." Lord Derby, in his speech on the Government measure, says, " We find a fact which no novelist would have ventured to introduce into a fiction, namely, that a letter was addressed to the Colonial Office, and that three years after, in 1859, an answer was returned, beginning 'With reference to your letter of the 7th of March, 1856.'' The fact was, the Government was naturally unwilling to face the state of the case. Thus England purchases a nominal dominion at an enormous cost, and "educates" the Colony in Repudiation. In Canada, in the West Indies, and in Australia, the name of Repudiation has been heard.

self under the shadow of the same institutions which have made him happy here. But the truth is that in these days, as in the days when men emigrated for conscience sake, some are driven from home by the wish for a change; some fly from the workhouse, as some fled from Laud.

To a class in England, the possession of Canada, like the other dependencies, yields matter for unreasoning pride. To England, it yields endless expense, perpetual danger, conscious weakness, and the humiliation which conscious weakness, though hidden under a lofty bearing, brings.

To a class in Canada, the connexion with England yields the hope of baronetcies and the hope of subsidies. To Canada, it yields a protection which quenches the spirit of self-defence, which must be withdrawn whenever we are engaged in a great struggle in Europe, and which, while it is continued, makes the protected country the mark of hatred and aggression, and has now brought it to the verge of a ruinous war.

Some Canadians have told us that Canada cannot be independent. It is the voice of a province that utters those humiliating words. Switzerland, in the midst of armed and aggressive empires, stands secure and inviolable as a nation. Even a settlement of Englishmen may be governed till they despair of self-government, and defended till they despair of self-defence. But grant that Canada cannot stand as a nation by herself, it is with a nation in America, not with a nation in Europe, that she must ultimately blend. Hatred of the Americans, however strong, will not dry up the Atlantic, or reverse the laws of nature. And while she remains a province, Canada is, in fact, insensibly blending with the United States. She uses coin with their image and superscription. She takes their political impress, like a mass of unfashioned clay, having no distinct figure of her own. As a province, she cannot form the independent character or assume the clear lineaments of a nation.

Statesmen fancy that they can set this right whenever they think fit. They who despise chimeras, themselves nurse the greatest chimera of all, imagining that they can give paper institutions whenever they please to an adult nation. What "philosopher," if he has at all corrected his philosophy by reference to the experience of history, does not know that institutions, to command the hearty allegiance of a nation, must be planted in its young heart?

Every day's delay will also render more difficult the fusion of our other North American Colonies with Canada, with which they are naturally destined to make one nation. Separate interests will be formed and national jealousies will spring up between the several Colonies and the political leaders of each. The fusion of the thirteen American Colonies into the United States was not accomplished without great difficulty, though in this case the stubborn metal had been melted in the furnace of revolution.

The Canadians shrink from the dangers and the burdens of independent existence. No wonder. What child, if the future could be revealed to it in infancy, would not shrink from the dangers and the burdens even of the most prosperous and heroic life? But nature, if left to herself, kindly veils the future from the child. The infant nation finds itself on the lap of earth, conscious only of the wants of the hour, tries its young limbs, falls it knows not why, rises thinking never to fall again, and is embarked in the battle of life before it knows what the battle of life is. Canada has been kept in the cradle till thought has awakened in her, and fear with thought. She has learned to scan her future without learning to face it. Yet, after all, she must face it. She, too, will have to play her due part in the progress of humanity, as we have played ours before her. We by long and hard effort have made the will of kings subject to the law. It is her task to make the will of the people subject to the law of reason. Her work once achieved will be worthier and more solid than ours. But it will not, any more than ours, be achieved without an effort. It was as the scene for such efforts, apparently, that the world was made.

She has the experience of the States before her, and may use it. She is not bound to copy their errors. She is not bound to set up every four years an elective presidency as a prize for factious intrigue and unprincipled ambition; to give a vote to every houseless wanderer; to fill the judgment seat with the tools of party, or to strip lawful authority bare of every vestige of reverend state. She will not, if she parts with us in good will, part from us, like the States, with a violent bias towards extreme democracy as most opposite to

the institutions which she has left. Our rulers have
not riveted on her, as they riveted on the Southern
States, Slavery, the deep cause of all the ruin and
misery now before our eyes.

. What do the Canadians gain by our tutelage? Has
the withholding of full responsibility taught them self-
control? Have they escaped any of the political vices
which are supposed to attend democracy? Have they
escaped extravagance in finance? Has not a nominal
restraint rather encouraged them in violence? Has
not a factitious credit rather encouraged them in expense? Let those be witnesses who, while in one
column they represent the Colonies as a "noble fabric,"
which it is profanity to touch, denounce them as swind-
ling anarchies in another. The system of local and
municipal self-government, which should have formed
the basis of the whole edifice, and might have been
a check on central jobbing, was not given to Canada
by us, but borrowed too late from the United States.
The greatest difficulty of Canadian statesmen is the
division between the two races; and we aggravated
that difficulty by the Quebec Act, which riveted French
law on Lower Canada to cut off our subjects there from
the rebel Colonists of the States.

England has been of all imperial countries most
liberal and wise to her dependencies. Their unwillingness to part from her is the crown of her policy; their
lasting affection, if they part from her in kindness, will
be its sure reward. But England cannot do for Canada
that which no nation can do for another. No nation
can live another's life. We have our hands full of work

of our own. We have yet to solve the problem of extending civil rights to the great mass of our people. The distribution of wealth among us is fearfully unequal. We have a vast pauper and criminal population. In the State, the relics of feudalism lie heavy on us. In the Church, a great conflict, touching the very life of the nation, is being waged between medieval authority and liberty of thought. From these things Canada is free, though she is not free from the coarseness and rawness of a young democracy, or from the unscrupulous lust of money which is the barbarism of commercial settlements. I see motes in her eye which need to be taken away, but none which need so much to be taken away as the beam in ours.

If it is always hard for one nation to guide the development of another, it is hardest of all in the case of nations radically differing from each other in their social structure. England is an aristocracy, while the whole frame of society, to which political institutions must conform, is in Canada democratic. The aristocratic ministers of England would be not only sensible and high-minded men, they would be more than men, if they could love a society founded on equality; and they cannot be good foster-fathers of that which they do not love. There lurks in their hearts, and transpires in all they say, a belief that this great group of commonwealths, founded on social equality, the native growth of the New World, is a monstrous and unnatural birth, which, if we will only wait a little, will creep back into the womb. Wait a little, they say to themselves, and in Canada, perhaps in the United States also, nature and the Divine law will assert their sway; and an aristocracy, with a monarchy and an established Church, will happily arise. Some Canadians seem to share this belief. A Canadian writes me word that if Canada is to be a separate nation she must have a king to prevent the highest places of Government from being occupied by the unworthy. Suppose she had a king like George IV., or like that king of Naples who was always trying to put his leg over a horse in the tapestry on the wall?

Statesmen usurp the privilege of professors when they act, or delay action for a dream. Do they really think it possible, and do they really intend, to plant in the New World a feudal aristocracy, with its indispensable basis, the rule of primogeniture and great settled estates? If they do, in the name of practical wisdom let them be quick. For while they pause, equality and independence are every day striking their lawless roots more deeply in the soil in which the sacred tree of privilege and dependence ought to grow. Let us see, in a working form, the plan by which a people of freeholders is to become a people of tenants, and a people tenacious of self-government is to bow its head to a house of peers? Are there to be, as among us, game-laws to preserve feudal sports in an industrial age, and to tempt the feudal lord to reside on his estate, and do his duty to his dependents? Is the Canadian aristocracy to be exported from this country, or created on the spot? If it is created on the spot, where will be its title to reverence, and its social superiority? It may corrupt, and that deeply, but how will it refine?

Grant that Canadian society is, in its rude beginnings, somewhat rough and coarse; is it not better to trust in the power of education for improvement, than with conscious, and therefore most abject idolatry, to set up such a golden calf as this?

Pitt, in the Act which established the Canadian Parliament, took power for the Crown to create hereditary peers. The power never was used, even in those aristocratic times. Large grants of lands were made to persons of quality, in order to found a territorial aristocracy, but that system of disposing of the public lands, after doing some mischief, was abandoned for the American rule of public sale to the highest bidder. Lord Egmont, as we learn from Horace Walpole, drew up a plan, which the English council in its wisdom and providence was near adopting, for introducing the whole feudal system into St. John's. The same nobleman, with perfect consistency, built for himself in England a feudal castle, which he prepared to defend itself with crossbows, against the day when gunpowder should be disused. Not only in America, but wherever the power of our Government has extended the same battle has been waged. Territorial aristocracy of the sacred English type was forced on Celtic Ireland with fire and sword. The native farmers of the revenue in India were taken by force to their own great astonishment and turned into squires. Man without a squire, in the eyes of these politicians, is an unhappy outcast from the pale of a divine law. If they did but know how imperfectly in the various phases of humanity the divine law has been fulfilled!

As to the Established Church, Pitt gave it to the
Canadians, with a great endowment of land, in the
form of clergy reserves, and the Canadians have renounced it, and turned its endowments to the purposes
of the State. We, in an old country, may still wear
the grave-clothes of the Middle Ages from fear of
change ; but no nation which has put them off will
ever put them on again. Our attempts to propagate
the Church of England as a State Church in the Colonies serve only to create prejudice against that Church,
and even against religion. As a free Church the
Church of England flourishes not only in the Colonies,
but in the independent States of America, and draws to
her all that she, a single fragment of shattered Christendom, with her Tudor faith and formularies, can reasonably expect to draw ᵉ.

Our constitutional monarchy is feudal, like our aristocracy and our Church. It is the apex of the system
of which they are the base ; and it would seem that to
attempt to set up in a new land the apex of the system
without the base would not be the part of the wise.
But if any one thinks it would, let us see his plan for

ᵉ " While State aid has been almost wholly withdrawn from the service of religion in the Colonies, the zeal of the several denominations
has supplied the deficiency to an extent which it would then have been
deemed wild to conjecture. The Church of England, in particular, has
now more than thirty Colonial Bishoprics ; of these only one or two in
North America derive from Great Britain a small income, limited to the
lives of the present incumbents, and a few, in different parts of the
world, are partially supported by the Colonial revenue. But, speaking
generally, they are maintained on the ' voluntary system.' "—*Merivale on
Colonization*, p. 607.

The attempt to establish the Church of England in Virginia totally failed.

a constitutional monarchy, without an aristocracy or an established Church, drawn up in a practical and intelligible form. What powers does he propose to give the King of Canada? What royal revenues, what civil list does he expect the frugal Canadians to supply? Of what honours will the Crown be the fountain? Is the Royal Marriage Act to be extended to Canada? Is the rule of the Protestant succession to be kept up in a nation half of which are members of the Church of Rome? At least make your scheme intelligible to us and to yourselves, if, for its sake, we are to bring war upon two nations.

In England Monarchy has a root, and it has a use. It binds the unenfranchised, ignorant, and indigent masses of the people by a tie of personal loyalty to the constitution. In the New World Monarchy has no root; and it has no use where the masses of the people are enfranchised and bound to the constitution by property and intelligence.

If any one doubts that Constitutional Monarchy of the English type is feudal, and imagines it to be good for all nations, let him look at Greece, where feudalism did not exist, and at France, where it had been abolished, and see how Constitutional Monarchy of the English type has flourished there.

And even supposing this aristocratic reverie capable of being accomplished, what interest have the English people in its accomplishment? Why should they desire to plant among the communities of the New World a hostile outpost of feudalism and privilege, the source of division, jealousy, and war? What reason have they

to fear the sight of great commonwealths based on free
reverence for equal laws, and prospering without lords
or dependents? Why should they look with jealous ma-
lignity on the mighty development of the Anglo-Saxon
race emancipated from Norman bonds over a continent
which its energy and patience have made its own? Why
should they desire to thwart the manifest designs of Providence, which has willed that a new order of things
should commence with the peopling of the New World?

In the race as in the man the moral and physical life
are so closely knit together that the progress of the one
is the progress of the other, and everything falls into
the general plan. The great migrations by which the
earth has been peopled have at the same time unfolded
the great scenes of history, and carried man through
the successive phases of social and political existence.
Old England has failed to shake off feudalism; but the
founders of New England left it behind, and planted
a realm beyond its sway. The knell of privilege struck
when they, at the foundation of their State, bound themselves in a voluntary covenant to "render due obedience
to just and equal laws framed for the general good."
They from the first renounced the Norman law of
primogeniture in succession to land, and returned to
the old Saxon law of just division, under its Saxon
name of gavelkind. When hereditary aristocracy offered itself in the person of certain Puritan peers, who
wished to retain their privilege in New England, they
calmly, but firmly put it away f. From the State

---

f " Several of the English Peers, especially Lord Saye and Sele, a Pres-
byterian, a friend to the Puritans, yet with but dim perceptions of the

Church they were hunted and persecuted exiles; and if they did not reach at a bound the doctrine, then unknown, of perfect religious liberty, they reached it soon, and embraced it without reserve, while intolerance and penal laws reigned here. To the Crown alone, which, like the Pope, had presumed in its fatuous arrogance to grant away the New World, they unhappily remained attached by a slender thread of allegiance, which in time drew after it encroachment, resistance, and fratricidal war, the source of mortal division and long hatred between the Old England and the New. By the issue of their enterprise,

true nature of civil liberty, and Lord Brooke, a man of charity and meekness, an early friend to tolerance, had begun to inquire into the character of the rising institutions, and to negotiate for such changes as would offer them inducements for removing to America. They demanded a division of the general court into two branches, that of assistants and representatives,—a change which was acceptable to the people, and which, from domestic reasons, was ultimately adopted; but they further required an acknowledgment of their own hereditary right to a seat in the Upper House. The fathers of Massachusets were disposed to conciliate these powerful friends: they promised them the honors of magistracy, would have readily conferred it on some of them for life, and actually began to make appointments on that tenure; but as for the establishment of hereditary dignity they answered by the hand of Cotton, 'Where God blesseth any branch of any noble or generous family with a spirit and gifts fit for government, it would be a taking of God's Name in vain to put such a talent under a bushel, and a sin against the honor of magistracy to neglect such in our public elections. But if God should not delight to furnish some of their posterity with gifts fit for magistracy, we should expose them rather to reproach and prejudice, and the Commonwealth with them, than exalt them to honor, if we should call them forth, when God doth not, to public authority.' And thus the proposition for establishing hereditary nobility was defeated."—*Bancroft's History of the United States*, vol. i. pp. 384, 385.

victorious though chequered, victorious though now
wrapped in storm, man has undoubtedly been taught
that he may not only exist, but prosper, without many
things which it would be heresy and treason to think
unnecessary to his existence here. It is a change, and
a great change; one to be regarded neither with childish exultation nor with childish fear, but with manly
reverence and solicitude, as the opening of a new page in
the book of Providence, full of mighty import to mankind. But what, in the course of time, has not changed,
except that essence of religion and morality for which
all the rest was made? The grandest forms of history
have waxed old and passed away. The English aristocracy has been grand and beneficent in its hour, but
why should it think that it is the expiring effort of
creative power, and the last birth of time? We bear,
and may long bear, from motives higher perhaps than
the public good, the endless decrepitude of feudalism
here; but why are we bound, or how can we hope, to
propagate it in a free world?

I have read, sir, a mass of articles and speeches, but
I have failed to discover a single argument for the
present system except that of " prestige "—" prestige "
being, in plain English, a false appearance of strength,
known by everybody to be false, which, it seems, has
come to be thought the true life of the greatest of nations. As for the imposing dogma that " Providence "
has put the Colonies into our hands, and that it is our
duty to keep them, we must regard it not as an argument, but as a renunciation of argument, unless those
who propound it can shew us that Providence has re-

vealed its will to them by some other channel than that of reason. But the system does not rest on argument. It rests on unreflecting pride, ignorant of the true sources of English greatness. It rests on class interests and prejudices, ever triumphant, by their concentrated energy, over the public good. It rests on the routine of offices which we fondly imagine to be the seats of a superior intelligence, while in fact they are apt to become, except for mere administration, the most mechanical of all machines. It rests upon patronage, that foundation of adamant, upon which the puny assaults of reason and justice have so often spent, and will long spend, themselves in vain.

I am, &c.,

GOLDWIN SMITH.

August 27, 1862.

X.

NEW ZEALAND.

SIR,—Few people, except those whose minds prejudice has closed against the plainest teaching of experience, will fail to conclude from the correspondence between the Colonial Minister and the Governor of New Zealand, a portion of which you lately gave us[a], that our Colonial system must be changed, and that soon; whether the change they prefer be the simple and obvious one of political separation, or the less simple and obvious one of a federal union, the working plan of which has not yet been put forth, between two nations at opposite sides of the globe.

In the case of New Zealand, as of other dependencies, that which is officially styled the "Empire" is patronage to a few, but to the nation expense, weakness, humiliation : while to the Colony it is a protection which cannot last for ever, and, so long as it lasts, stifles self-defence and kills the root of national virtue.

With danger lowering on our own shores, with the war income-tax almost hopelessly fixed upon us—with France mistress of the destinies of Europe, and trampling international rights under her feet—with the

---

[a] See the extracts at the end of this Letter.

defence of the Canadian frontier on our hands—with
a cotton famine to cripple our resources as well as to
afflict our people, we are keeping up an army of 5,000
or 6,000 men, at an expense of more than half a million, to carry on a war against a horde of naked
savages in New Zealand.

There are in New Zealand 100,000 Europeans and
50,000 natives[b]. But of the natives only 11,000 are
hostile. These 11,000 send out at most 3,000 fighting
men; and to keep down these 3,000 men we are employ-
ing 6,000 regular British soldiers and a ship of war.
Even a civilian may venture to hazard the conjecture
that the solidity and perfect alignment of British regu-
lars must be rather wasted in fighting with Maories in
the bush. In General Cathcart's campaign at the Cape
in 1852, a good many of the 12th Lancers were lost.
One who took part in the campaign deposes, that it
was a very rough country for Lancers and one in which
that force was not of much service. The same witness
deposes that English Infantry, tightly buckled up and
the heavy knapsacks[c] on their backs, found it difficult
to get about through the most impenetrable thorn-bush
in the world.

To this exertion and this expenditure on our part
the Colonists respond by discontinuing the annual
training of their militia. Our Colonial Secretary is
"surprised" at such a want of energy. But surely he
might as well be surprised at seeing an apple fall to

---

[b] In the original letter I greatly understated the case in saying that
"the natives did not exceed the Europeans in number."

[c] Report of Committee on Colonial Military Expenditure, p. 100.

the ground. How many more experiments, and how many more millions of wasted expenditure, will our statesmen require before they are convinced that very money-loving people, so long as they can be provided with armaments by the Mother Country, will not be at the expense of providing armaments for themselves?

The Colonists, it seems, would not be unwilling in the abstract to contribute something towards the army kept for their protection; but, unluckily, they cannot do it without imposing additional taxes on themselves, and to pay additional taxes is, as they quietly assume, the function of the Mother Country alone. No doubt of our unlimited liability seems to cross their minds. A New Zealand financier, in answer to the appeal of the Home Government, satisfactorily proves that the local revenue is already devoted to local objects, including public works and colonization. "It does not appear to occur to him," says the Duke of Newcastle, "that the revenue itself might be increased by the imposition of fresh taxation; that the portion of that revenue which is so applied as to relieve municipalities from the necessity of imposing local taxes might be applied, in whole or in part, to the more pressing needs of the Colony, and that the portion of the revenue which is devoted to public works and colonization may in times of disaster, and particularly in times of civil war, which is disaster, be diverted to the paramount object of averting absolute ruin. No doubt in steps like these the Colony would be making sacrifices. But this is exactly what the British Government has a right to expect from them." With submission to the

Duke's judgment, the British Government has no right to expect this. It has no right to expect anything but the injustice and contumely which it receives. It has taught the Colonists to draw on the resources of others, and it has no right to expect that they should feel the duty of paying for themselves; it has taught them to lean on us, and it has no right to expect that they should know how to stand alone.

While our arsenals and even our capital are proclaimed by the Government to be in danger, the Colonists of New Zealand, revelling in the luxury of an unbought security, plant outsettlements in dangerous places, and call upon us to send out troops enough to protect them. The Duke of Newcastle suggests that if it is not worth the while of the Colony to protect the outsettlers, it can scarcely be worth while to retain the outsettlements. Again I must say I think the Duke is wrong. A gross of green spectacles may be a very bad purchase if bought with your own money; but it may be a good purchase if bought with the money of other people. Prudence is not the common attribute of minors drawing on the purses of their mothers.

The Governor of New Zealand has formed splendid schemes for his government. He proposes (1) the maintenance for several years of a large military force at the expense of the Mother Country; (2) a machinery for civilizing the natives, partly at the expense of the Mother Country; (3) the construction of roads by the help of the troops in the pay of the Mother Country; (4) military commissioners to be posted in the several districts, each paid by the Mother Country. The large

military force is to be maintained partly that the outsettlers may enjoy their farms in peaceful security
without lifting a hand in their own defence; partly as
"a standing exhibition of strength," and of the "determination" of the Colonists not to yield an inch to
the enemy while a penny remains in the Mother
Country's purse. An Irish absentee proprietor, being
a man of spirit, wrote to his resident agent, who had
been threatened by Whiteboys, "Tell them they are
very much mistaken if they think that they will in-
timidate me by shooting you."

My critics in New Zealand, as well as in England,
find my views very deficient in "sentiment." I do
not know, nor, to tell the truth, do I much care, on
which side the claptrap may be, but I submit that
some at least of the sentiment is on mine. The proposal to lay fresh burdens on this overburdened country
—to tax the few comforts of the poor labourer here—
in order to protect the "outsettlements" of prosperous
and unencumbered Colonists, excites sentiments which
are natural, if they are not refined. It is, perhaps,
a coarse thing to say, but the statesmen of sentiment
will find in the long run, that as poetry itself, to be
genuine, must be founded on common sense, so political
sentiment, to be lasting, must be founded on common
justice.

"A taxpayer's yell" was the name given by a Colonial journal to Mr. Adderley's vigorous protest against
the wasteful folly and iniquity of the present system of
military expenditure in the Colonies. Yes, the "yell"
of some English clerk whose scanty salary is charged

with income-tax, or of some peasant whose ounce of tea is reduced to half an ounce that Colonial opulence may go untaxed, and who in return for the money wrung from him receives unlimited "prestige."

The Governor of New Zealand proposes to prolong and increase our expenditure, and at the same time he proposes to do away with the last excuse for it. He proposes to take the protection and management of the natives entirely out of the hands of the Home Government, and to place them, like other local affairs, in the hands of the local Government and Assembly. The Duke of Newcastle sanctions this most important step. He does so, partly, he says, in reliance on the knowledge and judgment of Sir George Grey, but partly because "he cannot disguise from himself that the attempt to keep the management of the natives under the control of the Home Government has failed." Words as true as they are magnanimous, and as momentous as they are true! Not only in New Zealand, but in all our Colonies, the attempts of the Home Government to exercise a special protection over the natives have failed ; and bright visions, the incitements to those attempts, have found a dark fulfilment. Where the natives have escaped the worst fate, it has been either through the sense of moral responsibility on the part of the Colonists themselves, which the intervention of the Home Government impairs, or through their fears, which the military support of the Home Government dispels. The only saviour of savages is the missionary [d]. I believe

---

[d] Mr. Herman Merivale has some striking remarks on the influence of Religion in civilizing native races, On Colonization and Colonies, lect. xix.

this may be proved conclusively by historical induction. But what would historical induction avail, compared with the admission of an honest statesman? Let us welcome this admission, that millions have in different Colonies been expended in vain, as a ray of truth breaking through the clouds that surround the Ministerial Olympus, and consider whether there may not be still more light behind.

In these attempts to make the Home Government the guardian of the natives we see in the clearest light the inability of Parliamentary Ministers, with their feeble powers and ephemeral tenure of office, to carry on a paternal policy in the Colonies. The truth is, if we are to have an Empire we must have an Emperor.

The Colonists are, as a matter of course, told they "must expect though not an immediate yet a speedy and considerable diminution. of the force now employed." They were told, when the force was sent out, that it should not be employed at all unless they would pay for it : yet they have managed to employ it, if not in fighting, in making their roads; this country, with its 900,000 paupers, paying £100 a-year per man for their road-makers. They understand the coyness of the Colonial Office, and know the talisman which will bring the troops back again even if they are withdrawn. Let us hope that this threat of the Colonial Secretary will produce no effect, for if it does, the effect will be a Maori war.

A witness, lately Under-Secretary for the Colonies, is asked by the Committee on Military Expenditure in the Colonies, "Whether he thinks that there would be

any difficulty in announcing to the Cape Colonists that
it was intended to reduce their garrison, and that they
must take measures for their own defence?"   "It has
been announced," is the reply, "over and over again."
"Has not that announcement," ask the Committee,
"been followed by action?"   "It has been followed
by diminishing the force; but that force has been increased again upon apprehension arising.   There has
been a continual succession of diminution and expansion
at the Cape ever since I had anything to do with it [e]."

How is it possible that such a system of sponging
and cozening should fail to lower the public spirit and
corrupt the public honour of the Colony?   And what
pecuniary advantage can make up to a young community, the character of which is just being formed,
for the lowering of public spirit and the corruption of
public honour?   It has been plausibly argued that the
tutelage of the Mother Country is a good thing because New England, the founders of which were left to
fight the Indians by themselves, grew up slowly, while
New Zealand, defended by the troops of the Mother
Country, is growing up very quickly.   But into what
is New Zealand growing?

The case of New Zealand, be it observed, is a crucial
instance—an instance by which the system must stand
or fall.   The New Zealanders are the very flower of
our Colonists, tainted by no convict ancestry, but sent
out under the highest auspices and with the highest
aims.   If we have reason to expect just and liberal
treatment from any Colonists it is from them.   With

* Report, p. 183.

them, if with any Colonists, we might hope to remain united by an unfailing tie of sympathy and affection. Yet we are receiving at their hands not justice or liberality, but the reverse, and a dispute is open by which, if it proceeds, the tie of sympathy and affection may be strained to breaking.

This is the fault of neither party. It is the fault of the utterly irrational and untenable system by which nations with Parliaments of their own are treated as provinces to be governed and defended by another country. To give a nation a Parliament of its own is to give it independence. Two Parliaments under the same Crown never have produced, and never can produce, anything but clashing of interests, contradictions of policy, discord, and confusion; and, at last, angry separation, the grave of that glory which belongs to England, the mother of nations. When we have given people free institutions we have decided that they are fit to govern themselves. Let us, then, accept the consequence of our own decision. Let us accept it quickly, or we shall imperil the highest prize ever placed within the reach of any nation.

In the next column to the New Zealand correspondence I read the account of the public meeting in New South Wales for contributing to the relief of the sufferers in Lancashire, and of the noble liberality which was then called forth. These are the spontaneous, unofficial fruits of the sympathy, deeper and surer than any political connexion, which unites all men of English blood; a sympathy which the presence of a Governor General with the veto does not create, and which his departure would not destroy. This generosity, I am told by the correspondent of *The Times*, is "the practical answer to my proposal that the Australians should cease to be Britons." It is the practical answer to much indiscriminate obloquy which *The Times* has heaped on the Australians. It is the practical ratification of my proposal to take the final step in the course which has hitherto proved so prosperous. The gift of partial independence to the Colonies has produced this affection between them and us; let the gift of perfect independence make it sure for ever. Will men by becoming perfectly free "cease to be Britons?" Cannot they be their own masters and yet be generous to their friends?

I may be sanguine, but I think that this question is making way; that the film of official phrase and unreasoning tradition is passing away from the eyes of the nation; and that it begins to see the difference between an "Empire" which is power and wealth, and an empire which is nothing but waste, peril, and humiliation. Nor need we despair that the Colonists themselves will soon awake to a sense of their highest interests, and perceive that a precarious protection and a temporary relief from expense are too dearly purchased by a loss of self-reliance, the only sure source of national security and greatness.

I am, &c.,
Goldwin Smith.

Sept. 13, 1862.

"No. 14.
"Copy of a Despatch from the Duke of Newcastle, K.G., to Governor Sir George Grey, K.C.B.

"(No. 53.)   "*Downing-street, May* 26, 1862.

" Sir,—I have had under my consideration your Despatches noted in the margin *, informing me of the language which you have held to your Ministry, of the plans which you propose to yourself and them, and of the course which you desire the Home Government to pursue in regard to the management of Native Affairs and the cost of the war in New Zealand.

" 1. In the first place, you inform me that you propose hereafter to conduct Native Affairs like all other matters, with the advice of your Executive Council ; and you deprecate any attempt to set up either the Governor or any special body between the natives and the General Assembly as a protective power.

" 2. You propose to establish a machinery for the government and improvement of the natives, which you suppose will eventually cost about £50,000 a year. Half of this sum, you state, is already provided by the Colonial Legislature, and you have led the Local Government to expect that the other half will be virtually supplied by the Imperial Government in the shape of a reduction from the Colonial contribution of £5 a head to the expense of the Imperial force stationed in New Zealand.

" 3. You propose the maintenance for some years of a large military force, partly as a standing exhibition of strength and determination, partly in order to afford to the outsettlers that protection and sense of security which is essential to enable them profitably to occupy their farms.

---

* "No. 3, Oct. 9, 1861, page 1; No. 8, Oct. 26, 1861, page 5 ; No. 16, Nov. 2, 1861, page 21; No. 36, Nov. 30, 1861, page 27; No. 38, Dec. 6, 1861, page 28."

" 4. You suggest that roads should be made by the troops (still supported, I presume, at the expense of the Imperial Treasury) in conjunction with natives ; and

" 5. You propose that military men should be employed as commissioners in the native districts, continuing, while so employed, to receive Imperial pay and allowances.

" With regard to the increasing debt, due from the Colony to the British Treasury, you state that to exact payment would be to ruin the Colony, and you transmit a memorandum drawn up by the Colonial Treasurer proposing the following course : ' Not to attempt to meet these various demands, or to provide for this excessive expenditure, at present, but to wait till the existing native difficulty is removed, to ascertain with accuracy what proportion of the expenses the Imperial Government would, after due deliberation and a full knowledge of the facts of the case, charge the Colony with, and then to apply for a guaranteed loan of the requisite amount.'

" Now I must, in the first place, observe that I see in the papers before me no adequate apprehension on the part of the New Zealand Government of the obligation under which the Colonists themselves lie to exert themselves in their own defence, and to submit to those sacrifices which are necessary from persons whose lives and property are in danger. Mr. Reader Wood states that the annual revenue of the Colony (independently of the land revenue) is £272,000. He mentions that £90,000 of that sum are paid to Provincial Governments, and he observes that the land fund is Provincial revenue, and expended in colonization and public works. But it does not appear to occur to him that the revenue itself might be increased by the imposition of fresh taxation; that the portion of that revenue which is so applied as to relieve municipalities from the necessity of imposing local taxes might be applied in whole or in part to the more pressing needs of the Colony, and that the portion of that revenue which is devoted to public works and Colonization

may, in times of disaster, and particularly in time of civil
war, which is disaster, be diverted to the paramount object
of averting absolute ruin.

" No doubt, in steps like these the Colony would be making
sacrifices. But this is exactly what the British Government
has a right to expect from them. Those who are expending
half a million a-year in the defence of the Colonists and their
property (a very appreciable item among those which fix on
the British tax-payer the burden of an income-tax) are entitled to expect from these Colonists that, instead of having
recourse to the momentary relief of a loan, exhausted it would
seem almost before it was raised, they should, by some immediate, general, and lasting sacrifice of the kind which I
have indicated, give some pledge of their readiness to take
their share, as far as their means will allow, in the defence of
their country. And, in connexion with this subject, I cannot
pass without remark that passage in the Colonial Treasurer's
financial statement of 23rd July 1861, in which he charac-
terizes as ' most unfairly charged against the Colony' demands properly made against the Colonial Government by
the Commissariat, nor the very strong animadversions made
in the Colonial Legislature on the conduct of the commissariat officer in bringing forward these claims in the simple
discharge of his duty.

" Little, however, as I am satisfied with the contents of
your Despatches in these respects, I am earnestly desirous to
afford the Colony in a time of undoubted trial the utmost assistance which can be given with any justice to this country.
I therefore proceed to communicate to you, as explicitly as
is now possible, the decision of Her Majesty's Government
upon the questions which you have raised.

" I am ready to sanction the important step you have
taken in placing the management of the natives under the
control of the Assembly. I do so partly in reliance on your
own capacity to perceive, and your desire to do, what is best
for those in whose welfare I know you are so much inter-

ested. But I do it also because I cannot disguise from myself that the endeavour to keep the management of the natives under the control of the Home Government has failed. It can only be mischievous to retain a shadow of responsibility when the beneficial exercise of power has become impossible.

" I cannot hold out to you any hopes that a large military force will for any length of time be kept in New Zealand. It is for the Colonists themselves to provide such a military police force as will protect their outsettlers. If it is not worth while to the Colony to furnish such protection, it would seem to follow that it is not worth while to retain these outsettlements. You must therefore expect, though not an immediate, yet a speedy and considerable diminution of the force now employed.

" I doubt whether, under present military regulations, an officer can be detached from his regiment to serve as commissioner in a native district; but in case this should prove practicable, Her Majesty's Government can only assent to such an arrangement on the understanding that the whole pay of the officer shall be defrayed by the Colony.

" I can hold out no prospect that this country will consent to bear any part of the expense of the local militia and volunteers. All existing and future liabilities on this score must be defrayed by the Colony. This sum appears to have amounted on the 29th of October last to £193,180.

" The agreement so lately entered into by the Colonial Government for the contribution of £5 per man to the cost of the troops stationed in the Colony must also be fulfilled up to the close of the year 1861.

" But, in consideration of the present difficulties of the Colony, and in compliance with your advice, Her Majesty's Government will be prepared, under the following conditions, to reckon as military contribution all sums shewn to be expended in a manner approved by you on native government, or other purely native objects, in excess of £26,000, which I understand to be the amount now paid from the Colonial revenue towards these objects.

"The conditions subject to which I am able to authorize this concession are the following :—

" 1. The amount furnished by the Colonial Government shall not be less than £26,000, and that furnished by the Imperial Government must not exceed the amount of military contribution due from the Colonial to the Imperial Government, calculated at the rate of £5 a head for every soldier employed.

" 2. No other Imperial funds are to be employed, nor any advances procured from the Treasury Chest towards paying the expenses of the scheme.

" 3. An account of these expenses must be furnished to the Controller of the Treasury Chest, for the information of Her Majesty's Government and of Parliament, shewing the amount and application of this Imperial contribution.

" 4. The present arrangement is to last for three years, that is to say, from the 1st January 1862 to the 31st December 1864, when it is to be hoped that the Colony may be in a position to provide for the well-being and government of the natives, so far as the institutions which you propose to introduce shall not have been self-supporting by means of local taxation, a result which you will keep steadily in view, and the importance of which I cannot too earnestly impress upon you.

" 5. In giving up for a limited period the claim of this country to a portion of the present military contribution, no pledge is to be implied as to the continuance of that contribution as a permanent arrangement, but it is clearly to be understood that the aid to be required from New Zealand for military protection shall remain subject to any general measure which Parliament or

M

Her Majesty's Government may adopt with regard to the maintenance of Imperial troops in the Colonies.

"You will not fail, I trust, to recognise in these concessions the desire of Her Majesty's Government to co-operate in a spirit of liberality and confidence with yourself and the Colony in the important and hopeful attempt which you and your ministers are now making to introduce such civilizing institutions among the native tribes as may, under the blessing of Providence, save both races of Her Majesty's subjects in New Zealand from the miseries of civil war, and the Imperial and Colonial Governments from the heavy burdens which it entails.

> "I have, &c.   (Signed)   NEWCASTLE."
> "Governor Sir George Grey, K.C.B.,
>   &c.   &c.   &c."

Affairs have since taken a singular turn. The New Zealand Legislature, learning from the Duke's Despatch that they were no longer to have the English troops, have repudiated the management of the natives, which they had themselves previously demanded. They tell the Home Government that it must take the responsibility on itself, as it will not furnish them with the money. Upon this *The Times* of January 19th, 1863, makes the following just remarks :—

"The result of this despatch is a solemn address to the Queen from the New Zealand House of Representatives of a nature totally unexampled in Colonial history. Instead of accepting with gratitude the right conceded to them by the Colonial Minister, the New Zealand Assembly respectfully decline to undertake the task imposed upon them. They recognise the difficulty of governing the two races by two agencies responsible to different authorities, but they cannot accept the power offered them if it is to be attended with

THE EMPIRE.

any greater liability than at present for their own defence.
They ignore the fact that the proposition came originally
from their own responsible Ministers, and they quote the
unsatisfactory condition of affairs in New Zealand at the
present moment as a reason why the system under which
that unsatisfactory state of affairs has arisen ought to be in-
definitely continued. We have never seen a public docu-
ment less convincing in its statement, or more entirely di-
vested of the graces of modesty and self-respect. The simple
meaning is that the Colonists have got a good thing, and intend to keep it. They alone of all the people of the earth
have the privilege of making war at other people's expense.
The quarrels which arise with the natives are their quarrels,
not ours. The expense of fighting out those quarrels they
claim should be our expense, not theirs. Those on the spot,
who have in their hands the power of war and peace, are to
have no responsibility; we, separated by the whole bulk of
the globe, are to have the whole of it. Hitherto the responsibility has been thought to be a salutary check on power.
Henceforth, as far, at least, as New Zealand is concerned,
those two things are to be studiously kept apart from each
other. We have no wish that the Colonists should be called
upon to contribute to the expense of the Imperial force maintained in New Zealand, but we confess the very strongest
desire that our forces should be materially reduced. The
Colony has now the management of native affairs. If war
does not bring troops from England to carry it on, and a large
commissariat to keep up prices, the settlers will find some
means to remain at peace, or, which is the next best thing,
to defend themselves. There will be no peace so long as
war is attended with gain and immunity from military service. We have a right to demand on behalf of the heavily-
taxed people of this country that this burden shall be removed from their shoulders, and we therefore rejoice to find
that Sir George Grey, in his speech to the New Zealand Parliament, announces that he has hitherto had no occasion, and

hopes to have none hereafter, to employ the military forces in any active field operations. Our policy in New Zealand towards the natives is comprised in a single word—wait. Temporizing expedients, delays, dilatory negotiations, all manner of devices which are of little avail in ordinary cases, are of the greatest use when we have to deal with a race that is continually decreasing on behalf of a race that is continually increasing. It is easier to grow into the undisturbed sovereignty of New Zealand than to conquer it."

XI.
COLONIAL EMIGRATION.

TO THE EDITOR OF THE "DAILY NEWS."

Sir,—I should abandon my case if I omitted to reply to the important paper on the "Utility of Colonization," by Mr. Herman Merivale, read before the British Association, and reported in your journal[a]. Mr. Herman Merivale is not only a writer of the highest distinction on Colonial subjects, and one to whom all students of those subjects are deeply indebted, but, as Under-Secretary for the Colonies, he was long the chief administrator of the present system. If he fails to give sound reasons for the continuance of the system, it is because there are no sound reasons to give.

I must, in the first place, guard against a fallacy as to the views of Mr. Merivale's opponents which is implied in the title of his paper. As I have said before, nobody can doubt "the utility of Colonization." To doubt the utility of Colonization would be to doubt the utility of every inhabited country on the earth, except the original seat of man. What is doubted is the utility of keeping Colonies in a state of dependence on the Mother Country when they are capable of self-government and self-defence, and when their fitness to manage their own concerns has been formally acknowledged by the gift of Parliamentary institutions.

[a] *Daily News*, Oct. 7, 1862.

The argument now adduced by Mr. Merivale for the
continuance of this costly and dangerous system is an
economical argument, but one of a very special kind,
and unknown either to the Colonial Secretary, who de-
fends the system on economical grounds the validity of
which Mr. Merivale would not admit, or to *The Times*,
to which it is evidently a discovery as new as it is welcome: so that we are again led to remark the diversity of pleas adopted by the different advocates of
Colonial dependency, and the difficulty they have in
determining among themselves on which plea they
shall take their stand.   I say Mr. Merivale would
not admit the validity of the economical grounds on
which the case is defended by the Colonial Secretary.
In the new edition of his work, " On Colonisation and
Colonies," published last year, some passages of the
original text are qualified in the notes; but I am not
aware that he has qualified the passage to which I
referred when I was meeting the argument in favour of
dependencies drawn from the amount of the Colonial
trade.*   It is in truth merely the statement, in forcible
and telling language, of an historical fact.   Speaking
of the American Revolution, he dilates on the great
economical advantages gained by both parties when
the American Colonies "exchanged the tie of subjection for that of equality," which he describes in the
words of a Greek poet as the surest bond of friendship
and alliance between nations.   " No one," he proceeds,
" now really doubts, notwithstanding the hostile tariff
of the States, that the separation of our North American
Colonies has been, in an economical sense, advantageous

to us. And yet precisely the same arguments are current at this very day respecting the superior profit of
Colonial commerce, and the wealth arising from Colonial domination, which were in every one's mouth before
that great event had occurred, and, by its results, con-
founded all such calculations. So easily does our reason
contrive to forget the strongest lessons, or to evade their
force, when prejudice and the love of power warp it in
the contrary direction."

Mr. Merivale uses in the course of his present dis-
sertation some incidental expressions which shew that
he is a little inclined to slide back into the commercial
argument. He intimates "that ships, *Colonies* (by which
he means *dependencies*), and *commerce* may be a little
more nearly connected than it is now the fashion in
some quarters to suppose them." But his own words,
as I have cited them, give, I think, a sufficient answer to
this intimation. He also suggests the fear of "hostile
tariffs" in case the Colonies are released from a state
of dependence. But, not to mention that the tariff of
Canada is already hostile, he himself, as we see, takes
into account the hostile tariff of the States when he
pronounces that the American Revolution was a source
of great economical advantages to both parties.

Mr. Merivale's present argument consists of a peculiar view of the happiness of nations, combined with
a peculiar view of the necessary agency of dependencies
in promoting it. He lays it down, in effect, that those
nations are the happiest in which the restrictions of
prudence on the increase of population are least opera-
tive; and in which there is a constant pressure on the

means of subsistence, relieved by copious emigration : while for emigration he holds that dependencies are the only sure outlet. The conclusion is that our Colonial dependencies are never to be permitted to " exchange the tie of subjection for that of equality," or to be bound to us by that "which is the surest bond of friendship and alliance between nations."

I should shrink from encountering so eminent an economist on a great economical question, and I am therefore glad that I am not called upon to discuss his ideal of national happiness. The two nations which at first sight seem most nearly to correspond to it are Ireland and China. These are the two great colonising countries in Mr. Merivale's sense of the term, though not in that sense in which we proudly apply it to England as the mother of free nations.

Granting Mr. Merivale's first position, that a state of things involving constant emigration is the ideal of national happiness; his second position, that dependencies are the only sure outlets for emigration, is at variance with the fact that the emigration from these kingdoms to the independent states of America is greater by two-fifths than to all our dependencies put together. Emigrants of the upper classes may generally prefer a country under British dominion : though even emigrants of the upper classes are sometimes, in these days, as in the early days of New England, active spirits, seeking for a freer air. But to assume that what an Irish peasant desires to find in a new land is another Ireland, or even that what an English peasant desires to find is another England, might be graceful but would not be in accordance with the truth. Possibly if this fact were more distinctly impressed on the minds of our statesmen, it might lead them to turn their attention to matters of nearer and more urgent concern than the regulation of sturdy and thriving communities at the other side of the globe.

But Mr. Merivale suggests that the States of America will be " closed " against our emigrants, at least for a long time, by the effects of the Civil War. Hence he infers that it is necessary to keep Canada in a state of dependence. " Canada," he says, " as long as it remains connected with us, affords a certain and regular place of resort for no inconsiderable portion of our overflow. How long Canada might do so if we were to follow the advice of a modern political school, by leaving her to independence—that is, to forming connexion with the States, or with some neighbouring portion of them—no wise man, with the Civil War now raging before his eyes, will venture to anticipate."

Now, in the first place, before we jump to the conclusion that the Civil War will stop emigration to the United States, let us look at the facts. The number of emigrants from these kingdoms to the United States in the whole year 1861 was 49,764. The number in the six months ending June 30, 1862, was 33,822. At this rate, instead of the falling off which Mr. Merivale assumes, there will be a large increase in the present year [b], in spite of the aggravated confusion and ravages of the Civil War.

[b] This anticipation has been fulfilled. The number of emigrants from these kingdoms to the United States during 1862 was 58,706.

It may be said that the increase in the number of
emigrants during the first half of the present year was
caused by recruiting for the Federal army. But, in
the first place, it does not appear that there is any
disturbance in the proportions of the ages and sexes
among the emigrants warranting this presumption.
In the second place, supposing this to be the case, it
would not really affect the question. In every labour
market, war makes a difference in the kind of labour
demanded. But an emigrant who goes out to be a
soldier or a cannon-founder is an emigrant still, and his
departure relieves our surplus population just as much
as if he went out to be a ploughman or an ordinary
artisan.

It is true there was a great fall in the amount of
emigration to the States in 1861, the first year of the
Civil War; and it is natural to suppose that this fall
was partly due to the war. But, as Mr. Merivale is
aware, the data from which we reason on this subject
are very fallacious, owing to the mixture of different
causes operating, some at home, some abroad. We
must know the rate of wages in the two countries, and
several other things, before we can with any approach to
certainty determine how much of the fluctuation is due
to the calamities of the Civil War. The fall in the
amount of emigration to the States in 1858, when all
was calm, was nearly double as great as that in 1861.
In the case of our North American Colonies, not to go
back to the time of the Irish famine, the number of
emigrants fell from 43,000 in 1854 to 17,000 in 1855,
and from 21,000 in 1857 to 9,000 in 1858; which

shews, by the way, that emigration to dependencies is not exempt from sudden diminution any more than that to independent nations. In 1861 there was a fall in the amount of emigration to Australia, and all other places except British North America. There was a considerable increase in the emigration to British North America. But here we are perplexed by an uncertainty as to the ultimate destination of emigrants, many of whom pass on from Canada to the United States. Your correspondent at New York reports that emigrants are still coming into the States from British America, as well as from this country. They would be especially likely at this time to go by way of Canada, though their ultimate destination might be the States, because they would naturally rather prefer a neutral port to the ports of a country engaged in a maritime war [c].

As to the troubles in Ireland, which Mr. Merivale ascribes to an alleged decrease of emigration to America, I venture to think that they have their source in evils older than Columbus, and that their present occasion is to be sought partly in local distress, partly, perhaps, in the conduct of the present Government of this country.

That the Civil War will make a "permanent change" in the prosperity of America, or in its fitness as a receptacle for emigration, is an assumption contradicted by the whole experience of history, and notably by the history of the American Republic in the years follow-

---

[c] I have here endeavoured to meet some arguments advanced by Mr. Merivale in a correspondence in *The Daily News* which ensued upon the publication of my original letter.

ing the Revolutionary War; a war which raged for eight years with fearful havoc and terrible vicissitudes, and in the course of which the finances of the Republic were in such a state that a bill for £732 paper currency was paid with four guineas and a half in gold. When a nation is struggling for a great cause, the energies and virtues called forth by the struggle soon heal every wound. "Separated States," granting that separation will take place, would scarcely be less open to emigrants than those which are united. Otherwise what would be the guilt and folly of those who urge on the dismemberment of that "vast confederacy," which, as Mr. Merivale says, "has received our children into its bosom for half a century."

But supposing that the Independent States of America were ruined, that this door was closed against emigration for ever, and that Canada was our only hope for the future, would that be a reason for keeping Canada in a state of dependency? If Canada is in any danger, is it not solely on account of her political connexion with us? Mr. Merivale suggests that if she were left independent she might choose to throw herself into the arms of the United States. If she does choose to throw herself into the arms of the United States, we shall not be able to prevent it. But she will not be the more likely to choose it if, as Mr. Merivale expects, the United States should fall into such misery that an Irish peasant will shrink back from them to famine and eviction. The debt which the United States have now accumulated seems in itself enough to repel the Canadians from annexation.

These far-sighted speculations on the usefulness of Canada as a dependency, in case of the ruin of the United States, seem to me to fall within the scope of a sentence pronounced by Mr. Merivale in his book against the too subtle advocates of the "Colonial system." "There could be no more dangerous error," he says, "in politics, than to build up artificial fabrics, not with a view to present emergencies, but to that future which a thousand contingencies may alter in a moment; most of all, if they are built and maintained at a loss. But in point of fact this has never been done. The Colonial system, like every other system of the kind, was constructed with a view to the present gain of particular classes : once established, it has found ingenious advocates to defend it, on the ground of prospective utility." The artificial fabric of our dominion over Canada is maintained at "a loss" which will be reckoned by millions in the present year. The danger of a desperate war arising to both countries from the connexion is a "present emergency." The value of the dependency, contingent on the permanent ruin of the United States, is a consideration of "prospective utility." Judging from experience, we should say that the utility was eminently prospective.

Not only Canada but Australia would, in Mr. Merivale's opinion, cease to be equally attractive to our emigrants when it was no longer "under the protection of our flag." His reason is, that "the sense of security now caused by British institutions would cease to exist." The fact that most of our emigrants go to the United States, is, once more, the conclusive answer to these speculations. In the States our emigrants find the essence of all British institutions, self-government; though they do not find the institution, which is by no means essentially British, of subjection to a distant Crown [d].

The Times swells Mr. Merivale's note of alarm, and portends that these great communities of Englishmen, if left to independence, must in their abject helplessness "transfer their allegiance to some foreign power"—to China, I suppose, or to Japan. If they attempted to remain independent, "the paltry nation and its despised flag would be of far less account than the half-

---

[d] My friend and colleague Mr. Rogers, the Oxford Professor of Political Economy, in a letter to *The Morning Star*, (Oct. 17, 1862,) remarks on this part of Mr. Merivale's argument :—" Not more true is it that Colonies are under the same Government as ourselves. Identity of Government is not maintained by the reverent announcement of a few constitutional fictions, a vague and undefined dependence, or even by community of races and immediate ties of blood. No one knows better than Mr. Merivale that the Colonial Office is impotent against the Colonial will; that an appeal from Colonial Courts of Justice to Queen's Courts would not be endured except as an escape from a difficulty; and that the most rash and meddlesome Colonial Secretary would not venture on a veto upon Colonial acts. Canada is loyal to a proverb, even to the raising a regiment, but her Government has gone to the verge of repudiation in the affair of the Grand Trunk Railway, and has adopted that very hostile tariff which Mr. Merivale deprecates as the consequence of political independence. It is only in the great Oriental satrapy that the Home Government is absolute, and is able to retard, against the wisdom of able financiers and enlightened governors, as much activity and prosperity as would long since have obviated the crisis by which the great manufacture of the north of England is affected. India, however, in which the per centage of European mortality is double that of England, where few children are reared, and no marriages in the second generation are fertile, is hardly an available outlet for British over-population."

caste communities of Central America, and the population would in all probability steadily diminish until
some other State took up the work of Colonization."
Such is the point to which our faith in the self-reliant
energies of Englishmen has been reduced by this system of tutelage and subjection. Did the writer in *The
Times* ever hear of the foundation of New England?
Does he know that a company of English peasants,
with no help but that which every honest and religious Englishman carries in his own heart, established,
amidst the horrors of an untrodden wilderness, and in
face of swarming tribes of hostile savages, a polity
which endured in unbroken order and happiness, drawing to it from the Old World the choicest spirits who
loved freedom, till the Crown asserted its phantom
rights, and by its wise and beneficent interference
brought on civil strife and revolution?

We have been speaking of private emigration. Dependencies might be more necessary, or at least more
useful, if Colonization was to be conducted on a grand
scale for the relief of our surplus population, or for
political objects, by the State. But the State neither
does, nor is likely to do, anything of the kind. The
only kind of Colonization which the State has in modern times attempted to conduct is transportation.

Our Government has indeed been frequently urged
to found Colonies after the heroic model, with a complete section of English society, including noblemen
and gentlemen as well as labourers, so that a miniature
England, perfect in all its parts, might be planted at
once in the new land. Such it was supposed was the

mode in which the famous Colonies of Greece were founded.

Archias, one of the high aristocracy of Corinth, being compelled to fly his country for an atrocious crime, collected a band of adventurers, sailed to Sicily, and dispossessed of their abodes a tribe of the native Sicels, some of whom probably became the slaves, while others became the dependents, of the conquerors. Thus Syracuse was founded, and such was the aristocratic element included in the foundation. This was probably the history of the Greek Colonies generally. They were enterprises undertaken by bold adventurers, outlaws, or refugees, more resembling the enterprises of Cortes and Pizarro, or those of the Saxon and Norman rovers, than the religious Colony of New England, or the agricultural and commercial Colonies of Australia. The Greek nobles who led them, like the Norman Sea-Kings and the Hengists and Horsas who led the Saxon bands, were military chiefs, who. maintained their ascendancy over their followers in the new land by their military prowess, not mere social decorations sent out by the moral taste of the Home Government, to form the Corinthian capital for the column of the new nation. Would the younger son of a Duke, supposing the Government could find one for the purpose, when stripped of all the social connexions, not to say of the habiliments, which make him the object of respect here, be able to preserve his ascendancy, and to exercise a beneficent influence among a community of ploughmen and shepherds? It is recorded of the race which sent forth the Saxon Colonies to England, that

they chose their kings by birth, but their leaders by
valour. Did they not take a practical view of the
matter, especially as regards the leadership of Colonization?

Besides, how is the Government to obtain the required section of English society? It cannot press
sons of dukes and squires. Let any projector of
schemes of this kind try to present clearly and in
detail to his own mind the course which the Colonial
Office would take to collect and organize the materials
for an heroic Colony : his vision will probably melt at
once into air. To take the sacred fire from the hearth
of Downing-street is no doubt an easy process, but in
other respects the proposed imitation of a Greek Colony
seems not so easy. It might prove something like
the imitation of a Roman banquet in Peregrine Pickle.
Even the priest who accompanied the sacred fire would
be very apt, judging from experience, to turn up again
at the hearth of the Mother Country in Pall Mall.

The foundation of Canterbury, in New Zealand, was
an attempt to realize the heroic idea. It has failed, and
in place of the Anglo-Catholic community of noblemen
and gentlemen, with their High-Church priesthood
and their loyal train, the coarse and practical race of
commercial adventurers is fast usurping the room.
The Neo-Catholicism of the Anglican Church was not
strong and fervent enough to do what Puritanism did
in New England. Yet the Colony being a private
enterprise, and drawing into it real private sympathy
and effort, has not been without a good result; it has
left in Canterbury the germ of a religious and moral

N

nation, and a hope above that of the mere commercial settlements, much more of the convict Colonies, which cover the surrounding shores.

Government, when it has undertaken to found Colonies, has been obliged to use materials far below the heroic standard. To Virginia it sent a cargo of broken gentlemen, vagabond serving-men, and goldsmiths without work in search of imaginary gold. Nature rejected once and again this evil seed of a new nation, but it was obstinately forced upon her, and the original settlement was recruited from the same auspicious sources. The result was such a nest of felons and vagabonds that, according to a most competent witness, convicts literally preferred being hanged to being transported to Virginia. Hence has sprung the Slave Power, from whose deadly domination the hope of the New World is just struggling to get free.

Again, after the rebellion of the American Colonies, our Government thought at once to repair that loss and get rid of their felons by founding Convict Settlements in Australia. They meant well, but they tainted the very sources of national life in a new division of the globe. "The whole man," says De Tocqueville, "lies in the cradle of the infant, and there is something analogous to this in the case of nations: each people retains the traces of its origin; the circumstances which attended its birth and assisted in its development exercise their influence on all the rest of its career." If this saying of the great political philosopher is true, what has Government done for humanity by founding penal settlements in Australia?

I confess that I do not regard with unqualified enthusiasm the rank growth of material prosperity which
is shooting up with the rapidity of a gourd in those
countries. I see nothing as yet among the Colonists
of Australia that marks the opening life of a great
nation. Does any Australian speak with pride and
affection of his country? Does any Australian speak
of his country at all? Is it not regarded merely as
a land in which money is to be made, and from which
a fortune is to be carried back to buy a great house
and dazzle the neighbourhood in England? There is
a purpose higher than this which rules, and, whatever
speeches may be made about Colonial prosperity at
Colonial banquets, inexorably rules, the world.

Is Government to carry on systematic Emigration for
the purpose of relieving the pressure on the means of
subsistence among our population? And are dependencies to be retained for this purpose? In the first
place, Emigration does not relieve the pressure on the
means of subsistence : it carries off those who press
least on the means of subsistence, the young, the
healthy, and those who are fit, or will soon be fit, for
labour. It leaves the old, the sickly, and the helpless. When Mr. Merivale speaks of emigration as a
regular provision for one child out of six in this country, and one out of three in Ireland, he must mean
children who have arrived at the age of labour, unless
he intends to send the parents with them. In case of
such a calamity as the Irish famine, Emigration at
the expense of Government, that is, at the expense of
the tax-payer, may possibly be the best mode of giving

immediate relief to the mass of suffering. But bleeding, though it may save from instant death, will not work a permanent cure. A permanent cure can only be worked by a radical change in the habits of the people; and nothing will effect a radical change in the habits of the people but the power and hope of acquiring property, the source of all self-restraint, frugality, and industry among men.

Writers are accustomed to speak of Government as doing everything out of a fund of its own. They forget, though they cannot fail to know, that when Government sends out emigrants, it sends them out at the expense of those who remain. And when an emigrant has gone out to another country he ceases in any way to contribute to the burdens of this. He pays no English rates or taxes; he has slipped his shoulder for ever from under the load of our National Debt: therefore to those who still bear these imposts and these burdens, his departure is, fiscally speaking, a dead loss, though they may rejoice to think that he is gone to a happier land.

Perhaps there may be room for a few more people in England yet. Has Government reduced the burdens of the nation to the utmost possible extent? Has it retrenched every item of needless expenditure? Has it cut down the Establishments as low as the safety of the country will permit? Has it solemnly abjured all needless wars? Has it repealed all laws which interfere with the fair distribution of wealth or prevent the productive- powers of the soil from being fully called forth by labour? If it has really done all this,.

it may be permitted to entertain the mournful thought
of saving a few out of the general misery, by imposing
additional burdens on those who are left to suffer.

We are not now dealing with political or ecclesiastical questions, but the sentence of the economist will
not be doubtful on a Government which keeps up the
Irish Church Establishment, and expatriates the Irish
people.

As to the question about the employment of capital
in Colonization so far as the State is concerned, it is
enough to say that the State has no capital to employ.
No one probably would propose that the Government
of this country should raise money by taxation, to be
invested in the speculation of cultivating waste land in
Australia. It need hardly be said that the working of
silver mines in America by the Spanish Government,
or the farming of Java by the Dutch, affords no parallel
whatever to such a speculation.

The main object of nature in Colonization is not
economical object. She does not intend to create
an extraordinary and, perhaps, treacherous demand for
certain manufactures of the Mother Country. She does
not intend to provide a loophole for the consciences
of bad rulers, and permit them, after misgoverning a
country as Ireland has been misgoverned, to look lazily
for relief to the banishment, after dreadful demoral-
ization and suffering, of great masses of the people.
Her high purpose is to sow the seed of new nations;
destined to serve, in their turn and in their place, the
ends for which the world was made. And left to herself she has chosen her seed well. She has chosen the

brave Frank, the brave Anglo-Saxon, the brave North-
man, the crew of the "Mayflower" pious as well as
brave. Governments have chosen the convicts who
have left their taint on the origin of Australia and
those "gentlemen" of Virginia, to whose society felons
preferred death, the worthy progenitors of that portentous incarnation of heathen hard-heartedness and
lust, the great Slave Power, whose advent we are
welcoming with jubilant ecstacy into the civilized and
Christian world.

. A company of exiles for conscience' sake landing on
a distant shore, struggling unaided with the horrors
of the wilderness and the attacks of the savage; tilling
the land by united efforts, and having all things in
common till the victory over the wilderness was won;
braving hunger and suffering, decimated by disease,
but at last laying the deep foundations of a great
people; such is colonization conducted by the hand of
nature. "We are well weaned," said the founders of
the settlement, "from the delicate milk of our Mother
Country, and inured to the difficulties of a strange
land. The people are industrious and frugal. We are
knit together in a most sacred covenant of the Lord, of
the violation whereof we make great conscience, and
by virtue whereof we hold ourselves strictly tied to all
care of each other's good and of the whole. It is not
with us as men whom small things can discourage."
"Let it not be grievous to you," said the Puritans at
home to their brethren in New England,—"let it not
be grievous to you that you have been instruments to
break the ice for others. The honour shall be yours till

the world's end." The settlement was not a commercial speculation, nor did it answer as a commercial specula-tion to the settlers. " It concerneth New England al-ways to remember that they were originally a plantation religious, not a plantation of trade. If any man among us make religion as twelve, and the world as thirteen, such an one hath not the spirit of a true New Eng-landman."

We need not such a platitude as to imagine that the heroic story of the Puritan settlement is to be repeated in these times. Yet even Economy may still find in it matter for meditation when she is engaged on problems touching the exportation of capital to Colonies and the division of Colonial land. And poli-tical science, exploring the causes which form the cha-racter of infant nations, will often compare the moral results of this "plantation originally religious" with those of " plantations of trade."

The Stuart Government hated New England, and tried to stop the emigration to it. The heirs of the Stuart principles hate New England still. They love more that Colony of the other England, a Governor of which could boast, at a pretty late period of its history, " I thank God there are here no free schools nor print-ing, and I hope we shall not have them these hundred years." Yet if the Governments of the Old World were aware what New England has done for them they might feel towards her, if not affection, yet some kind of constrained gratitude. What would have been their fate if the masses of want, misery, and discontent of which she has relieved them, for which she has found homes and schools, and which she has turned into the customers and feeders of Europe, had been thrown back hopeless upon their hands! What would be their fate even now if their prayers were granted by the anger of Heaven, and this great vent for social misery and political difficulty were closed! And how strong must the foundations of the great Transatlantic Commonwealth have been, since they have received year after year this flood of alien vagrancy and distress without being submerged or loosened by its turbid tide!

Has the protection of the Home Government favoured Emigration by increasing the productiveness of land in the Colonies? It seems to have done the reverse. The artificial security given by it has led the Colonists to scatter their settlements widely, instead of concentrating them, condensing the population, multiplying the mutual facilities which a condensed population affords, and bringing out thoroughly the productive powers of the land. The Government has itself admitted that such dispersion of the settlers is an evil; and it is an evil which the protection given by the presence of our forces to outsettling and squatting tends directly to increase.

The interference of our Government in the distribution of land, again, has apparently led to evils, both economical and political, of a grave kind. It was conducted, till irremediable mischief had been done, on the system, evidently derived from the landlord system of this country, of large grants and leases of land. In some parts of Australia an agrarian struggle between the wasteful occupants of great tracts of country and

the new comers has been the result. I had a letter
the other day from an inhabitant of one of our pattern
Australian Colonies, one of which the name has of
late been always in the mouths of those who defend the
present system. " You are doubtless conversant," he
says, " with the legal tenure of land given in Australia
to persons employed in grazing pursuits, or squatters.
These form a class who are in possession by lease of
immense tracts of land, which they, in the majority
of instances, very inadequately occupy. The produc-
tion of wool is entirely in their hands, but as has been
pointed out by Dr. Lang and others, years ago, the
quantity of wool they raise is but small when compared
with what it would probably be were the land acces-
sible to persons of small means and in small quantities.
There is, in fact, in Queensland and the other Australian Colonies, absurd as it may seem, and perhaps unintelligible, a monopoly of land. A class is there
formed whose interests are obviously adverse to the
growth by immigration on an abundant scale, of a
numerous class of small freeholder agriculturists. This
class has always avowed its readiness to employ any
kind of labour, cheapness being alone sought for. They
fought for convict labour to the last; and are now in
a rather sinister manner seeking for Coolie labour."
Whether this writer's view of the question be wholly
just or not, here are plainly the seeds of discord; and
they have been sown in this young community by
a distant Government interfering under the sense of
a fancied responsibility in affairs with which it has no
manner of concern. And now Government seems to

be going, under the influence of capitalists, to interfere
in the Colonial labour market, as it has interfered in
the division of Colonial land, and, if Political Economy
is a true science, with every prospect of as happy a result. "The one aspect," says the correspondent whom
I have just quoted, "in which Coolie labour is to be
viewed, with reference to Queensland and the Australian Colonies, is this. All these Colonies have a responsible Government, and are similar to Canada in
their present and future prospects. Towards the Australian Colonies the minds of people thinking of emi-
grating are now turning with an interest and decision not observable before. Queensland, more than
any other Australian Colony, as being the youngest,
has employment to offer to the surplus population of
the Mother Country which is practically inexhaustible.
None of our public works are begun, our roads are
unmade, our bridges unbuilt, our lands untilled, and
our political institutions from sheer want of population
are apparently too liberal. This is a state of affairs
which points surely to the necessity of filling up the
Colony with those who can appreciate the political
structure, and help each one to promote all that is enlightened, progressive, and British. To bring hither
a degraded race who can do nothing but mechanically
labour is to inflict a deadly injury upon us, by separating classes into Indian fixedness, and thus stunting
all that is most desirable in the Colony." This writer
does not stand alone, as public meetings in the Colony
prove. Is there any answer to what he says? And if
there is not, is this importation of a servile caste to be

persisted in, against the prayers, and to the evident
degradation of the yeomen and free labourers who are
the heart of this young nation. We have founded
slave states already in America and in the West Indies.
Is not this responsibility enough?

My correspondent says that "the institutions of his
Colony are apparently too liberal from sheer want of
population." Too liberal, in the sense of being too
free, they cannot be: but they may be quite unsuitable
nevertheless. A Constitution was framed for Carolina
by the English proprietaries of the territory, on a plan
devised by Shaftesbury and Locke, with four Estates,
two orders of Nobility, a Grand Council, an intricate
system of legislation, Constitutional checks and balances,
Courts of ceremonies and pedigrees, baronies and ma-
nors, and an Established Church. This Constitution
was the theme of general applause. "The model," it
was said, "is esteemed by all judicious persons without
compare." "Empires would be ambitious of subjection
to the noble government which deep wisdom had projected for Carolina." The people for whom this "model"
of "noble government" was designed were a scattered
population of refugees, living deep in the woods, far
apart from each other, and with no roads between
them.

Mr. Merivale states in his present paper only what
he conceives to be the advantages of dependency, even
as regards this country. He says nothing of the great
expense, or of the still greater peril of an empire spread
over the world, and exposing us everywhere to wounds.
He does not tell us how he thinks our power and in-

fluence in Europe are affected by the dispersion of our
forces from Canada to New Zealand. While he ad-
vises us to keep Canada perpetually dependent on us,
for the sake of emigration, he does not give us any
reason to hope either that the Canadians, while they
are in a state of dependency, will undertake their own
defence, or that• we shall be able to defend that vast
frontier against the Americans, especially if we should
have a European war on our hands. He does not
notice the danger, which yet is but too apparent, of
quarrelling with our Colonies on the subject of military
and commercial policy, and of thereby breaking those
natural ties which independence, as he has himself
eloquently shewn, makes stronger and more secure.
If, as those who applaud him say, he has in his present argument been descending to the low level of
his opponents in order to defeat them on their own
ground, let us hope that he will now try to raise us to
his own level, by arguing on whatever grounds he
thinks highest. If a man were to tell me that he did
not care for economical considerations, I should take
him for a fraudulent stockjobber; but I fully acknowledge the superiority of moral and political considerations, when sincerely urged, to those of an economical
kind.

As to the Colonies themselves, Mr. Merivale's arguments leave their interests out of view. We have seen
that he holds "equality" to be better than "subjection."
Yet he proposes to hold the Colonies in perpetual subjection because, as subjects, they will be more con-
venient receptacles for the overflow of our population.

In a future argument, which he half promises, I trust he will shew that this subjection will not stunt and distort the political growth of the young communities, or quench the spirit that should make them great nations.

In his book, Mr. Merivale says of British statesmen that "though prepared to recognise Colonial independence as the natural ultimate result of modern Colonial policy, none of them wish to see the revolution commence in their own day." That I apprehend is the real state of the case. We are "drifting," and drifting towards a dangerous shore. England may look to her statesmen, if ever a nation could, for the able and upright administration of the current business of the State. For organic change, however necessary and however urgent, she must look to herself.

I am, &c.

GOLDWIN SMITH.

Oct. 13, 1862.

XII.

MR. ADDERLEY ON CANADIAN AFFAIRS.

TO THE EDITOR OF THE "DAILY NEWS."

Sir,—The crisis in our relations with Canada has led Mr. Adderley to re-publish his letter on the Colonies, with a special preface on Canadian affairs. He will be heard with interest and deference by all who desire to form a fair judgment on the subject. He adverts to the letters which I have addressed to you, and says that he "deplores my conclusions." Yet I venture to think he strengthens the premises from which those conclusions are drawn. Not only so, but, if I am not mistaken, he practically leads up to them. If I understand him rightly, he would withdraw all our forces from the Colonies, and leave them to provide each for its own defence. When he has done this, I believe he will speedily find himself landed in the conclusions which, as propounded by me, he now deplores.

As to the present state of things, his language is frank and strong. "Canada and England cannot long remain together on terms of disadvantage to either. If you wish for permanent friendship with anybody, its terms must be fair and equal on both sides. Romantic patronage on one side, and interested attachment on the other, is not friendship, but mutual decep-

tion. When we find out that we are paying too much
for our pride, or they that they are receiving too little
for their dependence, the rottenness of our present connexion will be detected. As I value Canada, I seek
for the earliest possible exposure of her false friends
who would cherish her present relations. Let not a
free country like England dream of maintaining Colonies in equally free government with herself, by the
bribe of undertaking their protection. Their freedom
is corrupted, and its spirit dies, in the very act of receiving the boon, while its form mischievously remains,
for we cannot recall their Constitutions. England undertakes a task of protection which she cannot always
sustain, and saps the strength of freedom which would
ordinarily sustain itself." Men of sense have long been
convinced that the present connexion is noxious to both
parties. There is nothing new in these letters of mine
but the proposal that as the connexion is noxious it
should be dissolved.

To the allegation that the withdrawal of the troops
from Canada would be a penal treatment of the Colony,
Mr. Adderley vigorously replies:—" Surely a Colony
has become the most fastidious of tyrants. We may
not ask it to arm, for fear of its taking offence and
separating from us. We may not agree with its own
decision that there is no need of arming, because it
would be penal treatment to withdraw troops whose
presence they say they don't need, while they like to
retain it. Such terms of friendship compose no friendship, nor alliance, nor community, nor solid intercon-
nexion of any sort; but a fool's paradise of mutual

promise and expectation equally visionary and eva-
nescent."

Nor does Mr. Adderley entirely shut his eyes to
" the inevitable defect of dualism in distant Parliamentary Government." But he says "there are
also gaps in the system of Constitutional Government
at home—gaps which are rather bridged over by compromise and management, or avoided by foresight and
prudence, than constructively filled up." No doubt
there are gaps in the English Constitution; perhaps
there are lurking dangers in those gaps which time
may reveal. But what gap is there in the English
Constitution at all approaching in its vastness to that
between two independent Parliaments, one in Europe,
the other in America, one (as Mr. Adderley allows)
representing an aristocratic, the other a democratic
society, and each dealing, in its external relations, with
a totally different group of nations? The Governor
General must be "judicious" indeed who, by any
wheedling, could bridge over such a chasm as this.

"Our American, African, and Australian Colonies,
naturally free, have also representative institutions, and
the representative of the Crown on the spot. They are
complete transmarine Englands. They have all the
equipment of English self-government; only in separate establishments, because their distance renders their
representation in Westminster impossible. It is but
creating confusion to give them entire nationality, and
supply them with an external Government besides."
Surely this last sentence hits the mark and carries home.

If our Colonies cannot possibly be represented at

Westminster, how can they take part in the councils of
Westminster? And if they cannot take part in the
councils of Westminster, how can they be expected to
take part in the acts which flow from those councils?

In this matter of arming against the Americans, for
instance, what hope is there of permanent agreement
between the two Parliaments? The Canadians have
no aristocratic antipathy to the American democracy;
they are intimately bound up with it by commercial
and social relations; and in case of a war with it they
would be in the most imminent danger of a desolating,
invasion. Their Parliament and ours deliberate under
entirely different conditions, and are morally sure to
decide different ways.

There is a circumstance still more fatal to agreement in questions of military expenditure. The mass
of the tax-payers are represented in the Canadian Parliament, while they are not represented in ours. If
the fiscal burdens of the Canadians are to be regulated,
directly or indirectly, by the estimates of the English
Parliament, the Canadians have a right to press upon
us parliamentary reform.

To put the same thing in other words, the state of
society in which we still linger, and are likely to linger
long, is one that loves great standing armies. The
state of society in which the Canadians are placed is
one to which great standing armies are utterly re-
pugnant.

The Canadians, Mr. Adderley will remember, abjure
all interest in English quarrels. The theory of the
matter of course is that they are as much a part of

O

England, and as much affected by all that affects England, "as Middlesex." The fact is that Mr. Rose, the great Canadian advocate of the present connexion, confounds his partisans on this side of the water by declaring that the Canadians had no concern in any of the questions between us and the Americans, not even in the Oregon question; and that if Canada were drawn by us into any of these quarrels she would be immolating herself in a spirit of romantic devotion to the honour of the British flag. Mr. Adderley has an •understanding above cant, and he knows how far mere romance will carry a thrifty people in military expenditure or in bearing the ravages of a desperate war. A "militia," indeed, is the utmost he seems to expect from the Canadians. And what is a militia against the great army of the Northern States?

As to Imperial compulsion, in this or any other matter of Colonial government, Mr. Adderley frankly admits it to be out of the question. And as the Colonial constitutions have been granted past recall, the day for stipulations is gone by. We have only the free votes of the Canadians to look to, and we begin to see what their free votes will produce. They talked of "the last man and the last dollar," but up to this time neither men nor dollars have been forthcoming. Dollars, indeed, as we have seen before, there are at present none to come forth.

Suppose the Canadians, or any other Colonists, are obstinately frugal, and refuse to provide themselves with armaments on our scale, what is Mr. Adderley's last resort? He must look this contingency in the face.

"Let America only decompose and reconstruct herself in the neighbourhood of Canada. There is no cohesion in the constitution of Canadian connexion with England sufficient to resist the mere impact of any fragment from the ruins of the Union." Do not these words, spoken by an Imperialist, shew us at once the desperate nature of the task which we have imposed upon ourselves in making it our duty to keep Canada in Europe? Do they not warn us, as with the voice of a trumpet, that America has destinies of her own which we may mar, but cannot guide: and that our duty is to the community of nations to which we belong?

It has been held, as a sacred tradition of our policy, that the union of the whole of North America in one nation would be very dangerous to our interests; and that we must continue to hold Canada in order to keep the Continent divided. Why did we not in the first instance leave Canada to its French Colonists, who would have fulfilled the behests of nature by making it a separate nation? The policy of promoting divisions as a source of weakness in rival communities is not only less genial but less sound and less feasible than that of promoting unity as a source of strength in your own. And our only motive for wishing America to be divided and weak is in fact our fear for the safety of these very possessions. The Americans are not likely to meddle with Europe, and therefore the consolidation of their power would threaten no other interests of ours. But whether this policy be sound or unsound, grand or mean, its object is effectually fulfilled in another way by the breaking up of the great American federation:

and if it is only to prevent the unity of America that
we have been staying, we are now, if we find it otherwise desirable, at liberty to retire.

The advantages derived by England from the present connexion, which are to countervail to her its
perpetual difficulties and dangers, are set forth by Mr.
Adderley, who is thoroughly master of the subject, in
these words :—" England has a direct interest in the continuance of her North American connexion. She would
rather have the vigorous natives of those shores recruit
her own than a foreign naval power : however inde-
finitely, we feel that there is power, as well as weakness,
in extent of empire, and we know also that our emi-
grating instincts have more certain if not larger scope
under the same allegiance." 'I am not sure that I understand the first of these three arguments ; but it
cannot mean that the vigorous natives of Canada at
present recruit, to any considerable extent, our naval
power.   For the emigration argument Mr. Adderley
cites Mr. Herman Merivale, whose reasonings I have
already endeavoured to meet.   In truth, it is not easy
to understand how that argument can be put forward in
face of the fact that the main stream of emigration, even
now, in the midst of the Civil War, sets, not towards
our dependent Colonies in Canada or elsewhere, but towards our independent Colonies in the United States.
As to the "indefinite feeling" that extent of empire
is a source of power, it is easily accounted for without
supposing it, in defiance of daily experience, to have
any real foundation.   It is a delusion not so much of
the pure fancy as of the memory ; a notion once true,

which has survived the state of things that gave it birth. The time was when conquering and imperial nations—Rome and Spain for example—drew military force and revenue from their provinces, and when extended empire might be justly regarded as a source of strength as well as of weakness. We draw from our provinces neither military force nor revenue; but, on the contrary, dissipate our own military force and waste our own revenue in retaining them. To us, therefore, an extended Empire is a source of weakness alone. But the old notion still remains, and governs the actions of nations and of statesmen who will not be at the pains to inquire into the reasons of the policy which they pursue. It is, as Mr. Adderley justly says, an "indefinite feeling" and nothing else, that leads us to keep up these costly and unremunerative establishments, and to incur the constant risk of still more costly wars. A little clearness and definiteness of thought on the part of those who manage our affairs would render all further argument superfluous, save the two nations from a great peril, rivet for ever the attachment of the Colonies to the Mother Country, and relieve from a heavy burden the resources of an over-taxed and suffering people.

Mr. Adderley, indeed, can scarcely feel that his own arguments in favour of the connexion are irrefragable when he tries peremptorily to put an end to the discussion. "Secession and abandonment," he tells us, "should be inadmissible questions on either side. *Nemo potest exuere patriam* should be the recognised maxim of both. ᶜ To contemplate divorce is to imperil union. The

Canadians would be rebels if they abjured their allegiance, and the Queen would repudiate inalienable responsibilities by abdicating her functions of sovereignty. Imperial disintegration cannot be legitimate matter for discussion within any Empire." I need not draw out this principle into its consequences or recall the sinister illustrations which it has received from history. I will not even pause to ask Mr. Adderley why, when he implicitly admits that the substance of Imperial power over the Colonies is gone, he holds it such treason to discuss the utility of the shadow. It is enough to say that we now regard all discussion as more than legitimate which can promote the interests of the nation ; and that Her Majesty knows no responsibility so inalienable as that of doing, on all occasions, whatever is for the good of her people.

Mr. Arthur Mills has worked with Mr. Adderley in the investigation of this question, and I believe there is a good deal of sympathy between them. In the Introduction to his work " On Colonial Constitutions," Mr. Mills pronounces that " the past has furnished irresistible evidence of the instability of those principles of Colonial policy which were once deemed to be the pillars of our national greatness." " To retain," he says, " for the longest possible period, at the smallest possible cost, with the greatest possible advantage to ourselves, a permanent dominion over the dependencies of our Empire, was once the problem which occupied the minds of British statesmen. To ripen those communities to the earliest possible maturity—social, political, and commercial—to qualify them by all the ap-

pliances within the reach of a parent state, for present
self-government, and eventual independence, is now the
universally admitted object and aim of our Colonial
policy [a]." The universally admitted object and aim of
our Colonial policy, according to Mr. Mills, is that
which Mr. Adderley denounces as Imperial disintegration, and puts beyond the pale of legitimate discussion. If my views are treason, there are, if Mr.
Mills may be believed, a good many traitors.

To so sensible a man as Mr. Adderley one may talk
sense without fear. If the maxim *nemo potest exuere
patriam* means that a man ought never to put off the
allegiance of the heart to his native country, it is
rational and true : but if it means that men cannot go
forth from their country to found an independent state,
it is a political absurdity and an historical falsehood.
Occupancy confers a good title to new territory, but it
confers it on the occupants. The Queen would no more
detract from the honour of her Crown by renouncing
for the public good her title to dominion over communities in America and Australia, than the Pope
would detract from the honour of his tiara by renouncing the imaginary power which he once exercised, of meteing out to his different liegemen the
realms of an undiscovered world.

Mr. Adderley tells me that I need not be at the
pains of discussing the alternative of federal union.
To him I dare say the discussion of such an alternative
is needless, but the plan has found advocates, and was
gravely propounded not long since by a Canadian of

[a] Mills on Colonial Constitutions, p. lxix.

eminence. For the groups of American and Australian Commonwealths, federation is a political instrument of inestimable value. It may give them at once the peace of great Empires, the active intelligence of small communities, the mutual education and discipline of a cluster of independent nations. But a federation of England, North America, and Australia is a chimera which Mr. Adderley may well decline to discuss.

And yet what is his own scheme? He has not yet given it to us in a working form, and I confess the principle on which it is to be founded eludes my grasp. How does he propose to ensure the harmonious action of a set of independent legislatures representing con- stituencies of the most different character, and scattered literally all over the globe? How does he meet the arguments against a connexion which gratuitously in- volves nations widely separated, not only by distance but by interest, in each other's quarrels and wars? The palmy days of sound Colonial relations according to him were the days just before the American Revolu- tion. But those were the days when, because European Kings had fallen out with each other in the middle of Germany, "black men fought on the coast of Coro- mandel, and red men scalped each other by the great lakes of North America." They were the days when Adam Smith bitterly complained of the expense and uselessness of the Colonies, charging them with being the perpetual source of quarrels between us and other powers, and with having cost us ninety millions in a single war. The American Revolution itself was rather a sinister result of a perfectly sound state of things; and, as Mr. Adderley is aware, that Revolution was not a sudden and accidental event, but the climax of a long train of disputes and quarrels, one of which had come to the very verge of civil war.

I would beg Mr. Adderley to consider whether there is not some truth in what I have said before; whether these cravings for a grand unity are not destined to find their fulfilment in the moral and intellectual, rather than in the political sphere. There may be—there is—a great Council of England and all her Colonies, and the deliberations of that Council may influence, and do influence, the action of all its members. But it is the great Council of the Press.

Our first Colonists were practically independent, though they owed a nominal allegiance to the Crown, as the fancied grantor of lands beyond its sway. And while independent they laid, with their own strong hearts and hands, the foundations of a great and happy nation. Even their relations to the natives at that time were on the whole better and more Christian than those of any Colonists have since been. The increase of their trade, and the prospect of a lucrative monopoly, led the Crown to exercise its imaginary rights: and then speedily ensued quarrels, revolution, and disastrous severance between the Old England and the New; the New England carrying away with her a revolutionary bias which has perverted her political course, and the bane of slavery, which the fatal selfishness of the Home Government had fastened upon her for its own ends. From that time to this it would, I believe, be difficult to shew that the Colonial Office has

done, or could have done, anything but mischief. Its
interference with the politics of the Colonies has been
unsystematic, aimless, and, from the constant changes
of ministers, self-contradictory, bringing on a rebellion
in Canada, and everywhere injuriously impeding the
free action of those powers of self-government of which
every Englishman is the heir, and which, wherever
two or three Englishmen are met together, make a
nation. Its attempts to propagate the Church of England as an establishment have not only failed, but
injured the prospects of that Church, of the clergy,
and of religion in the Colonies. The errors which it
is now acknowledged to have committed in the distribution of land, partly under the impulse of aristocratic
prepossessions, have entailed no small amount of political as well as economical evil on the communities.
By transporting felons to Colonies it has done mischief
to Colonization, of which it has at last itself become
aware. Its military protection has stifled self-defence,
and induced the Colonists in some places to plant themselves in dangerous out-settlements, whence have sprung
savage wars. Finally, its attempt to act as the guardian of the natives and the regulator of their affairs
has proved, by the honest confession of the present
Colonial Minister, an expensive failure. Such, I think,
has been the general course of a history which Mr.
Adderley knows well. That the Colonial Office has
done good acts must be and has been acknowledged;
but they are chiefly those by which of late years it has
wisely restricted its own interference and magnanimously retrenched its own power. The blame lies not

on the men, some of whom have been the flower of English statesmen, but on the system, under which the same affairs are managed by two Governments, representing communities widely differing in their political character, at opposite sides of the globe.

I am, &c.,

GOLDWIN SMITH.

Nov. 12, 1862.

XIII.
GIBRALTAR.

SIR,—*The Times*, in its answer to my letter on New Zealand, tells me that I have "tempered the extravagance of my former rhapsody," as to what I said about "Gibraltar and Aden." I have not said a word about Aden. I will now, with your permission, say a few words more about Gibraltar. England is great enough to desire honest counsel from all her citizens. And her voice is not heard in the censures of journals or men who have never foregone a moment's popularity to secure her lasting strength and honour.

We are, no doubt, about to lift a sacred veil; but we have already lifted one almost as sacred with a result which encourages us to proceed. Our inquiries have already brought us pretty nearly to this, that the sum annually spent on our Colonial Empire, a sum which, in this year of distress, will not fall short of four millions, is, as far as we are concerned, pure waste. The sinews of English labour have hitherto borne the crushing weight of Imperial extravagance: the time may be at hand when they will be able to bear it no more.

The honour of the nation can suffer no disparagement by frankly discussing the value of any military position. The Duke of Wellington did not tarnish our honour by falling back, when prudence gave the word, from Busaco on Torres Vedras. We may do what is wise at present without renouncing the glories of the past. Gibraltar is, and always will be, a famous monument of English valour. So are Calais and Dunkirk. But who wishes that Calais and Dunkirk were ours now?

Calais was occupied as a landing-place for our invasions of France. When those invasions became hopeless, and had been virtually abandoned, the landing-place became worthless. Yet ambition clung to the possession with an obstinacy, and resented its loss with a fury, at which it is easy to smile now. "To men," says an historian, " who weighed the trivial advantages which had been derived from the possession of the place against the annual expenses of its garrison and fortifications, the loss appeared in the light of a national benefit; but in the eyes of foreigners it tarnished the reputation of the country, and at home it furnished a subject of reproach to the factious, of regret to the loyal." The loss of Calais tarnished the reputation of the country because it was taken from us by force instead of being given up when it had become useless. Yet an eminent journal tells us that though the usefulness of Gibraltar to us is doubtful, and the expense and danger of keeping it are beyond doubt, there is "no precedent" for giving up anything without compulsion, and that by so doing we might shew weakness. This is the very form of argument satirically put into the mouth of the fatuous maintainers of useless dependencies by Lord Brougham : and, as he truly says, is identical with the now discarded and derided reasoning of Lord North. Surely "Empire" must be one of those strange intellectual spheres in which "two and two make five," or people could never argue that we should wait to be kicked out of the window in order to avoid the unprecedented humiliation of walking voluntarily out of the door.

The ignominious manner in which Calais was lost could not fail to tarnish the reputation of the country in the eyes of foreigners : but if foreigners imagined that the strength of the country was diminished by the loss of a useless fortress, they were speedily undeceived when they encountered in arms the England of Elizabeth.

That Calais must have been lost at last, no one will now dispute. A powerful and united nation intent on its object and watching its opportunities has never failed in the long run to expel the invader, even an English invader, from its own soil.

As the value of Calais ceased with the French wars, so the value of military posts occupied to force a way for our trade is ceasing with the reign of monopoly. Commerce no longer needs cannon to clear her path : she is becoming everywhere a welcome guest. We have embraced the principle of Free Trade, the most powerful principle perhaps, and the most fruitful of consequences, political and social as well as economical, that ever was introduced into the affairs of men. Is it likely that this principle should have no effect on the value of maritime outposts planted with reference to the exigencies of a totally different state of things?

It is said that Cromwell thought of taking Gibraltar. Cromwell took Jamaica, but he took it not to extend our territories, or to indulge the empty pride of distant sway. He took it to break the dominant monopoly of Spain by giving a footing to his race in those waters; and having taken it, he proposed to make it over to the Colonists of New England, whom, with a true insight into the real sources of our greatness, he treated in effect as an independent nation.

Immense improvements have recently been made in artillery, and great changes have consequently taken place in the conditions of war. It is reasonable to suppose that these improvements may in some degree have affected the value of our maritime fortresses. The fate of Sweaborg seems to point that way. And in fact, those who plead for the retention of all these fortresses appear pretty plainly to admit that they are strong only so long as we command the sea. This is putting their value as strongholds rather low. That the system of outlying fortifications has been carried to an absurd extent is proved by the fortifications at Corfu, on which a vast sum of money has been spent, and which are now, it seems, allowed on all hands to be useless. "I totally disapprove," said Earl Grey, "of the whole policy of large expenditure upon fortifications in the Colonies. The experience we have had of the past seems to me to lead to the conclusion, that almost the whole of the money we have spent upon Colonial fortifications has been so much absolutely wasted; and that with respect to some of those fortifications, erected at great expense, the

wisest thing we could now do would be to blow them
up again[a]." Who will assure us that it is only to Colonial fortifications and not to other outlying fortresses
that this applies?

Be it observed that I do not presume to propose the
abandonment of Gibraltar or of any particular station.
As a civilian I am of course wholly incompetent to
form an opinion on any military question. I merely
advocate inquiry and deliberation in place of a blind
adherence to things as they are. The military dependencies are a strategical position, each part of which
was taken up with reference to circumstances that may
change, and of which some have changed. Is the position never to be reviewed? Is not a single post to be
relinquished to the end of time, however untenable or
useless it may have become? A Member of Parliament
said the other day that "not a rock on which the flag
of England had ever been planted should be given
up." One would think one was listening to some bom-
bastic Oriental flattering the Brother of the Sun and
Moon, not to an Englishman giving upright and manly
counsel to the great English nation.

Of course it is a severe test of a statesman's greatness to counsel retreat, however wise. The true Chatham, in his glory, could afford to give up Gibraltar
when he saw that to give it up was for the real good
of England; but a mock Chatham could not afford to
give up Heligoland.

Once in the estimates always in the estimates, is the
principle on which at present we really proceed. If

the slave trade were extinguished to-morrow, we should
hold every pest-hole on the coast of Africa as tenaciously
as before. "We occupied Sierra Leone," says Mr.
Adderley, "for the purpose of importing free blacks,
and Gambia for exporting slave blacks under the As-
siento treaty, and we continue to sacrifice Englishmen
there in hopes of discouraging the slave trade. In the
possession of St. Helena we have no apparent object."
Touch St. Helena, and you will find at once that it is
essential to the greatness of the nation. There is no
real power of revision or control in the Government.
The nation has no security against the continuance
of utterly useless expense and perfectly gratuitous
peril. Grant us fair inquiry from time to time : let us
know that we have good reasons for keeping each
military or maritime station; and reasonable men will
be content.

I have not questioned, nor do I desire to question,
the legality or morality of our conduct in holding
Gibraltar; and therefore the replies which have been
made on those grounds to what was said on the subject
in my first letter are beside the mark. It may be indeed
that it was not very chivalrous in us in the first instance, when we had professed to go to war in support
of the just rights of one of the two claimants of the
Crown of Spain, to keep part of the inheritance in our
own hands : nor is the treaty of Utrecht one to which
we should refer as an infallible canon of English honour.
But whatever doubts may have rested on the morality
of the original acquisition were afterwards cured by
solemn and repeated cession. If nations could not

make a valid cession of territory, wars would be inter-
necine. We have a good title to Gibraltar by conquest, and a full right to hold it, if we find it our interest to do so. And on the same principle we have
a right, in case we think fit to cede it, to require a full
equivalent by way of compensation. But at the same
time the Spaniards have an equal right to wrest it from
us if they can. Title by conquest always implies such
a right on the part of the conquered. Strafford pleaded
in justification of his arbitrary government of Ireland,
that Ireland was a conquered country. Pym replied
with overwhelming force that this plea warranted rebellion. "If the King, by the right of a conqueror,
gives laws to his people, shall not the people, by the
same reason, be restored to the right of the conquered,
to recover their liberty if they can?"

I own, however, that I differ on the point of morality
with some of my opponents in refusing to measure the
value of the possession to us by the anguish and humiliation which it inflicts on Spain. The wish to retain it
on that ground seems to me as senseless as it is malig-
nant. I dare to avow myself an admirer of a policy
the opposite to that which, under the influence of certain teaching and certain examples, we are beginning
to identify with our greatness. I wish to see my country
bearing herself towards other nations as an English
gentleman bears himself towards other men—I wish to
see her careful of their rights and feelings, as well as
of her own; more desirous of their esteem and confidence than of their fear; ready to interfere where
justice requires it, but not meddlesome or intriguing;

reserved towards those of doubtful character, towards others, frank and open in all her dealings; a little high to the strong, but never insolent to the weak. There are advantages in such a policy besides those of mere feeling. There is an end and a limit to the concessions and courtesies necessary to win the good-will of nations. There is no end and no limit to building fortresses against their hate.

I will go further. The fierce animosity which the religious struggles of the sixteenth century bred between the nations of Christendom has partly abated. Through the estranging barriers of State Churches something of a common Christianity has worked its way. Science and literature have exercised a reconciling power. Monopoly is giving way to free trade; and with one harvest the nations are beginning to have one heart. The old statecraft and the old diplomacy still prevail in high places, but rulers can no longer reckon on the same fund of mutual hatred in the people. This may be degeneracy and weakness, but it is nevertheless a fact which practical men will not disregard. "A sagacious ministry would always employ Gibraltar in dividing France from France, Spain from Spain, and the one nation from the other." Such was the language of Fox, still cited with applause by the advocates of aggression and domination. But to say nothing of the nonsense, the sentiment has now become somewhat alien even to hearts to which the honour of England is most dear.

The Duke of Wellington did not tarnish the honour of his country by falling back on a strong position at

Torres Vedras; nor did he by that movement prematurely proclaim the millennium. England, however, though she has not proclaimed the millennium, has, by her International Exhibitions and in other ways, proclaimed the hope of greater good-will, and of a stronger sense of common interest among nations; as well as her own desire of becoming the great benefactress and instructress, rather than the great tyrant of the world. She has also taken the lead, and has been followed by other nations, in creating a new armament of a purely defensive kind, in opposition to those great instruments of aggressive ambition, the possession of which has hitherto made war the game of Kings. It is true that the military passions are very far from having died out. It is true that they have even to a certain extent drawn new life from the satiety of civilization; and that a craving for adventure and daring has in some degree taken the place of the coarser motives for mutual destruction which prevailed in more barbarous times. But it is nevertheless true that the motives for peace are gradually gaining, and those for war are losing, power, and that there is on the whole a sensible increase of good-will among mankind.

We have, moreover, given up the idea that truth and civilization are to be propagated by force. Spain is not yet so far advanced as we are in her course towards perfect liberty of conscience. She sank deeper than we did in the abyss of Ecclesiastical tyranny, and in her return up the steep ascent she has only just reached the point which we had reached eighty years ago. But if her re-ascent is gradual, so was ours; and if she is yet far from the summit, we, with our Heresy Courts and our Irish Establishments, have not yet reached it. We shall not quicken her progress up to tolerance and charity by treating her with harshness and insolence. She will not be attracted towards religious liberty, or liberal principles of any kind, by seeing the flag of a liberal nation flaunting in her face from a hostile fortress on her own soil.

We have in Malta a Mediterranean fortress at once strong and inoffensive. Do we really require Gibraltar also? Is it worth the price paid for it in money and hatred? Let our rulers, as they desire to rule for the good of all, give us a fair answer to this question.

Gibraltar cost in money during the five years 1853— 1857, £1,854,852. Set off the cost of this fortress, Malta, the Ionian Islands, and the Mediterranean fleet, against the profits of our trade to the Mediterranean, and the profits will not cut a very good figure. In the two years 1854-5 the three military stations alone cost us between them upwards of three millions and a half. Besides this, our commercial interests in Turkey were alleged as partly the cause of the Crimean war. What were the clear profits of our export trade to the Mediterranean in those years?

But money will not measure the cost of Gibraltar. Its price is the implacable and undying enmity of Spain. " Gibraltar," says Lord Stanhope in his History, " was a question nearly touching the Spanish pride. It is almost incredible what deep and deadly resentment had been raised in that haughty nation, who had extended their conquering arms so far, to see a fortress upon their own shores held and garrisoned by England. They viewed it with still more bitter feelings than the French had formerly our possession of Calais, and there was scarcely a Spanish statesman of this period who might not have applied to himself the saying of Queen Mary, and declared that when he died the word 'Gibraltar' would be found engraven on his heart." As the proud heart of England would feel if the flag of Spain were flying in insulting triumph on the cliff of Dover, so feels the proud heart of Spain while the flag of England flies in insulting triumph on her Rock. When she was sinking into the abyss of ruin she dragged the last remnant of her departing strength again and again to the assault. From the hour of the capture she was arrayed against us and on the side of France, in every European war, till the tyranny of Napoleon drove her by force to accept our alliance and our protection. Even then her gratitude was quenched by the inveterate hatred. Talk of Gibraltar "dividing France from Spain!" It is the bond of steel which has bound them together, and will always bind them together whenever, by attacking us with France upon her side, Spain may have a chance of recovering her great fortress and (what to do her justice she has desired more ardently) laving the stain upon Castilian honour. Our Foreign Ministers, seeing her growing strength, have left off hectoring to her, and begun to assure her that "it is a fundamental maxim of British policy to wish well to Spain and earnestly to desire her welfare and prosperity." These blandishments will not avail.

Is it to the lasting resentment and the reviving power of Spain that *The Times* alludes when it says that "we may look upon the time as close at hand when the expense of Gibraltar will be reduced to a sum small in comparison with the outlay of former years?"

Not to Spain only but to other nations Gibraltar in our hands is a cause of offence. It is the symbol of that insulting domination under which all nations have smarted in their turn. It is the throne in their eyes of the old tyrant of the seas. We may defy their resentment, and even prize it. The hatred of your neighbours may, in the mystic sphere of diplomacy, be a source of strength, though in common life it is a source of weakness. But as we have constantly to deal with the effect, we may as well keep in view the cause.

Such being the cost, what is the return? Captain Sayer, who holds an appointment at Gibraltar, in the valuable History of the place which he has recently published, thus sums up the reasons for retaining the possession:—"To cede Gibraltar would be to renounce our freedom of navigation in the Mediterranean; our commerce in those seas would be paralysed; we should forfeit the safety of the overland route, depreciate our power in the East, and lose all influence in Morocco." As a place of trade Captain Sayer admits that Gibraltar has sunk into insignificance since the banner of England has ceased to float in its pride over a smuggling station.

It did not occur to Captain Sayer, when he was writing about freedom of navigation in the Mediterranean, that the next greatest commercial nation to England is America; and that the Americans navigate in perfect freedom the Mediterranean and all other seas, not only without fortresses, but without a war navy worthy of the name. In the days of monopoly, when it was the object of all nations to exclude and destroy each other's trade, there was a reason, though a wretched one, for posting ourselves in arms all over the globe; and the statesmen of those days had at least a solid object in seizing and keeping Gibraltar, while their successors have nothing but fancy and tradition. But in these days of free trade commerce is its own support and its own safeguard. It wins its way by a diplomacy more prevailing than that of the Foreign Office, and a force more prevailing than the force of arms. Let the Masters of Thirty Legions vex and tax the world if they must; but let them do it in the name of ambition, not of commerce. Commerce has nothing to ask of them but their most beneficent neglect.

Originally Gibraltar was desired not only to secure the freedom of the Mediterranean to ourselves, but to enable us to interfere with the freedom of others. "Deprive yourselves of this station," said Fox, "and all the states of Europe which border on the Mediterranean will no longer look to you for the free navigation of that sea." "The Mediterranean becomes to them a pool, a pond in which they can navigate at pleasure and act without control or check." Such was

the sense of the Government and the nation in those
times. Such may be the sense of some of those who
influence the Government still. But such, it may be
hoped, is not the sense of the nation.

A "paralysis of trade," which Captain Sayer portends in case Gibraltar is abandoned, would be a fearful disaster; but happily experience shews that while
nations stand in need of each other's commodities, and
are not forbidden by the paternal wisdom of rulers,
freely to interchange them, no such paralysis is likely
to occur.

Captain Sayer, and not he only, appears to write on
these subjects under the impression that the trade is
our trade alone, and that we alone are concerned to
defend it, while it is the interest of all other nations, if
they can, to destroy it. Is not our export trade their
import trade, and is not our import trade their export
trade? Why should the butcher wish to destroy the
baker's bread on its road to his own house, or the baker
to prevent the butcher from sending his meat in return? These things are the same on the large scale
as on the small. Every nation round the Mediterranean
is interested in protecting the trade in every article
that it wants. Every nation is interested in protecting
the general trade, the benefit of which comes round to
it, as a sharer in the aggregate wealth of the world.
And trade will be protected if nations are allowed to follow their natural tendencies, undisturbed by diplomacy.
It is with the greatest difficulty that they are induced
now to abstain from interfering with the combatants
in America to get at cotton. In relying on the action

of these motives we do not dream about a coming millennium or the brotherhood of man, we reckon on the regard of men for their own palpable interest; and men will in general be moved by a regard for their own palpable interest, if their rulers do not take pains to inflame their passions and to blind their eyes.

Spain and her dependencies take from us annually goods to the value of five millions and a half, and they send us annually goods to the value of ten millions. Why should the Spaniards be "envious" of this trade, or desire to "destroy" it?

I quite agree with my opponents that we have a "great interest in the Mediterranean;" and I wish to secure that interest in the only way now rational or feasible, by cultivating the good-will, respecting the honour, and promoting the prosperity of the Mediterranean nations.

It will be time to discuss the necessity of keeping Gibraltar as a protection to the "overland route to India," when we are assured by competent authority that it would be possible to use that route at all in time of war with the Mediterranean powers. But, in the meantime, let it be observed that if Gibraltar is kept up at the expense of England for the sake of India, we must not be told that India pays for herself.

"The East" does not change, and till it changes there is little fear lest force, if it is great and real, should ever be "depreciated" there, even when disencumbered of a useless appendage. As to our influence in Morocco, the climax of Captain Sayer's case, it is one of those subtle diplomatic essences of which people

out of the Foreign Office can hardly presume to speak,
and the value of which, I fear, is much more strongly
felt there than among the labouring masses, the sweat
of whose brows supports diplomatists in the luxury of
intrigue.

These considerations, as well as the safety of the
overland route, be it observed, are after-inventions to
bolster up the falling case for retaining a fortress which
was originally occupied for close trade and " the honour
of his Majesty" alone.

The question, once more, is not whether we should
cease to hold a great fortress in the Mediterranean, but
whether one great fortress there is not enough. The
present statement apparently goes to prove that Malta
is a cypher, which would neither save our trade from
paralysis nor our influence from depreciation. Yet
that place cost us more than two millions and a half
in two years.

If it be said that Gibraltar commands the Strait and
is the key of the Mediterranean, and that therefore the
retention of this place is essential to the retention of
Malta, the answer is that there are six good miles of
sea-way beyond the effective reach of its guns. But if
a fortress on the Strait is indispensable, Ceuta, or some
other place on the African coast, which would be held
without violating any nationality, could no doubt be
obtained in exchange. Some would prefer as the equivalent for the cession, a treaty of commerce giving a
perfectly free entrance for our manufactures into Spain.
And most people would be disposed to require, as a
condition, the payment by Spain of her just debts.

Captain Sayer, however, rests his case on higher grounds than those of our interest. " Were England to give up Gibraltar, she would be committing a far more serious political immorality than she can be guilty of by keeping it. She would drop the apple of discord among the nations of Europe, and infallibly inaugurate an era of war. Restore the fortress to Spain to-morrow —how long would she retain it? Just so long as France might choose to leave her in possession of it."

Why, here is an " impregnable" fortress which cannot be held by the united force of a nation with sixteen millions of inhabitants, a revenue of 21,000,000*l.*, a respectable fleet, excellent naval arsenals, and an army of 160,000 men! Moral arguments of a certain kind are apt to prove double-edged.

"The history of the past century and a half shews that not only was Spain at no time strong enough to retake Gibraltar, but that she was unable to hold it against attack." It was taken from her by surprise at the period of her greatest decrepitude, when the fortifications were almost in ruins, and there was hardly any garrison. It has never been in her hands since. And this is the historical proof that she is unable to hold it against attack!

France is ambitious, but she is not mad. And mad she must be to vault, even if she had the power, into our seat of odium at Gibraltar, or not to see her advantage in the present arrangement, which, to prevent her having a Spanish fortress, gives her Spain. The Mediterranean a French lake! who can make it so but ourselves?

If we cannot trust Spain with Gibraltar, can we trust Denmark with Elsinore? Can we trust Turkey with the Dardanelles?

Supposing, however, that Spain is really too weak to hold her great fortress, and that all the accounts we have heard and the appearances we have seen of her reviving fleets and armies are unfounded and delusive, a simple remedy remains. Instead of handing over to her the fortress of Gibraltar, hand over to her only the bare and inoffensive rock. Let the fortress be dismantled, and let Spain be bound by a covenant never to arm it again. Let this stronghold of ancient hatred, and ancient monopoly, be numbered with the castles from which feudal robbers once threatened the highway of commerce, and wrung black-mail from the trader on every strait and river.

Spain was once, what England is now, the mightiest of European nations and the terror of the world. She sank into impotence under the weight of despotism, a dominant priesthood, and a multitude of dependencies. Spanish historians begin the reign of Philip II. with the resounding roll of the kingdoms, provinces, Colonies, and fortresses of which he was lord in all parts of the globe. " He possessed in Europe the kingdoms of Castille, Aragon, and Navarre, those of Naples and Sicily, Milan, Sardinia, Roussillon, the Balearic Islands, the Low Countries, and Franche Comté; on the Western Coast of Africa he held the Canaries, Cape Verd, Oran, Bujeya, and Tunis; in Asia he held the Philippines and a part of the Moluccas; in the New World the immense kingdoms of Mexico, Peru, and

Chili, and the provinces conquered in the last years of Charles V., besides Cuba, Hispaniola, and other islands and possessions. And his marriage with the Queen of England placed in his hands the power and resources of that kingdom. So that it might well be said that the sun never set in the dominions of the King of Spain, and that at the least movement of that nation the whole world trembled." It is needless to rehearse the tale of decay, ruin, and degradation which is opened by this proud page. It is needless to say that the world had little reason to tremble at the magnitude of an empire which, as Spanish historians now perceive, was draining the life-blood of the nation.

The despotism has passed away, though for a moment it has been succeeded by a military government. The power of the priesthood has been broken, and its wealth is gone. Almost all the great dependencies have been lost. Spain is rising again, not at the slow rate of ordinary progress, but with the speed of sudden resuscitation, and the pulses of life are awakening through every part of that once mighty frame. We have seen her again send forth an army not unworthy of the days of Gonsalvo. We shall soon see her fleet again powerful on the seas. Her population, her revenue, the value of her land, are rising with extraordinary rapidity. The railways necessary to concentrate her forces, as well as to promote her internal prosperity, are in full course of construction. The appearance of books of great merit in different departments attests the revival of her intellectual life. Her public men and military chiefs are still of that turbulent, unscrupulous, and intriguing race which always springs from revolutions and civil wars; but they are not devoid of the restless and daring ambition which gave birth to the marvellous enterprises of Cortes and Pizarro; and each of them knows well that there is one achievement which would place him for ever far above all his rivals, and that this achievement may become possible when England is involved in a desperate war.

A policy of strength, economy, and moderation, in place of the policy of blustering and prodigal weakness, will not be suddenly embraced by ministers whose ideas were formed in a state of things which has now passed away; but it will be embraced by the rising statesmen of England before many years are past.

I am, &c.,
GOLDWIN SMITH.

Sept. 27, 1862.

XIV.

THE PROTECTORATE OF TURKEY.

TO THE EDITOR OF THE "DAILY NEWS."

Sir,—It is evident that England is about to be committed more deeply than ever to the regeneration of Turkey. After having shed torrents of her best blood, lavished an enormous sum of public money, and added five millions to her public debt under the name of a guarantee, in the cause of the Turks, she is now about, under the same auspices, to embark an immense amount of private capital in the same cause. She is in fact adding to her dominions and responsibilities the Protectorate of the Ottoman Empire.

The Prime Minister takes the unusual course of recommending capitalists to invest their money in the Turkish funds. He is confident that Turkey will revive. Hitherto, he admits, the symptoms of revival have not been great. "It is well known," he says, "that for some time past, from various circumstances, the finances of Turkey have been in the greatest possible confusion and disorder. Troops have been for months without pay, public servants have received no salary, engagements of all sorts have been contracted which there have been no means of fulfilling: and the evil had increased to such an extent that the Turkish Government had become most anxious to have

matters placed on a fair footing; and Her Majesty's
Government felt that till that was done there was no
solid foundation for the stability and prosperity of the
Turkish Empire." Now, however, Her Majesty's Government have taken such effectual measures that matters will henceforth " be placed on a fair footing," and
the "stability and prosperity" of the Turkish Empire
will rest upon "a solid foundation." "We are told,"
proceeds the Minister, "that the gentleman was sick.
Well, he was very sick. We were asked to assist in
supplying a remedy, by putting him on a regimen.
I trust we have done so. I trust that in a time not
far distant we may find that this friend of ours is
not more sick than some of his neighbours, who have
hitherto boasted of the strength of their constitution
and the vigour of their health." When shall we hear
again the voices which, while England was in her
loftier mood, were heard from the place of Chatham,
Pitt, Canning, Peel, speaking in worthy accents of
great affairs?

Such is the assurance upon which the public hasten
to put down their money, which will be lost if the
assurance proves false. At least it would be rather
sanguine to expect that if the Turkish Government is
overturned by insurrection or invasion, the insurgents
or invaders will undertake the payment of its debts.

When we come to the grounds for these hopes, we
find they are—(1) the great resources of the country;
(2) the vigour and reforming tendencies of the new
Sultan.

The great resources of the country, instead of being

Q

an encouraging feature in the case, are the most damning evidence against the character and government of the Turks. How abject must the race be under whose dominion a land once teeming with wealth and swarming with population has sunk to such a state of wretchedness as the provinces of Turkey present at the present day. If the country were naturally poor there might be some hope for its lords. Its natural fruitfulness bids the advocates of their rule despair.

A new Sultan with reforming tendencies is a thrice-told tale. We know its sequel by heart. But upon this new Sultan all depends. It is clear from the pass things have come to that there are no reforming tendencies anywhere else, and therefore the bondholders had better pray hard for his Highness's life. The Prime Minister admits that this destined regenerator of his nation is, "from his former habits of life, not perhaps so fully versed in matters of detail connected with his Government as other persons might be." His Lordship cannot be charged with overstating the case. The ruler upon whose activity and vigilance the recovery of this money depends, is doomed, by the inveterate customs of his race, to remain in entire seclusion, both before and after his accession, worshipped like a Lama in his shrine, but seeing nothing with his own eyes beyond his palace walls. A few years will shew whether the present Sultan will be able to break through this seclusion, to defy the influences of the harem, to contend triumphantly with the vast hierarchy of corruption by which he is surrounded, and to combat with

success the fanatical bigotry which is as fatal as corruption to radical reform.

If we wish to form a rational opinion as to the
chances of Turkish regeneration, we must look, not to
Turkey alone, but to the group of similar phenomena
to which Turkey belongs. If we had seen only one
corpse, we might take the contraction of the muscles
after death for the return of life.

The Turks are one of several conquering hordes
which have from time to time descended upon the
rich countries of the East, and founded temporary
empires. While the horde is in its conquering state,
the warlike passions and qualities predominate over the
sensual appetites. But when the conquest is over, and
the horde is settled in the unbridled enjoyment of the
riches which it has won, the sensual appetites gradually
obtain unbounded sway. Habits of industry, which
might counteract these appetites and arrest decline,
are not formed, because the conquerors have come
into the possession of wealth not created by their
own labour. Of course the chief, having the greatest
means of indulging his sensuality, is the first to sink
into the abyss of corruption. The despotism, the only
form of government of which such hordes are capable,
then becomes enfeebled and breaks up. The rulers
of provinces, through whom the government of a
Sultan secluded in a harem is necessarily carried on,
cast off their allegiance, and set up for themselves;
and thus the Empire falls into that state of dissolution in which the Mogul Empire was found when we
commenced the conquest of Hindostan.

In the case of the Turks the period of war and of
the ascendancy of the warlike passions was exception-
ally prolonged owing to their being brought into contact
with the military nations of Christendom. They had, in
fact, not ceased to be a conquering race much before
the middle of the last century. The institution of the
Janissaries, recruited from kidnapped Christian youth,
also enabled the warlike element to hold out longer
than it otherwise would have done. But now the reign
of sensuality has hopelessly set in. As usual, it attacked
the centre of government first; and the process by
which the Empire is broken up into rebel satrapies,
the precursor of a still more complete dissolution, had
been commenced by Mehemet Ali, when it was arrested
by the interposition of European powers.

Fiscal disorder is not the root of the evil. The root
of the evil is abject sensuality, which utterly precludes
the existence of such self-devotion, such public spirit,
such aspirations as are necessary to regenerate a nation.
Turkey is not a nation, but a horde—a degenerate,
utterly corrupt, and dwindling horde. The hordes of
Franks and Goths might have been as the Turks are,
had not a better religion combated their sensuality,
and implanted in them the true germ of national life.

The Prime Minister says that "financial reform is the
basis and foundation of all national strength." I venture to think that judicial reform, which is equally
needed in Turkey, is just as much so. But the root of
both is national morality, which in the present case is
utterly and hopelessly wanting. A Turk will make
considerable efforts, as well as commit the greatest

crimes, to get money for his pleasures; he will make
no effort to pay his debts, much less to pay the debts
of the State.

No such thing as respect for industry, the sole source
of permanent wealth and the sole basis of sound finance,
has ever existed among the dominant race. Their chief
men have simply passed from living by the plunder of
the conquered population to living partly by plunder
and partly by corruption.

Of course a poor Turk has the negative virtues of
poverty. But raise him, set him to rule, and all the
evidence goes to prove that he will become at once the
victim of sensuality, and seek the means of indulgence
by corruption. He has no other object in public life.
Of course the Sultan is in a certain sense a reformer,
because it is his property that the viziers and pachas
steal. And he may, by a spasmodic effort, for a moment partly arrest the peculation, when it falls under
his own eye. But he cannot infuse into the servants
of the State that sentiment of honour which is the
only thorough and lasting cure.

There is overwhelming evidence that the numbers of
the Turks are diminishing at a rate which will soon
render them incapable of holding down the subject
races. Vicious habits, and the infecundity of women
living an unhealthy life in a harem, seem to be the
principal causes. Another cause is the pressure of the
military conscription on the dominant race, who are
of course afraid to arm the oppressed nations. If our
Minister thinks he can extirpate these causes, he may
hope to arrest the fall of the nation.

One quality resembling a national virtue the Turks have—and that is their pride. This quality we are now carefully extinguishing by the exercise of the most humiliating tutelage. The organs of the Government tell us that nothing is being done for Turkey but " what one independent nation may do for another." It is a hypocritical fiction. Turkey is undergoing at our hands that which no independent nation ever under-went at the hands of another—which no nation ever underwent while any drop of national life lingered in its veins. A Government helpless in itself has called in the foreigner to help it amidst a putrid mass of cor-ruption and despair : in receiving this help it resigns the last vestige of independence into the foreigner's hands.

The Minister's object in making these representa-tions, and in drawing English money to the Turkish exchequer, is plainly a diplomatic one. "No one who has paid any attention to contemporary history, or cast his eye on the map of the country, can fail to see that the maintenance of the Turkish empire is essential to the balance of power in Europe." I confess that I for one fail entirely to see, either from contemporary his-tory, or from the map, how the existence of a mere im-potence can support " the balance of power" in any way whatever. I must however at the same time con-fess that, being no diplomatist, I think " the balance of power" a less solid and feasible, as well as a less genial object of pursuit, than justice and good-will among nations ; and that I am unable to perceive how justice and good-will among nations can be promoted by the maintenance of a fetid cesspool of diplomatic jealousy, trickery, intrigue, and lying, which is the perpetual source of quarrels, and has just been the source of a dreadful war.

The population of the Turkish empire is not, as the Minister says, a "mixed" race. It consists of two separate and hostile elements—a race of conquerors who, degenerate and decimated by their heathen vices, are about to lose their conquests—and the conquered races, whose nationality has been preserved by their religion, and who are about to have their own again. Nor is there the slightest reason to believe that in consequence of our interference with Turkish finance "the religious hatreds which have for many ages agitated the Turkish empire will henceforth be softened, and ultimately disappear." St. Sophia was a Christian Church. It is now a heathen mosque. It is destined to be again a Christian Church, and that soon. We have more reasons than one for deprecating the policy which would give England, a Christian nation, cause to mourn instead of rejoicing at that change.

I am, &c.,
GOLDWIN SMITH.

April 5, 1862.

XV.
THE IONIAN ISLANDS.

TO THE EDITOR OF THE "DAILY NEWS."

Sir,—The revolution by which Greece recovers her freedom will render more odious and probably more difficult than ever our retention of the Ionian Islands. So evident is this, that the journals which, when the question was first mooted in your columns, warned "all Ionians," in Oriental style, that "England would not part with her transmarine possessions," now give the honours of large type to correspondents who advocate the annexation of the Islands to Greece. That measure would be in accordance with the will of the Ionian people, often expressed through constitutional organs, the authority of which we have ourselves allowed.

At the time when the Islands were placed under our protectorate, Greece was still a part of the Turkish empire. Having no nation with which to unite, and being incapable of standing by themselves, these small communities were entrusted by the Council of the Great Powers to our keeping. Our trust has been honourably and faithfully discharged, as the Ionians themselves, when launched into the stormy sea of Greek independence, will perhaps have reason wistfully to confess. But its object has been at an end since, with our sympathy and by our assistance, Greece has become a nation; and those who have counselled England forcibly or surreptitiously to turn a trust into a " possession," have counselled their country to her dishonour.

The desire of the Ionians to be no longer a dependency, but part of a free nation, may, in a commercial point of view, be injudicious, but it is English. It is the same desire which England is herself applauding and supporting with all her heart in the case of the Italians. We may think that our rule is beneficent in the Ionian Islands. The Austrians thought that their rule was beneficent in Lombardy, and they think that it is beneficent in Venetia. They fancy the Italian people, as we fancy the Ionian people, incapable of self-government; and by keeping them in subjection, they make them what they fancy them to be. We have constructed good roads in Ionia and kept up a good police; but England has testified in a hundred constitutional struggles that good roads and a good police are not the highest objects of national existence. The Ionians are forcibly held down by a foreign soldiery. When this is said, all is said, at least to hearts which owe allegiance to the cause of freedom.

To play the gaoler of a people struggling for national existence is a part which can no longer be pressed on a great and generous nation.

I shall not trouble you with discussing any subtle questions of ethnology as to the affinity or want of affinity between the inhabitants of the Ionian Islands and the Greeks of the mainland. The Ionians themselves have no doubt upon the subject. We must listen in these matters to the voice, not of the antiquary, but of nature.

Honour goes before expediency in the counsels of England. But the question of expediency is as clear as that of honour. The late Lord High Commissioner of the Islands himself proposed to relinquish them all except Corfu. They have been to us a mere source of expense, weakness, and that odium which, if there are such things as moral forces in the political world, is the worst of all weakness. They serve no purpose of commerce. And in case of a war they could neither be defended, as military positions, without a larger force than we could possibly spare, nor abandoned without loss of honour [a].

It is to be hoped that the diplomatists will respect the rights of an independent people and allow the Greeks to do that which they think best for themselves. The nations have suffered many things of diplomacy, not only in the matter of Greece but in other matters, without having their maladies healed. Is it not time they should think of taking their case into their own hands?

As to the Turkish Empire, which is threatened by this Greek movement, and which our diplomatists are evidently hastening to protect, I ventured some time ago, when our Ministers were preaching up the Turkish loan, to lay before you the reasons for believing that its days are numbered. It is going the way of all Eastern despotisms founded by conquering hordes,

[a] I have here omitted some paragraphs deprecating the nomination of an English prince, which is now out of the question.

which, when the impulse of conquest is spent, sink into
sensuality, corruption, and decay. It is incapable of
national regeneration—for it is not, never has been,
and never will be a nation. No national hope, no
national memory, nothing which can inspire that self-
devotion to public objects and that generous sacrifice
of the present to the future by which alone nations are
redeemed, has ever entered into the Turkish breast.
You may hold up the crumbling pile, as we have long
been holding it up, by main force, but it will never
stand by itself again. The man is not "sick," but
morally and politically dead. We are keeping a corpse
unburied, and the whole atmosphere of Europe is tainted
with its corruption. Those who live by the shallow
and evil craft of diplomacy alone have any interest in
prolonging the revolting scene.

The regeneration of a nation is not a financial or
military, but a moral process. To make the efforts and
bear the sacrifices which it demands, the people of the
fallen nation must be bound to each other by some
bond higher than that of mere self-interest : they must
believe in something above present gain and enjoyment : they must have an animating hope for the future
of their nation. These things often shew themselves
in very coarse forms, mingled with much alloy, so that
it may be difficult to distinguish them from ambition
or other selfish motives. But they must be present in
some degree if a nation is to rise again. Did any advocate of our Eastern policy ever see an approach to self-
devoted patriotism in a Turk?

Pour in your money. If integrity is absent, you will

only give new food and a fresh stimulus to peculation.
We poured some thirty millions of money into Turkey
in the course of the war. The consequence was that
in the great gulf of corruption there yawned a deeper
abyss still.

The Turks of Constantinople have been slightly var-
nished with civilization; but the race has not been
civilized in the slightest degree. Follow a traveller to a provincial city, and even the varnish is gone.
The Turkish correspondent of *The Times* tells us that
in the late war in Montenegro the Turks took no prisoners; every man who fell into their hands was put
to death "with horrible mutilations." They are still
a horde in cruelty. They are beneath a horde in lust.
They are a horde in the absence of any dawning ray of
intellectual life. If they have a military man of any
intelligence, he is sure to be a Renegade. Even their
warlike energies are at the last gasp, and their Empire
is held at bay in the Montenegrin war by the arms
of an undisciplined clan.

And suppose you could restore the strength of the
Turks, what would you restore but a vast reign of
cruelty and lust? Would it be a very signal gain to
humanity, if you could re-animate the prowess which,
in its glorious hour, was in the habit of flaying prisoners of war alive? Let the hopes of the Prime
Minister be fulfilled. Let the sick man grow well
enough to dismiss his physicians, or set their heads
on the Seraglio gate. The consequence will be that the
tyranny of the Mahometan over the Christian will revive in its full force. The nominal liberties and privi-

leges which we now extort for the Rayah will be given
to the winds. The slave-market will be re-opened at
Constantinople, if it has ever been really closed. And
perhaps the horde will feel again the lust of conquest,
and renew its ancient aggressions upon Christendom.

According to the latest and best accounts, even material civilization has made no way in Turkey. A wretched
peasantry still scratches a soil which might bear the
richest harvests. There are still no roads. The Turks
have no desire but to rot in peace. If any Europeans
propose to undertake improvements, they are thwarted by
the ambassadors of the other European powers, who are
afraid lest the success of the projected enterprise should
give influence to the nation of the projectors. It is the
same in all things. If a comparatively honest Turk
gets power into his hands he has all the ambassadors
against him but one. The energy of a Cromwell could
scarcely make head against such difficulties, much less
the energy of a Turk.

The system of centralization which reforming Sultans
have introduced in mimicry of the bureaucratic despotisms of Europe, seems in fact to have taken away the
last grain of saving salt from the putrid mass, by extinguishing the remnant of independent spirit and of
what might have passed for personal honour among the
old grandees of the Empire. There is nothing left now
but a dead level of baseness, with a central government
of roguery tempered by foreign intrigue.

The administration of justice, which, as was said before, is at least as important as finance, seems to remain perfectly Turkish. The prison is still the mint of

a Pasha. Without upright tribunals there can be no security for property; without security for property there can be no wealth. And while there is no wealth in a country, its finance, if it is to be set right at all, must be set right by diplomatists, commanding, for the purposes of their game, the purses of other countries.

To say that there is no improvement at all in Turkey would be untrue; but the improvement is not among the Turks. It is among the subject and oppressed races, who advance a little in spite of the Turk and his protectors. These people produce what wealth there is and so keep up the trade with us; and the interest of the money lent by us to the Turks for the oppression of our customers will be paid by imposts on our trade.

If I were to give the proofs of the hopeless degeneracy of Turkey, I should have to incorporate volumes into my letter. Mr. Senior goes to see the state of the case with his own eyes. If ever there was a keen observer and a competent witness he is one. As a profound economist, and a successful author of legislation on economical subjects, he thoroughly knows the symptoms of economical prosperity and decay. He is well fitted to feel the pulse of the sick man, and to tell us whether the patient shews any sign of returning health. He comes back and tells us that the corpse stinks. Why is no heed paid to his report? Why is the House of Commons, when a question touching six millions of English money is before it, satisfied with vague surmises eked out with stale jokes, instead of looking to the attested facts?

It is idle to think that the subject populations can be "trained" and "prepared" for freedom under the Turkish rule. Let us not, in supporting a detestable domination for diplomatic purposes, against all the principles of England, lay this flattering unction to our souls. The Turkish Government is, and must remain, one of the most jealous despotism, fatal to all free action, and therefore to all political training of every kind. The races over which Turkey rules are not subjects who might be gradually raised; they are enemies who must be held down. The only progress possible is that of increasing hatred, ending in deadlier war.

The last loan, though it has failed to regenerate corruption, has not altogether failed of effect. It has enabled the Sultan to increase his army, and has thereby insured that the last struggle, which might otherwise have been faint and short, shall be obstinate and bloody. It has also put off perhaps for two or three years the open shame which was on the point of overwhelming the policy of the Crimean war.

The Prime Minister, in recommending the Turkish loan, expressed a confident hope that the religious differences between the Mahometans and the Christians would cease to be a cause of political and social division among them. He appears to think that Mahometanism is like Christianity, a purely spiritual religion, unconnected with social or political domination; and that the question between the two creeds is one which no man of the world would allow to stand in the way of political convenience. His views have just received a curious illustration in Servia, where it has been found necessary to cart a Mahometan population bodily out of the way of the Christians, in utter despair of their ever living together otherwise than as mortal foes.

We have extorted a paper concession of religious equality in favour of the Christians, but we have not taken away the Koran out of Islam. One hears through private channels of more religious affrays and murders than are recorded in the papers. To prescribe tolerance to barbarism is in truth a charitable, but not a very promising course.

The end must come before long in the shape of an exhaustion of the military population. The numbers of the dominant horde are rapidly and steadily declining. Besides their bad habits, the conscription falls, and must continue to fall, wholly upon them. If they armed the Rayahs the game would be up.

A new Sultan, finding the roof falling in and the till empty, may introduce for the moment some administrative reforms; but he has to import his reformers from abroad. England is at this moment practically administering the Turkish Government, as well as supplying it, unhappily, with her money. We are reducing the Ottoman Empire to a semi-dependency, and taking its load of infamy on our shoulders. Our Government encourages, or affects to encourage, the movement of national emancipation in Italy, while, as the supporter of Turkish despotism, it represses a movement which is not only similar but actually the same among the oppressed Christian populations of the Turkish Empire. It helped to emancipate Greece, and now it struggles against the manifest consequences of its own work.

The Prime Minister shrugs his shoulders in contempt when people talk of the "independence" of the Pope. People may shrug their shoulders with equal justice when he talks of the "independence" of Turkey. He could himself scarcely read the history of Lord Stratford's reign over the Sublime Porte, and talk of the "independence" of those trembling slaves without a smile.

Has not enough of English money and of English blood been already squandered on an object not only utterly chimerical but flagrantly opposed to all our principles, to our morality, and to our religion? Why should the name of England be written in characters of hatred on the page that opens the history of the revived Greek nation? To say nothing of generosity, what can be more foolish than thus to make a mortal enemy of the future?

If the principle of nationality is a true principle, why should not England embrace it frankly, and take the strength and the greatness which a frank adhesion to a true principle never fails to bring?

The truth is, England has nothing to do with this business. In this cruel and shallow game of diplomacy, of which Constantinople is the favourite gambling-table and the subject races of Turkey are the victims, the cards are held not by the nations themselves, but by a knot of intriguing politicians in the name of the nations. These men set the world by the ears, shed the blood of the people, and squander

R

the fruits of their labour for objects merely factitious
and conventional, which, if the nation were really
acting for itself, its good sense and good feeling
would probably repudiate and discard. But as these
objects are unintelligible, we all take it for granted
that they must be profound, and are eager to shew
that we, too, are diplomatists and follow the moves
of the great game : like the courtiers in the story,
who, rather than confess their ignorance, saw the
cloth and descanted on its excellency of colour and
texture, when there was nothing at all before their
eyes. From time to time we are honoured, and our
grateful illusions are kept up, by a grand exposition of
diplomatic policy, in a speech of extraordinary ability
and several hours long, which we all vie with each other
in applauding, though none of us can give an intelligible
account of its contents. We repose in the belief that
our Government is perfectly constitutional, yet there
is a large part of the action of Ministers, including the
whole of their diplomatic action, which has not yet
been fairly brought under the control of the National
Council. If it were, the Foreign policy of England
would at least be English.

The great master of this craft is encouraged by a
recent writer of eminence, having pulled down one
"European system" by an intrigue, to set to work and
build up another. This he is told is to be "his last and
mightiest labour," the one on which his fame will have
to rest. And these august houses of cards, which are
thus built up and pulled down again, cost torrents of
blood and immense sums of public money, the main

fruit of which is the gratification of one diplomatist's vanity by a victory over the rest of the guild.

At a time when "the Eastern question" was in a very inflamed state, and we were in fact on the brink of war, the King of the Belgians went to see the Foreign Minister of England, whose "self-love" was "materially compromised" in the dispute. The King's report of the interview was, "I have opened the breach. A strong sentiment prevails of the importance of the situation; but the obstinacy is great; there is wounded self-love and restless personality: individual names are mingled with arguments and recriminations with reasons[b]." A little more, and this "wounded self-love" and "restless personality" would have plunged the world at that time, as they did plunge it afterwards, into a sea of blood. In case the Eastern question should again come to a crisis, it may be as well that the nation should recollect what influences are at work. And perhaps, when next the blessings of a Monarchy are complacently contrasted with the evils of a Commonwealth, the cost in blood and money of a secret diplomacy directed by "restless personalities" may not be left out of the account.

Peel, according to M. Guizot, was much behindhand in these matters. It seems that, properly speaking, he "had no foreign policy that was really his own, of which he had a clear conception, which proposed to itself a special plan of European organization, and the adoption of which he assiduously applied himself to secure." As a substitute for a foreign policy, however,

[b] Guizot, Embassy at the Court of St. James, p. 267. Eng. Trans.

THE EMPIRE.

it appears he had two feelings on the subject,—"he desired that peace and justice should prevail among nations." The irregular edifice which nature would build, if these two feelings had their way, would doubtless be very inferior as a piece of political architecture to "European systems" constructed by a master-hand, but it would not so often require to be rebuilt.

The day—not far distant, as I trust—on which Christianity shall once more stand triumphant over Mahometanism in the city of Constantine, will be a dark day for the professional intriguers of all countries. It will be a bright day for Christendom, and for civilization. It will be a bright day for England, unless England allows diplomacy to beguile her out of common sense, and make her forget that she is a free and Christian nation.

I am, &c.,

GOLDWIN SMITH.

Oct. 30, 1862.

XVI.
THE CESSION OF THE IONIAN ISLANDS.

TO THE EDITOR OF THE "DAILY NEWS."

Sir,—The cession of the Ionian Islands may now, I presume, be regarded as a settled thing, whatever difficulties of detail as to the mode and conditions may remain to be surmounted. One useless dependency is taken from our burden of empire; one issue of wasteful expenditure is staunched; one act of moderation has been freely performed; and now, I suppose, the prestige, the glory, the power of England are gone for ever. Those who love England and her cause hang down their heads; her enemies and the enemies of her cause exult. We are sunk in the scale of nations.

Let the advocates of aggrandisement tell us whether in the whole history of English diplomacy a more successful stroke has been made than this. People talk of moral force, of its superiority to physical force, and of the advantage of having it on your side. Now they see what moral force means. Now they see what it is, in an age when opinion is mistress of the world, to touch the heart and the reason of mankind.

"The case of the Ionian Islands," said Sir W. Molesworth[a], "is a capital instance of the manner in which public money has been thrown away upon worthless Colonies on the absurdest pleas. In 1815 the great Powers of Europe, not knowing what to do with the

[a] Speech on the Colonies, in the House of Commons, June 25, 1849.

free and independent states of the Ionian Islands, placed them under the protection of Great Britain. Lord Lansdowne and other distinguished statesmen remonstrated, on the ground that such possessions would be burdensome, expensive, and of no use; but Lord Bathurst maintained that they would be most valuable, that the country would gain immensely by them, and that they would defray all expenses incurred on their account. On such nonsensical pleas our Colonial Empire was extended."

The cost of the Islands for the five years 1853—1857 was £1,128,000; so that their cost for the whole period during which they have been in our hands, including the expense of fortifications, can scarcely have been less than eleven millions. This, of course, is besides their share in the expense of the Mediterranean fleet. The sum of £400,000 was spent on the fortifications at Corfu, which, in Sir W. Molesworth's opinion, were too extensive to be manned; so that the wisest plan in case of war would be to blow them up, and fall back on Malta and Gibraltar. And for this outlay we have received not one farthing of return in any shape whatever; for the small export trade to the Islands would have been just the same if they had been independent or a part of Greece. This nation has reaped nothing from the possession which Lord Bathurst assured us was to be so invaluable, but odium, moral weakness, and the twofold scandal which arises when freemen are forcibly held in subjection by a free people.

All this has dawned on the keen eye of diplomacy since the choice of the Greeks fell on an English prince.

It dawned on the eye of common sense and common justice long ago.

It is instructive to remember that not a twelvemonth has passed since the principal organ of this very Government was denouncing counsels of justice and moderation respecting the Ionian Islands in those tones of insolent swagger which we are beginning to confound with the majestic voice of English greatness. " We may as well declare at once, for the benefit of Americans and Spaniards, Russians and *Ionians*, Sikhs and Sepoys, that England has no thought of abandoning her transmarine possessions." So wrote *The Times* in February last. The Ionian Islands were a trust committed to our honour ; England was encouraged to play the part of a fraudulent trustee, by turning her trust forcibly into a possession ; and thereby to stain for ever the purity of her escutcheon, and forfeit that better empire which belongs to the protectress of justice and honour among nations. This was the advice given to their country by public instructors in the discharge of their duty to the nation. Even now the sight of the national acquiescence has not entirely silenced these promptings of dishonour. A Conservative journal opposing the cession, after avowing that our continued possession of the Islands would be forcible and fraudulent, informs us that, if we look fairly into the matter, no better title can be made to any territory than that of force and fraud. A holy text to write upon the broad phylactery of the party of "legitimacy and honour !"

The general bearing of the nation, however, on this

occasion may teach rulers that it is not so besotted with unreasoning prejudice and insensate pride as those who affect to play upon its foibles would lead us to believe; and that a statesman may hold his course with impunity through a good many phantom barriers, provided that his path be towards the public good, and that he has "a god in his own breast." After all, perhaps, more miscarriages in the affairs of this world are due to want of courage, and fewer to want of sense, than is commonly supposed.

Two hands are in the proposal of the Government. One, generous and wise, proffers the boon; the other, less generous and less wise, clogs it with evil and even impossible conditions.

The Greeks are told that before they can have the Islands they must again set up "a constitutional monarchy" in the person of a prince approved of by our diplomatists. A constitutional monarchy is that form of government under which a king "reigns and does not govern," while the government is carried on in his name by his constitutional advisers, with the support of a party in Parliament. If the king attempts not only to reign but to govern, as he is now doing in Prussia, the Constitution is overturned. This, it seems to be assumed, is a form of government not only universally applicable, but obligatory on all nations; so that those who omit to embrace it forfeit what would otherwise be their right. But the fact is, that of all forms of government it is the most peculiar to a particular nation, and the least capable of being propagated beyond the soil in which, through a singular series of historical acci-

dents, combined with political tendencies equally singular, it has grown up. Even in this country it has
enjoyed, in its perfect form, only a very brief and a
very precarious existence. William III. was not a constitutional sovereign in the full sense of the term,-for
he interfered constantly and actively in the government, was his own Foreign Minister, and put his
veto on a most important Act of Parliament. Queen
Anne was not a constitutional sovereign, for she overturned the Ministry and reversed the policy of the
country to please her favourite waiting-woman. George
I. and George II. were constitutional kings, in the full
sense of the term, because they were impotent; and
they were impotent because they were foreigners as
well as fools, and their title to the throne was disputed.
George III., not being a foreigner, and having an undisputed title, threw off the constitutional character
and began to govern, as we know to our bitter cost.
All acknowledge the debt of gratitude due to the late
Prince Consort for the wisdom with which he played
his delicate part in this intricate and delicate machine.
Constitutional Monarchy can scarcely be said yet to
have worked well, if it can be said to have worked at
all, anywhere but here. That it works here is owing
to the results of the long political training which the
nation has undergone, to its natural and acquired aptitude for practical adjustment, to its spirit of compromise, to experience teaching with terrible voices
from the past, to the peculiar balance in the mind of
the people between its affection for an ancient line and
its tenacious sense of public right. And this is the

constitution which is tendered with undoubting confidence, not only as the simplest and most natural arrangement, but as an article of political salvation, to a nation untrained, inexperienced, which has made only the first tottering steps in political life, with a keen undisciplined wit and warm impulses, sure to be impatient of compromise of any kind; which, moreover, has no great parties to support a cabinet, and can produce no substitute for such parties but unmeaning and selfish factions. It is tendered to them in the propitious person of an alien by race and by religion, destitute of any hold, personal or traditional, on their hearts, and under the happy star of recent and abject failure. We know how long it took to win the hearts of this nation, accustomed as they were to monarchy, for the Hanoverian line, though it was sprung from their ancient kings. To all this it is to be added that Greece is far too small and too poor to support the state and trappings of a monarchy, as her finances and the faces of her creditors plainly shew. The organs of practical wisdom have often, and very justly, reminded us, in the course of this discussion, of the difference between statesmen and professors. But did any professor, even in Laputa, ever dream a more chimerical dream than this of bestowing constitutional monarchy on all the nations of the earth—old and young, trained and untrained, whether monarchy of any kind has a root in them or not? Did ever an inhabitant of Laputa, having just tumbled headlong from his flying machine amidst universal laughter, mount with such serene confidence into another of the same kind?

Not only must the Greeks have an exact counterpart of our German monarchy, but they must have a German prince at the head of it; though this indeed seems to be becoming the one hope of humanity in all nations. But the German princes are not much inclined to take the place. Of course they are not: Otho has opened their eyes, and no one will take a place of great difficulty and danger with his eyes open but a fool or a great man.

Is there not in the whole Greek race a single man on whom nature has set something of the true royal stamp, and who could be trusted for a time not to reign only, but to govern, and by restoring order, redeeming credit, correcting abuses, and putting an end to ruinous and barbarous taxation, to prepare the way for liberal institutions; who would know how to hold power as a trust, and who would have greatness of mind enough to feel that, while the State was bankrupt, pomp and luxury were a dishonour to its chief, and that his best magnificence was simplicity of life? Is there no one in all the race fit to be the leader of a nation poor in revenue, but rich in hope? "Necessity," says Schiller's Wallenstein, "will have the man and not the shadow." It is a man and not a shadow that the necessity of Greece demands now.

What the nation in fact wants to carry it through the present crisis is something in the nature of a Dictatorship; but under the law, and with provision for the speedy restoration of a perfectly free constitution. A regulation King sitting still in his capital, and aping the buckram state of European monarchies, will be perfectly useless. A ruler is needed who will go over the country without equerries, see what is wrong with his own eyes, set it right with his own hand, and be always face to face with his people.

The first condition imposed on the Greeks is that they shall set up a constitutional monarchy. The second is, that their new ruler shall respect the policy by which England, the defender of Italian liberty, and the enemy of Austrian domination in Italy, is made for her imaginary interest to support the cruel, foul, and degrading domination of the Turkish horde over a part of Christian Europe.

To this policy, infamous as it has always been, palpably absurd and impracticable as it is daily becoming, some of the present Government are bound by a terrible pledge. Between them and a return to the path of reason towards the Turks and of justice towards their victims, there runs the impassable river of the blood shed in the Crimean War; that fatal war which, besides its own waste and carnage, broke the sacred spell of the long peace, and let havoc loose again upon the world.

And now it has become plain that the dreadful influence of Russia over the Greek race is, after all, in the main the result of our own policy. We support the Turkish despotism, and the victims of that despotism look to Russia for deliverance. They have evidently no wish, on any other ground, to put themselves under the ominous patronage of the Czar. .

If Russia desires an unwieldy extent of territory, she desires mere weakness, of which her enemies need hardly grudge her the possession. If she desires merely a sufficient maritime outlet on the South as well as on the North for the produce of her vast inland Empire, nature and the general interest of humanity sanction her desire. The world has been frightened into the belief that the invasion of the Northern Barbarians which overthrew the Roman Empire is about to be repeated in our times. People forget that the irruption of the Northern Barbarians was not an invasion but a migration. It is not very probable that the nobles of St. Petersburg will put their wives and children in their waggons and descend upon us like the Goths and Huns. Perhaps if they did they would find that the warlike nations of Modern Europe were different enemies from the Romans of the Lower Empire.

We need not here discuss again the prospects of Turkey, or inquire into the hopefulness of the enterprise in which our Government is now engaged, of regenerating an Empire, sunk in depravity and corruption, by the hand of a Treasury clerk. Events are very fast ripening; and we shall soon see which will prevail, the deep and universal causes which draw Turkey to her doom, or the arrangements of diplomatists which prescribe that she shall live and flourish to maintain the balance of power. No friend of the Greeks would advise them to plunge into a crusade before the hour; or dissuade them from listening to counsels of peace and moderation, even when uttered by the authors of the most reckless wars. But if they are called upon in any way to renounce the hopes of their race, and those of the other victims of Turkish oppression, either in deference to the factitious objects of diplomacy, or out of regard for the personal reputation of particular diplomatists, let them remember that above the "great Powers" there is, even on earth, a greater power in the good sense and generous sympathies of mankind. The world has been long in the hands of the Metternichs and Talleyrands, and the other intriguers of their school, the lowest offspring of modern civilization, whose only quality was a low cunning, alien to all grandeur, to all generosity, and to all true wisdom; who have cantoned out the world on the principles of a shallow selfishness, more foolish than the dreams of any honest enthusiast, without regard either to morality or to the great interests of man. But the yoke of this clique, if it is not broken, is loosened; and among other things the truth has dawned, though dimly perhaps and not always on wise minds, that no balance of power, or other object of a selfish diplomacy, can be worth half so much to the community of nations as the accession to their brotherhood of a new member, bringing fresh treasures of industry and thought, and of social and political experience, to the common store of man. In the progress of sound morality and generous ideas we are fast leaving behind the statecraft which would oppose the resurrection of a nation; and if diplomacy commands the Greeks to repudiate a hope which is not theirs alone, but that of Christendom and civilization, they have, I trust, only to appeal from the cold and silly dictates of diplomacy to the warm heart and the good sense of the English people.

I am, &c.,

GOLDWIN SMITH.

Jan. 13, 1863.

XVII.

THE CESSION OF THE IONIAN ISLANDS.

TO THE EDITOR OF THE "DAILY NEWS."

Sir,—I am sorry that accident prevented your receiving before the very few words which I have to say in answer to the severe strictures passed on my views respecting the cession of the Ionian Islands by Mr. Disraeli, in his speech on that subject the other evening.

I will not enter into the considerations of morality involved in the question, because Mr. Disraeli appears to regard such considerations as offensive *.

Taking the political line, the sum of Mr. Disraeli's argument against the cession of the Islands is this, that the source of wealth is power, and that the way to secure power is to occupy with arms strong places on the routes of commerce.

If Mr. Disraeli will post a sentry for a year at the doors of his baker, butcher, and grocer, and add the expense to his yearly bills, he will find, I believe, by experience, that the armed occupation of strong places on the routes of commerce is not necessarily a source of

---

* So I interpret the epithet "prigs." The Right Hon. gentleman and his organs industriously fix this epithet and its equivalents on all who advocate the observance of common honesty in political affairs and in public life.

wealth. But as the Right Hon. gentleman has not yet quite made up his mind on the subject of "unrestricted competition," it is premature to argue with him respecting the influence of Free Trade.

That the Ionian Islands, however, are "a strong place," seems to be an assumption which requires qualification. They appear to be a strong place so long as we have a fleet in those seas powerful enough to prevent their being attacked. The Turkish Government, on an occasion when hostilities were impending, being short of men for its army, raised by forced enlistment a corps of ten thousand Jews. War having broken out, the Commander-in-Chief called on the brave recruits to march to the frontier and defend their country. They responded to his call with martial enthusiasm, but requested that they might be provided with an escort through a part of the road which was infested by robbers.

I am, &c.,

GOLDWIN SMITH.

Feb. 9, 1863.

XVIII.[a]

INDIA.

TO THE EDITOR OF THE "DAILY NEWS."

SIR,—India, as I said in my first letter, stands on a footing of its own, apart from the other dependencies of our Empire. There we have not only placed ourselves in a position from which it is hard to retire, but taken upon us duties which we are bound for the present to perform. If we were to leave India we should leave it to anarchy. There is no power, Hindoo or Mahometan, to which we could make over our trust. We have destroyed or degraded all the native Governments ; and we alone stand in their room. We are wedged in the oak which we have rent.

"The French and Germans," said Reschid Pacha to Mr. Senior, "think that the strength of England is in India ; that if you lose India you sink into a secondary power, like Holland." "There cannot," replied Mr. Senior, "be a greater mistake. If we were well quit of India, we should be much stronger than we are now. The difficulty is, how to get *well* quit of it[b]."

It is safer to put it thus than to say that we have a "mission" to keep India. Mission is a large word. All

---

[a] This paper was not actually published in *The Daily News* ; but it was thought best to cast it into the same form as the rest.

[b] Senior's Journal in Turkey and Greece, p. 117.

S

sorts of men and nations have missions, and some of their missions are of a very objectionable kind. Spain had a mission, undertaken in a most religious spirit, and sanctioned by the highest religious authority, to send bucaneering expeditions into the New World, and fill it with misery and blood. Prince Louis Bonaparte had a mission to strangle French liberty in its sleep. France herself has a mission which keeps all her neighbours under arms. "A mission," historically speaking, is little more than another name for a tendency to rapine. Providence no doubt puts conquered territories into the conqueror's hands; and Providence puts the stolen purse into the pocket of the thief.

"Responsibility" is another word of the same kind. It is perhaps more frequently used than "mission" to defend the retention of what you have got in those special cases where the retention is very unprofitable to the nation at large, but profitable or agreeable to a class. In these cases, the class feels that, on whichever side the balance of political and economical advantage may be, it has "responsibilities" of a higher kind which it is not at liberty to resign.

No one can justly impeach the morality of England in conquering India. Our early acquisitions of territory there, which almost inevitably drew after them the rest, were made in an age when the morality of all European nations sanctioned conquest; at least the conquest by those whom the European nations were pleased to style civilized men, of those whom they were pleased to style barbarians. If we had not conquered India, France would. That she failed and left the prize to us was owing not to her superior moderation, but to her inferior power. Dupleix had not more honour or more scruples though he had less genius than Clive.

It is sufficient, when we are arraigned for our conduct in this matter before the court of nations, to say that the foundation of our Indian Empire was laid in the days when France was seizing Corsica, and when Austria, Russia, and Prussia were partitioning Poland. I should be sorry to maintain that the practice of the Great Powers constituted justice; but it constitutes a good answer to their own hypocritical accusations.

We did not mean to conquer India. The conquest was not a national design: the character of our statesmen cannot be charged with it; nor can their wisdom be pleaded for it. A Company of traders, formed after the commercial fashion of that day, which was all for protection and companies, planted, under a charter from our Government, a factory in the East. Their servants found that honest trade was a slow way of making a fortune; and that they could fill their pockets faster by breaking up and plundering the decrepit Empire of the Mogul. Then followed an exhibition of courage, energy, and genius in war and council by those adventurers, which has shed imperishable lustre upon their country; of rapacity, corruption, intrigue, treachery, and cruelty which have left indelible stains upon her fame. Spain scarcely owed more glory or more infamy to her Cortes and Pizarro than England to her Clive. The Company, though it tried, could not control its high-handed subordinates, fleshed with booty and intoxicated with ambition; its arm was not long enough to reach so far. Government was obliged to interfere; it was obliged to interfere more and more, till by the act establishing the Board of Control it virtually took the power and the responsibility into its own hands. Still India was not incorporated with England. It subsisted as an Empire apart, subject immediately not to the Queen but to the Company, having its bureaucratic office in this country, but resting on a native army of its own. That army mutinied and ceased to exist: a British army took its place. The Company was abolished, and India was incorporated with England.

Our Government, when they began to take India into their hands, intended to arrest the career of conquest. They solemnly declared that intention, and the declaration was sincere. But India was a long way off. Of the proconsuls, through whom it was ruled, some were honest and moderate, but some were intriguing and ambitious. It was always easy to sow the seeds of war. When war had once begun, the honour of England required victory; and victory always brought conquest in its train. Wise men fixed upon one boundary after another as the limit of our Indian Empire. The Duke of Wellington said we were never to go beyond the Indus. Nevertheless we have gone to Peshawur and tried to go to Cabul. We have gone to Birmah, and we are going still further east. Fate, a fate which, like all that compels humanity, was originally of our own creating, has driven and still drives us on. We had given a mortal blow to the strength and majesty of the native Governments, as we have now given a mortal blow to the strength and majesty of the Government of China. They sank as that of China is sinking, and as they sank left, like that of China, an anarchy on our borders. An anarchy on our borders we°could not bear : we quelled it with arms, and added the territory in which it had broken out to our dominions. The potentates who surrounded us, half barbarous and ignorant of international right, were always affording us technical causes for war, of which we took advantage with legal strictness, and which gave them and their kingdoms over into our hands. Our Empire went on eating into the native sovereignties without any formed design, by the mere tendency of strength to grow amidst weakness. Rome did not mean to conquer the world, but once launched on her career she came perpetually into contact, and coming into contact she came into collision, with comparatively barbarous and comparatively lawless powers. One after another they provoked her or sorely tempted her to attack them. One after another she conquered them ; she went on conquering ; she became absorbed by the devouring greed of conquest, till herself overpowered by the enormous mass of Empire, she staggered, and sank in ruin.

And even in their hour of Empire the Imperial • people of Rome were not happy. They were not even rich as a people, though their great nobles and farmers of the revenue were. "They fight," said a tribune, "to maintain the luxury and wealth of others, and they die with the title of lords of the earth, without possessing a single clod to call their own." In this Imperial people of ours, on whose dominions the sun never sets, how often will you see a peasant tilling his own land ? How often will you find a peasant who has any hope of possessing property, or any notion of an Englishman's rights, except the right, for which he struggles hard, to a share in the public alms ?

We have now turned over quite a new leaf in India, and are beginning again with a fresh system of Government and fresh hopes. This question may therefore be said, perhaps, to be rather one of the future than of the past or the present. It may be said to be one which the result of an experiment yet to be made can alone decide. Still it may be useful to lay down the lines of observation and thought as to the utility of a dominion of this kind. .

It may be the more useful since, whatever we may profess or resolve, we are more than ever in the conquering vein ; and we are now carrying on our arms from India to China. As in the case of India, the system of conquest is begun by merchants, with a touch of a different calling. From the smuggling trade in opium, these men are creeping on to enterprises of a more extensive kind. Their interests are no more identical with those of English commerce than their conduct is identical with English honour; but they have succeeded in getting themselves recognised as " *Cives Romani*," who are to be supported in every quarrel, into which their aggressiveness or their covetousness may get them, by the whole force of the Empire. We have made progress in these matters, as it was natural that we should. The statesmen and peers of the last century with difficulty brought them-

selves to grant a pardon under the name of an acquittal
to Warren Hastings. The genius and valour of "the
great proconsul" barely covered, in their eyes, the stain
which he had brought on the honour of England by his
crimes against feeble and unoffending Indians. Pitt
could not help consenting to send him to trial, though
party interest pointed the other way. The public men
of those days, though they squandered the public money
and made unjustifiable wars, were men of spirit and
honour; they would not have stooped to take part in
filibustering, and they had no taste for the butchery
of Hindoos. Now a Minister in quest of popularity
runs at the head of the filibusters, and rivals them in
dignity and regard for the truth [c]. And as the nation
begins to flinch from using its own army in the
work, Her Majesty is made to play the part of recruit-
ing-serjeant for the Emperor of China, and to invite
her subjects by an Order in Council to sell themselves
as mercenary soldiers to a barbarian prince. Surely if
there is one thing from which more than another civilized morality recoils, it is the hiring of men to ply
the trade of the mercenary soldier. War made by
hirelings is not war, but murder. All war would be
murder if it were not redeemed by the duty which the
soldier owes to his cause. This is true of all mercenaries; it was true of the German mercenaries who were
hired to fight the battles of England in the Crimean
war. But what is to be said when gallant Englishmen

[c] See Lord Malmesbury's Letter to Lord Palmerston on his Speech
at Tiverton respecting the China War, published in *The Times*, March
24, 1857.

are bidden to become the mercenaries of a prince who puts his prisoners to death by cutting them slowly to pieces on a cross? Thus it is that we fulfil the mission which Providence has, in consequence of our transcendent virtue and piety, and in spite of our unambitious hatred of aggrandizement, imposed upon us, of diffusing civilization and Christianity over the East.

We are told by the Prime Minister, that having overturned the Government of China by a filibustering war, we must now take it into our hands and set it on its legs again, by way of making it amends. We are told this in language of the utmost levity and insolence, seasoned with scoffs at the idea of a just Providence which inflicts retribution on those who commit wrong. The House of Commons responds with a courtier's laugh to the king's jest; and thus we take a second India on our hands.

In this matter of Eastern aggrandizement the nation has had a terrible warning to look to its own interests and its own honour. A plan was formed by an ambitious Government much in need of an increase of reputation, for the invasion of a country on the confines of our Indian Empire. But our agent in that country being, as the authors of the plot say, a man "of great simplicity of character," or, in other words, an upright servant of the public, sends to his employers information shewing that the proposed invasion would be alike impolitic and unjust. His information, as it stands in the way of glory and aggrandizement, is set at nought. The plot goes on; the invasion takes place; it ends in utter disaster; many thousands of Englishmen find an ignominious grave, and the honour of England receives a stain worse than that of defeat. The passages in the Envoy's despatches dissuading the invasion, if they were made known to the public, would bring down condemnation on the authors of a criminal and calamitous war. But in the copies laid before Parliament these passages are struck out without marks of omission, and a turn is even given to a part of the mutilated documents which makes them seem to countenance the invasion. It leaks out that the papers have been unfairly dealt with; but the Government when pressed to produce them is able, by the aid of its party and the free use of assurances, to defeat the demand. The Envoy himself has perished, and his name is at the mercy of his chivalrous employers. Years pass away before the genuine despatches come to light. A voice of indignation is then raised, but it is feeble from the lapse of time, and a powerful Minister at the head of a majority is able to bluster down justice. For the blood wasted and the misery produced by the criminal folly of the Government, not a pang of generous remorse is felt; the only thought is how to shift the blame from the living authors of the calamity upon the guiltless dead[d]. If this were greatness, some of us would be ready to pray that the greatness of England might depart for ever.

Moreover, if we are keeping India only in the interest of the Indians, to prevent the anarchy which would ensue on our departure, and not for any ad-

[d] See the debate on Mr. Dunlop's motion for the Afghanistan Papers, March 19, 1861.

vantage of our own, it is as well that the world should
know this; and that we should not be envied or in-
trigued against, as though we were holding a rich possession for our own ends.

In considering the interest of England in this matter,
that of India is, of course, always to be kept equally in
view.   Indeed, the one is inseparably mixed up with the
other.   If one man or nation enters into relations with
another, it must be for the good of both or for the good
of neither : this is as true in regard to economical matters as it is in regard to the other affairs of life.

It will not be disputed that our original object in
establishing ourselves in India was to grasp the lucrative monopoly (as it was supposed to be) of the Indian
trade.   But that monopoly has now been entirely abandoned.   The ports of India are open to all the world.
If we have still the lion's share of the trade, it is because, from the maritime genius and energy of our people, we have the lion's share of trade everywhere.   The
monopoly is practical, not legal; and it would not be
affected by the abandonment of the Empire.   The English residents in India form, no doubt, in themselves
a good market for the productions of this country.   In
this respect our political dominion may be useful to our
commerce.   But we derive from it no other commercial
advantage whatever.

While the monopoly lasted, it was a scourge to both
countries and to the whole commercial world.   It pa-
ralyzed, as all monopolies must paralyze, the industry,
and it blighted, as all monopolies must blight, the fer-
tility of the country on whose products it was imposed.

It made Indian goods dear to the mass of the people in the country which imposed it, for the fancied benefit of a few. It diminished the general wealth of the world; and as a consequence, the wealth of each nation, including our own. By a just, but common, retribution, it failed to enrich the monopolists themselves. The Company never throve by the way of trade, though many of their servants throve to a fabulous extent by robbery and corruption.

This monopoly, when questioned in the public interest, was defended by the Company with arguments which displayed the wisdom of Protection in its most naked form. A free trade, they protested, would so raise the price of articles in the Indian market by the increased demand which it would produce, and so lower the price in the English market by the increased supply which it would bring, that there would be no longer any profit in the trade. In other words, it was nothing but the existence of this wise and beneficent restriction that saved India from the evils of prosperous industry, and England from the evils of abundance. However, the East India Company were not sinners in this matter above all the Galileans. The Dutch burnt spices to keep the price high: not only so, but in the islands where they had no settlements they gave rewards to those who would strip off the young blossoms and green leaves of the clove and nutmeg trees, and thereby almost extirpated those trees [e]. Adam Smith, after denouncing the "savage policy" of the Dutch, proceeds to say :—"The English

[e] Adam Smith, bk. iv. c. 7.

Company have not yet had time to establish in Bengal so perfectly destructive a system. The plan of their government, however, has had exactly the same tendency. It has not been uncommon, I am well assured, for the chief, that is, the first clerk of a factory, to order a peasant to plough up a rich field of poppies, and sow it with rice or some other grain. The pretence was, to prevent a scarcity of provisions; but the real reason was to give the chief an opportunity of selling at a better price a large quantity of opium, which he happened then to have upon hand. Upon other occasions the order has been reversed, and a rich field of rice or other grain has been ploughed up, in order to make room for a plantation of poppies; when the chief foresaw that extraordinary profit was likely to be made by opium." Such was the spirit of cupidity, at once suicidal and cruel, robbing labour of its reward, and blighting the fruitfulness of the earth—a spirit accursed of Heaven and of man—under the influence of which these glorious conquests were commenced, and the foundations of this proud Empire were laid.

The private trade which the servants of the Company began to carry on in the early days of the Empire, was, while it lasted, more noxious, in the opinion of Adam Smith, than even the public trade of the Company. " The public trade of the Company extends no further than the trade with Europe, and comprehends a part only of the foreign trade of the country. But the private trade of the servants may extend to all the different branches both of its inland and foreign trade. The monopoly of the Company can tend only to stunt

the natural growth of that part of the surplus produce
which, in the case of free trade, would be exported to
Europe. That of the servants tends to stunt the natural growth of every part of the produce in which
they choose to deal, of what is destined for home consumption, as well as what is destined for exportation;
and consequently to degrade the cultivation of the
whole country, and to reduce the number of its inhabitants. It tends to reduce the quantity of every sort
of produce, even that of the necessaries of life, whenever the servants of the Company choose to deal in
them, to what those servants can both afford to buy
and expect to sell with such a prófit as pleases them."

We are much mistaken if we think that our conquest
of India, or the planting of our factories there, called
into being the Indian trade. There was an important
trade between India and Europe during the middle
ages, and in still earlier times. It was of course not
large in amount compared with modern trades, but it
was steady and active. It went by routes in which
it had to overcome great natural obstacles, and thereby
proved its force. What might this trade have become
in modern times with better carriage and more open
seas, and what might it have done for the industry of
India if it had not been sealed up by the monopoly
of the East India Company? In balancing the advantages and disadvantages of our dominion over India, we
have to set down this indefinite, but probably large item,
on the wrong side of the account.

We are now making railroads which will open up
the resources of the country; and in these and other

government works British capital, while India remains quiet, finds a lucrative investment. But is it certain that the native princes would not have done the same thing, and given the same employment to English capital and to English engineers? The native princes of Egypt have of late years freely adopted European improvements and given encouragement to the projectors of them. The native princes of India freely employed European architects to plan and decorate their mausoleums and palaces, European jewellers to cut their diamonds, and European officers to drill their troops.

At all events, so far as the investment of capital is concerned, our dominion gives no special advantage to its possessors. A capitalist of any country in Europe may invest in Indian railroads as freely as an Englishman; and the downfall of the British dominion, if it ruined either, would ruin both alike.

It will be admitted at once that we draw no military force from India. The employment of a few Sepoys in Egypt or in China is but a nominal exception to this rule.

It may be said, however, that India, though it furnishes no military force to this country, pays, unlike our other dependencies, for its own military defence. This is apparently, but it is not really, the case. The Cape was occupied, and is held by us, merely as a post on the road to India; and the expenses of that station, which have been enormous, must therefore be set down to the account of our Indian Empire. Other English ships may touch at the Cape, but these ships might

safely be left to the course of nature and the interest of
the Cape Colonists. It is our anxiety for the safety
of the route to India which compels us to keep the
place in our own hands. The same may be said of
Mauritius. But, moreover, our great force in the Mediterranean and our military stations there, are maintained partly on account of the necessity, or the alleged
necessity, of overawing the powers which command the
overland route. And, besides all this, our general
policy is influenced, and we are frequently entangled in
quarrels, and sometimes in wars, by causes in which
our alarm for the safety of the Indian Empire has its
share. The late war with Russia arose, not perhaps
in a great degree, but still in some degree, from this
source. As to the general envy and hatred of the
world, which attend vast territorial aggrandizement,
they are by most people, in reasoning about these matters, set down as a source of strength, though to others
they may appear to be rather a source of weakness.

The sudden calls of India for military assistance, if
ever they should recur at an awkward moment, may
lay a heavy pressure on the military resources of this
country. On a late occasion we sent out in a great
hurry 30,000 men, without whose immediate aid the
Empire would have been lost. The Indian Government
paid for this army, it is true; but to send out 30,000 men
at a moment's notice, if wages are high in this country,
and recruiting difficult, may be a very embarrassing
operation. It would be particularly embarrassing if we
happened to be at war with any European power at the
same time. And this is, in fact, very likely to occur;

for an European power at war with us would naturally
try to stir up revolt in India. The mutiny of the
Sepoys followed close after the war with Russia. It
might just as easily have taken place a short time
before, when the war with Russia was going on; and it
was suspected, though perhaps without much proof, to
have been fomented by Russian intrigue.

If it is admitted that we draw no military force, it
will be as readily admitted that we draw no revenue
of the ordinary kind from India. If we were Romans,
or Spaniards of the age of Cortes and Pizarro, no doubt
we should extort money from our subjects, but, as we are
a Christian, humane, and moral nation, we extort none.

There is, however, a revenue of a peculiar kind
which we derive from India, and which is probably
regarded by most people as the chief remaining advantage of the Empire. I mean the salaries which Englishmen receive for governing India, and the pensions
which they enjoy when they return from it. The experience of a few years will shew whether these salaries and pensions, on the strict and economical footing to which they have been reduced since the government of this country has taken India into its hands
and the heavy debt contracted in putting down the
mutiny has compelled retrenchment, will really repay
Englishmen for undergoing banishment to India and
all the sacrifices which it entails. A man is to quit
his country just as life is opening upon him; to be
separated perhaps for ever from his family; to forget,
or at least to be forgotten by, his friends; to spend
his days among aliens in a country to which he

has no attachment, with little European society, and that little not of his own choosing ; and this in a climate where the rate of European mortality is double what it is in England ; where life is but half life, and luxury is but a palliation of discomfort. He is to part with his children when they are a few years old, and send them to be reared in a distant country. Very likely he may have also to part with his wife. He is to return only when the best part of life is over, and the power of enjoyment is almost gone, to a land where his place knows him not. Will Indian salaries and Indian pensions on the reduced scale, and under a system of strict purity, which cuts off all indirect means of gain, long seem to Englishmen a sufficient reward for such sacrifices and privations as these? In the glorious days of India, the days of the Nabobs, fabulous fortunes were made by irregular means; and Clive stood astonished at his own moderation in having only brought home with him the wealth of an English Duke. In those days, too, fortunes were made with great rapidity, as well as to a prodigious amount, and there might be a prospect of living to enjoy them in England when they had been made. Do not the parting rays of that splendid epoch of corruption still shed their light over the present, and keep up an illusion which may presently pass away?

The Indian pensions spent in this country, if they were all, would be a very poor return to this nation for the sacrifice of much of its best ' blood, and of its best practical intellect, and for the liabilities and dangers which it incurs. It would be a very poor

T

return even if money spent in unproductive objects, as most of this money must always be, promoted the general well-being of the people; the reverse of which is the fact.

It seems doubtful, then, whether our dominion in India has done good, or is likely to do good, economically speaking, to either nation. Has it done good, or is it likely to do good, to either nation in a political, or, what must also be considered here, in a religious point of view?

To look at the question first on the side of India. Has our Government been, or can we feel assured it will be, a good Government for India? That it is now, and has for some time been, a benevolent Government, need not be doubted. So far as the people and the Statesmen of this country are concerned, it is a Government of unmixed benevolence. England wishes nothing but good to India, and would certainly embrace without a moment's hesitation any measure, saving the resignation of any part of her own dominion, by which the welfare of the Indians could be promoted.

Benevolence, sincere benevolence, guided the Indian administration of English statesmen even in less philanthropic times than ours. They did all that the wisdom of those days could suggest for the Indian people. To all of them who were, or by a liberal construction could be taken to be, their subjects, they gave English law, the perfection of reason, with its Black Acts and its Coventry Acts, with its profound distinctions between offences which were and offences which were not burglary and felony; with its clear and compendious pro-

cesses and its rational pleading system. The boon, en-
veloped in its shroud of dark and mystic language, is
described by the historian of British India[f] as hang-
ing over the head of the affrightened Hindoos like a
black and portentous cloud, from which every terrific
and destructive form might be expected to descend. A
Hindoo of the highest rank was, to the horror of the
whole people, hanged for forgery. It was a wonder, says
some one, that a Mahometan was not hanged for bigamy.
People were dragged five hundred miles to give bail
in cases which were to them utter darkness, and ha-
rassed out of their lives by writs of *scire facias*. The
majesty of the English Law, in the person of an at-
torney with his writ in his hand, forced its way into
the zenana of a Mahometan Prince. Lord Cornwallis
meant, if ever man did, to do good to the Indians and
to all mankind. In the height of his benevolence he
bestowed upon India the nearest approach that he could
devise to the class of English Squires. The poor barbarians had nothing exactly answering to the English
ideal; but the Zemindars, the native farmers of the
revenue, bore some faint resemblance to it, and were
made to serve the turn. The result was general ruin
and confusion.

This was ignorance. The ignorance has now passed
away. Corruption has been put down; and the benevolence remains. Will not the Government of India
henceforth be a good Government, perhaps the best
Government in the world? I fear there is a remark,
made nearly a century ago, but as true now as when

[f] Mill's British India, vol. iv. p. 270.

it was made, which is a sentence of death to these hopes. "It is a very singular Government," says Adam Smith ᶠ, "in which every member of the administration wishes to get out of the country, and consequently to have done with the Government, as soon as he ca, and to whose interest, the day after he has left it and carried his whole fortune with him, it is perfectly indifferent though the whole country was swallowed up by an earthquake." The reason why men sometimes govern a country well in spite of the tyrannical passions, the covetousness, the indolence, which tempt them to govern ill, is, that the country is their own, and that it will be that of their children after them.

Political mechanicians in framing their machines are too apt to leave out of consideration the motive power. The Chinese shipwrights, when a steam vessel was given them as a model, produced an exact imitation of her, with a truss of lighted straw to make the smoke.

We, sitting in England, are the fathers of the Indian people, and zealously exert ourselves in fancy and talk for their improvement, and for the promotion of their happiness. It is a different thing to exert yourself on the spot, in a climate which overwhelms you with apathy, without much hope of visible result during your own time, and without seeing the gratitude which we picture to ourselves beaming from the faces of the people. There are very few men in whom intellectual interests, unaided by strong desires, will overcome the

ᶠ Wealth of Nations, vol. iii. p. 85. The sentence is not quite grammatical, but its meaning is clear.

mere unwillingness to work; and the virtue of com-
petitive examination must be great indeed if it produces a service full of such men.

In the same way, we, sitting in England, pay the
most tender respect to the feelings of the conquered race.
But can we expect the same tenderness to be shewn
by the rude soldier, stalking as lord among a subjugated
people, of a different complexion from his own, and
with habits which, from their mere strangeness, must
move his ignorant contempt, and perhaps his disgust?
Can we expect this even of an officer or of a Government servant, unless he is a man of singular kindness,
comprehensiveness, and delicacy of mind? Did not
the mutiny bring to light facts which shewed that the
English in India behaved as conquerors among the conquered? And is not this human nature?

The servants of the old Company regarded it as their
duty to hold India, and they performed that duty in
a Roman way; their success being greatly aided by
a sort of corporate unity, depending partly on family
connexion, which in their case, as in the case of the
Roman Senate, preserved the traditions of Imperial
rule. They did not regard it as their duty to regenerate India. They were much blamed when their
hour of reckoning came for not having done so. It
is now to be seen whether the blame was altogether
deserved. It is to be seen whether, for the first time
in the history of the world, Philanthropy can successfully administer the heritage of Conquest.

A cheap Government the English Government of
India cannot possibly be, since all the officials, and,

now that the native army has failed, almost the entire military establishment, must be imported from the most expensive country in the world. The pensions must be fixed with reference to the scale and cost of living in England; so that indirectly India bears in some measure the pressure of our National Debt. If the salaries are cut down too low, the result will be corruption, the facilities for which in that country are very great. If the number of the officials is reduced too much, the result will be a defect of government, and a denial of justice, which are nearly as bad as misgovernment and injustice. Native officials may be employed at a cheaper rate. But honour is a rare quality among Orientals. In the Hindoo or Mahometan gentleman it may be found. But will the Hindoo or Mahometan gentleman ever take a petty office under an alien Government? The dominion of the foreigner almost inevitably excludes from public employments the real worth of a country, because the real worth of a country almost always dwells in the same breasts with its pride.

In considering what India can afford to pay for its Government, we must bear in mind that it is on the average a poor country. The dazzling character of some of its productions, and the concentration of these productions in the palaces of despots, begot in former times a fabulous notion of its wealth, which has even now not entirely died away.

It has been said that it matters nothing to the Indian tax-payer whether his taxes are paid to a Government resident in India, or to a Government resident in London. His native sovereign, it is argued, would take

just as much from him as we do, and it is all the same
to him whether the money is spent upon the spot or
elsewhere. But this reasoning shews that the political
philosophers who employ it have not thought the rude
organization and coarse functions of Oriental government worthy of their study. The money which an
Eastern despot sucks from his subjects runs partly to
waste in mere luxury. But part of it is spent in pageantry which gratifies the people ; part is spent in
works of magnificence which both gratify and in some
degree refine ; and part is spent in works of real
utility, such as tanks, quays, and public buildings. No
great public buildings for native purposes have been
erected since we became masters of India, and if we
quitted the country to-morrow the great works of its
old native lords would stand in triumph on the place
which would know our name no more.

"A large part of the habits of obedience to a Government," says Sir G. C. Lewis, "rests upon associations
with ancient institutions, and ancient names." If this
is true of the habit of obedience, it is still more true
of the habit of affection. And perhaps it may partly
account for the fact which Sir G. C. Lewis laments,
that "the Indian people have hitherto derived little
good from the acts of a Government, which has of
late years been perhaps the most benevolent in any
country." It is contrary to all experience to suppose
that a Government of strangers and sojourners, however powerful and however wise, can ever take root in
the hearts of the people. They may tremble, they may
partly appreciate, but they cannot love. Even to make

them thoroughly appreciate, their political intelligence must be raised to a much higher point than that at which the intelligence of the Indians is now. If we compare the loyalty which has been shewn to native rulers, even to native rulers whom we have branded as monsters, such as Tippoo Sahib, with any loyalty which the same people have shewn to our Government, the result of the comparison is not flattering to us. But this proves nothing against our Government, except that it is that of the stranger.

If the confidence of a people in their Government may be in any degree tested by their readiness to invest in its funds and speculations, the confidence of the Indians in their Government would appear not to be great. At least, if I am rightly informed, but a small amount of native money has been invested in our Indian Stock and Railways. In matters of this kind, however, we are commencing a new system, and the new system may open a new era.

If the English could be acclimatized in India so as to become a ruling class, attached to the country, instead of being merely successive relays of immigrants drawing incomes and pensions, much of this would be changed. But here, it seems, science bids us almost despair. The fact appears to be that over a great part of India few English children can be reared : that of those few the greater part are reared only to a life of disease and misery : that in Bengal the third generation of unmixed European blood is nowhere to be found : and that the proportion of European deaths compared with those of natives is frightfully large, and is traceable to diseases arising from the climate, not to causes which care or temperance might remove[h]. Appeals are constantly made to the behests of Providence as our warrant for keeping possession of a country which is not ours. How can Providence announce its behests more plainly than by sending childlessness and death?

Our Government has unquestionably extirpated some barbarous and cruel customs. It has put down Suttée, and the immolation of victims to Juggernaut; and it seems to have almost put down the self-tortures of the Fakirs. These lessons of humanity are of the highest value to the people. But there was a terrible counterpoise in the wholesale executions and other horrors which followed the revolt of the Sepoys.

Where we have supported and regulated dependent Princes, we have probably made their government rather worse than it would otherwise have been. Oriental despotism is the coarsest and lowest form of government; but in this as in other cases nature has her remedies, though of a rude and violent kind. When a dynasty is utterly decrepid, it is overthrown, and replaced by one of more vigour, which for one or two generations governs tolerably well. The revolutions are frequently revolutions of the palace, which do not bring much confusion or distress on the mass of the people. If we take native dynasties under our protection, and turn them into satraps of our own, we

[h] See a paper on Ethnoclimatology; or, The Acclimatization of Man. By Dr. James Hunt. 'Printed in the Report of the British Association for the Advancement of Science (1861), p. 129. ·

prevent nature's remedy from acting. The result will probably be, that to avoid being accomplices in abject misgovernment, as we were for some time in Oude, we shall in the long run have to take the government of the whole country, as we have that of Oude, directly into our own hands.

We have preserved India from external invasion. Had we not been her lords during the last half century, it is probable that she would have been visited by one of those inroads from the north which have marked the successive epochs of her history. Perhaps the Sikhs would have carried their arms southwards and founded a new dynasty at Agra or Delhi, instead of being arrested by our armies upon the Sutlej. On the other hand, it must be recollected that the progress of our own dominion has been marked by constant wars, ending with the war against the Sepoy mutineers. The state to which some provinces were reduced in the early days of our dominion by the profligate rapacity of buccaneering Englishmen, the wars which they excited, and the cruel tyranny which they exercised, was probably as bad as that to which any part of India has ever been reduced by wars between native Princes. It is of course extremely difficult to strike the balance, between the calamities which did, and those which might have occurred. In one respect the effect of European is worse than that of native wars. Native wars ravage for the moment, but leave no burden of debt behind. We have introduced into what we deem the barbarism of India one of the worst vices of civilized government, the practice of carrying on war with borrowed money, which ravages the harvests of posterity as well as those of the present time.   .

If the intelligence of the English people were diverted from its own concerns, and directed, under the influence of its benevolence, to the Government of India, there is no saying to what extent the people of India might benefit by our guardian care. But the fact is, the intelligence of the people of England can be very little directed to Indian concerns except when those concerns become entangled with the conflicts of English parties; and in that case India takes nothing but mischief from the interest which she excites. The India Bill of Fox was not thrown out on its merits as a measure for the benefit of the people of India; indeed, the bill brought in afterwards by its opponents was very much of the same character. It was thrown out because it was proposed by a ministry which, from party motives exclusively English, the King and the Tories desired to overthrow. The complete establishment of the Imperial Government in India by the abolition of the Company was immediately signalized by an incident of the same kind. A Governor General struggling with a great mutiny, and but just emerging from the extremity of peril, was attacked in a despatch published by a Government of the other party, which happened to come into power; and when the Government was called to account, a mere struggle of English parties, carried on with the utmost heat and excitement, but without any real reference to Indian interests, was the result. And so in the nature of things it must always be. India can scarcely ever be the

object of active solicitude to the Statesmen and the
nation who are supposed to be always occupied with
her welfare, except when they are impelled to attend to
her by motives which will prevent them from having
regard to her welfare alone.

The old Company had this advantage as an instrument for governing India, that it was in some measure
detached from English parties and exempt from their
party motives. And history will write on the tomb of
the greatest Corporation which the world ever saw,
that as regards the Foreign Policy of our Indian Government, the Directory generally inclined to the side
of moderation, peace, and justice. It opposed itself for
the most part to the restless ambition of Governors
General, often eager to signalize their Viceroyalty and
make a name for themselves in England by new conquests, for which there was always a pretext ready, if
there was no cause. Its hands were clean of the con-
spiracy which led to the Affghan war: and if it had
possessed the power it would probably have brought
the conspirators to justice for their crimes. Independently of any superior wisdom or morality, its
counsels were guided by a sense of special and permanent interest in the Empire, which was merely a temporary scene of personal ambition to a Governor General or a President of the Board of Control. But its
attempts to check rapacity and aggrandizement were
always futile, because the Governor General was supported by the Cabinet which had sent him out, and
by his party at home.

The commercial origin and traditions of the Com-

pany, which were so often cast in their teeth as rendering them manifestly unfit for governing an Empire,
in fact disposed them to a policy of wisdom and moderation; while the aristocratic Government in this
country, and its organs in India, were more often disposed to a policy of aggrandizement. Conquest had
been from the outset very injurious to the trading
interest of the Company, and they remained impressed
by this fact[1].

We have taken India out of the hands of the Company; but it is a mere illusion to think that we have
put it into the hands of England. We have simply

[1] Sir Thomas Roe, English Ambassador at the Court of the Mogul in
1615, besides his other services bestowed advice upon the Company.
" At my first arrival," says he, " I understood a fort was very necessary,
but experience teaches me we are refused it to our own advantage. If
the Emperor would offer me ten, I would not accept of one." He then
states his reasons: first, he adduces evidence that it would be of no
service in their trade; secondly, " the charge," he says, " is greater than
the trade can bear; for to maintain a garrison will eat out your profit;
a war and trafic are incompatible. By my consent you shall never
engage yourselves but at sea, where you are like to gain as often as to
lose. The Pourtugese, notwithstanding their many rich residences, are
beggared by keeping of soldiers; and yet their garrisons are but mean.
They never made advantage of the Indies since they defended them:
observe this well. It has also been the error of the Dutch, who seek
plantations here by the sword. They turn a wonderful stock; they
prole in all places; they possess some of the best; yet their dead pays
consume all the gain. Let this be received as a rule, that if you will
profit seek it a sea and in a quiet trade; for without controversies, it is
an error to affect garrisons and land wars in India.
" It is not a number of ports and residences, and factories, that will
profit you. They will increase charge but not recompence it. The
conveniency of one with respect to your sails, and the commodity of
investments, and the well-employing of your servants, is all you need."—
Mill's British India, vol. i. pp. 29, 30.

put it into the hands of a bureaucratic Office. The head of that office is involved in the party struggles, and he and his policy share the fate, of the party Governments of England; but he is not otherwise an impersonation of the English people, and, as his department is not constitutional, he falls, commonly speaking, very little under constitutional control.

On the other hand, English politics have also suffered, and perhaps are destined to suffer still more, from our connexion with India. The corruption of our manners by lavish expense and luxury, though very mischievous, was not the worst mischief done by the Nabobs in the days of the great Indian fortunes. These men carried on Parliamentary corruption on a great scale; they bought rotten boroughs, and formed a powerful faction, with interests separate from those of the nation; a faction which, in exerting its influence on English politics, kept its eye as steadily fixed on India as ever an Ecclesiastical Minister in the middle ages kept his eye fixed on Rome. ' When George the Third by a stroke of absolute authority turned out his constitutional Ministry, and for a time overthrew the Constitution, the whole power of the East India interest was put forth in favour of the Court simply because an India Bill which they disliked had been the occasion, though it was not the cause, of the King's treachery to his constitutional advisers; and we may set down in some measure to the account of our Indian Empire the consequences which flowed from the victory of George the Third over the restraints of the Constitution.

The West Indian connexion was a social and political nuisance of the same kind. The West Indian Slave-owners helped the East Indian Nabobs to corrupt our gentry, and ruin some of them, by introducing habits of lavish expense and vulgar ostentation : and, like the East Indian Nabobs, they formed a separate and very corrupt interest in the State, influencing English politics for unpatriotic ends. The amount of mischief which the two between them did to the legislation and government of this country was probably very great. No worse money ever came into England than that which came with the Nabobs and the Planters. But the fact is, that no money made by robbery, or conquest, or slave-owning, or by any other means but honest industry and fair trading, ever brought good to any man or nation.

The amalgamation of the Indian and English armies may also prove a fiscal evil to this country. It is essential to public economy that the nation should understand the public accounts, and the reasons for all important items of expenditure. But the mixture of the English and Indian armies is likely to produce an intricacy which may elude the scrutiny even of the House of Commons, especially as the service is regulated by an Office which, through some want of firmness in the representatives of the nation, has been very imperfectly brought under constitutional control.

Already the process of amalgamation itself seems to have given rise to infinite perplexities, out of which a Government deeply in debt, and feeling that its existence depends upon retrenchment, is naturally tempted to force its way, somewhat at the expense of justice.

It may further be said, generally, that the incorporation of a vast Empire such as India, which is not governed on free principles, with a free country, is apt to taint the political spirit of the free country, and to impair the vigour of its freedom. We may not be able as yet to point to specific evidences of this fact, but the influence is in its very nature impalpable, like a malaria in the air, and its pestilential effects may only become visible on looking back over a long range of history. Thus much, however, may easily be understood, that the principle of liberty can scarcely fail to be less sacred in a nation which holds despotic dominion over others. The despot is no more a freeman than his slave.

Does our dominion in India conduce to the propagation of Christianity? This is a question which cannot be left out of the present account. It is one, however, which we have not very trustworthy means of answering. The reports of the missionaries to their employers as to the number and value of the conversions are, no doubt, made in the most perfect good faith; but no man wishing to form a cool judgment on the matter would accept these accounts unchecked by the evidence of less enthusiastic witnesses. It would, no doubt, be equally irrational, on the other hand, to accept implicitly the counter statements of Indian politicians, who having the safety of the Empire chiefly in their minds, dread the disturbing influence of missionary zeal. The discrepancy is perhaps rather as to the value than as to the number of the conversions, but the value is of course the one important point.

Reasoning beforehand, we should probably say that our dominion would in some respects favour the progress of Christianity, and in other respects impede it. It cannot fail to favour the progress of Christianity by sheltering the missionary in the safe prosecution of his labours, and saving his harvest from being swept away by such outbreaks of barbarian fanaticism as those which destroyed the Christian community in China. On the other hand, this very security may tend to give the missionary calling less of the character of a spiritual enterprise undertaken from pure zeal, and more of the character of a paid profession; and when once the missionary calling has put on the character of a paid profession, the talisman is gone. No form so grand and winning as that of Xavier seems yet to have arisen among the propagators of Christianity in our Indian Empire, nor, taking the number of his converts at the most sober estimate, do we seem to have yet produced a parallel to his success.

Where the missionary goes by himself the native only sees Christianity arrayed in zeal, purity, and love. But in India he sees it in the far more questionable shape of a community of English officials, who would be more than men if, being removed from the influence of English opinion, they did not fall somewhat below the ordinary standard of English virtue; and if, being removed from the restraints which are imposed on Englishmen by the society of their equals, and placed among a subject race, they did not fall somewhat below the English standard of gentleness and kindness to those around them. Nor must it be forgotten that honest pride steels the heart against the religion of the conqueror; while, on the other hand, the religion of the conqueror has attractions for proselytes who disgrace a convert's name.

The religion of the conqueror, indeed, is a term which faintly describes the position of Christianity in India, when rebellious Sepoys after their submission were being butchered by thousands in cold blood; or when the Christian inhabitants of Calcutta were yelling for "revolutionary energy," that is, for promiscuous massacre and burning.

It is a further question, which need not be discussed here, how far a change has taken place in the most effective instruments for propagating the faith, since the time when the Apostles parted at the foot of the Cross to preach the Gospel to the world. At that time there was little intercourse between distant nations; the channels of thought were few; the amount of literature was scanty, and that confined to a few spots on the earth; no great scientific and intellectual forces were in action to shake the foundations of heathen creeds. There was, in general, no mode of overthrowing a false religion and planting a true one in its place but the personal presence of the Apostle and his spoken word.

The difficulty of raising enough English soldiers to guard all our dependencies, which I mentioned in my first letter as likely to affect the security of our whole Empire, is likely in an especial degree to affect the security of our Empire in India. It seems to be agreed on all hands that the plan of holding India with

Sepoys has broken down, and that it must be held
henceforth mainly by European troops. The number
of these troops at present thought necessary is seventy
or eighty thousand; but this is just after a great
blow, which has struck terror into the subject people.
Territories so vast can scarcely be held in the long run
by less than 100,000 good troops, especially as part
of our force is still employed, and is likely always to
remain employed, in frontier wars. There will be a still
heavier demand if the Roman spirit of our merchants in
China is to draw upon India for the means of their
conquests in that quarter. The waste of European
life, even with our greatly improved cantonments, is
double what it is in Europe, so that there will be required a double number of recruits. Should the supply
of soldiers fail, the Empire, which rests only on bayonets,
falls at once to the ground; and yet how is England
for ever to afford the supply? If our labouring classes
grow prosperous, as we all hope they will, what is to
induce them to enlist in a service which offers them,
and, while our Empire remains so large as it is, can offer
them, only poor pay, with a great chance of long exile
in a bad climate; and this added to the risk of being
shot on the field of battle, or, what is worse, dying of
gangrene in a military hospital? Already, if I am
rightly informed, the adventurous spirits among our
peasantry are beginning to emigrate instead of enlisting. The recruits are drawn more from the towns,
and a change is said in consequence to be coming
over the character of the soldiery. More than this,
as I have remarked before, our present command of

soldiers at a reasonable rate for the distant parts of
our Empire depends on an exceptional law regarding
the soldier's calling. When once the soldier has entered, or been enticed into, the service, he becomes,
according to our present law, for a long term of years
the slave of the State, so that he can neither quit his
calling like other labourers, nor demand an increase
of wages, however much the general price of labour
may rise. It is easy to see the convenience of this law
to the Government, and it is easy to trace its historical
origin. It is a remnant of a general system of forced
service, another and a worse remnant of which was the
press-gang. But the reason and justice of the law are
not so easily seen; and if it is not founded on reason
and justice, it is certain to be in the end overthrown, as
the power of impressment has been overthrown, by the
force of public opinion. Now, supposing you had to
go into a free market, to give the full market price
of labour, and allow the soldier to quit his calling
when he pleased, on giving whatever, under the circumstances of that calling, might be reasonable notice, I
ask once more what it would cost to keep the army of
India under the standards.

The principle of Colonial Emancipation does not
apply to India, because it is a conquered country,
not a Colony; and to throw up the government without making any provision for the preservation of order
when we are gone, would be to do a great wrong to
the people in addition to those which have been already
done. But the course of affairs, if it continues as it is
at present, seems likely in this case also to enforce

a change in the relation between England and her dependency.

It appears pretty clear from what has already happened that the two Governments, one in London the other in Calcutta, one acting from a distance the other on the spot, will not work together. It would be very strange if they did. The difficulties of carrying on the simplest form of government, where there is any room for diversity of views and policy, are great enough. No double monarchy of Brentford in the whole history of politics was ever so framed to produce inevitable clashing and collision as this double monarchy of India. The two Kings of Brentford were at least both resident at the same seat of government, and each of them saw the affairs which they regulated with their own eyes. They may have differed, and probably did differ, about their budget; but it is not likely that they ever edified their lieges by declaring, one that there was a large surplus, and the other that there was a deficit, and engaging in a sharp controversy before the public on that important matter of fact.

Scarcely is the budget controversy over between Westminster and Calcutta, when a new controversy breaks out between them about the settlement of waste lands, and it is perfectly clear, in the appeal to public opinion which follows, that the general confidence is not awarded to that one of the two Governments which is nominally supreme.

Is it not obvious to common sense that a London Office can only do mischief by meddling with the administration of India? Is not this especially obvious, when we remember that the real power of the Office is vested in the Secretary of State, and will be wielded by a number of men in quick succession, often without special qualifications for the Indian department? For every one knows that in the distribution of offices among the members of the Cabinet, party convenience must take the first, and personal aptitude the second place. Men are tossed from one department to another just as accident and the necessity of satisfying various pretensions may happen to dictate. The present Secretary for India has been Chancellor of the Exchequer and First Lord of the Admiralty, and he might just as well be President of the Board of Trade or Secretary at War.

While India belonged to the Company, it was necessary to have a Board of Control, because the Company had failed, and from the nature of the case could not but fail, to exercise the proper control over the acts of their India servants; but now that the Queen herself governs India by the hand of her Viceroy, the necessity for a Board of Control, or any London Office exercising the functions of a Board of Control, has ceased to exist.

Time, then, will probably shew that it is expedient to leave the Government of the Indian Empire to be administered on the spot by the Governor General, with full powers, for the proper exercise of which he will of course be held personally responsible by the Parliament of this country. If he proves incompetent, the proper remedy is recall; if he abuses his authority, the proper remedy is impeachment. The intermittent meddling of a bureaucratic office in this country is of no use in either case. It can only diminish responsibility, deaden the motives to vigorous exertion, and possibly afford a cloak for misconduct. It is not probable that had the Governor General of India stood alone to answer personally at the bar of English opinion for his own offences, he would have dared to enter into the Afghan war.

Such experience as we have had seems also to shew that it will be expedient to let the Viceroy of India have his own military establishment, pay his own price for soldiers, and raise them how and where he finds best, the whole being of course subject, like the Empire itself, to the British Crown.

In this way we shall at least give India a despotism carried on by a line of able and honourable despots, amenable in the last resort to the tribunal of a public opinion much higher than that of the Indians themselves. The evils of mixing together the politics and establishments of two countries remote from each other, and totally opposed in their political character, will be diminished; India will be less bound up with England in all senses than it is now. The means of holding it will be drawn from the country itself; and the measure of the resources which the Empire can supply will be, as it ought to be, the measure of the Empire. In case the Viceroy of India should find it necessary to contract his dominions, he will be able to do this without so much impeaching the power or tarnishing the majesty of this country.

I do not shrink from using the term despotism, because I am convinced that, provided the Viceroy be properly appointed; provided that he be chosen without reference to party or to rank, but solely with reference to his ability to govern India; and provided he be always liable to recall for incompetency and impeachment for misconduct, it is better that his authority should be really despotic. In a conquered country governed by the stranger liberty has no place, and to utter the name is a mockery and a profanation. In such countries the concession of oligarchic freedom to the members of the conquering race, only aggravates tenfold the slavery of the conquered. The sole chance of justice for the subject people is the existence of a power supreme over all alike, and capable of protecting the weak against the strong. The personal partiality of the supreme ruler for those of his own race is sure to be strong enough, without placing him legally under their irresponsible and unscrupulous control. A Parliament of English residents overruling the Governor General during the late mutiny would have filled all India with fire and blood.

In the case of India, the reasons against conceding oligarchical liberties to the members of the dominant race are peculiarly strong, because the English in India are not even permanent residents. They go there only to make fortunes as quickly as they can, and then return. They neither have, nor can have, any sort of patriotic feeling for India; they neither have, nor can have, any great anxiety for the lasting welfare of the people or the lasting prosperity of the country.

A grain of English interest would outweigh a ton of Indian interest in the balance of their minds.

In being denied liberty they would perhaps also be denied the instrument of suicide. Give them Parliaments, and they will have parties and party conflicts in the presence of the subject people. Probably as the party conflicts grow venomous, (and most venomous in so narrow a community they are sure to grow,) there will be appeals to the subject people; and appeals to the subject people are lighted matches applied to a mine. We have had some inkling of these tendencies already, and we seem to be in a fair way soon to have more.

To sum up the whole case in a few words. India is not a Colony or a nation but an Empire; and, as I have said before, if you are to have an Empire you must have an Emperor.

I am, &c.

GOLDWIN SMITH.

March 2, 1863.

APPENDIX I.

EXTRACT from an article in *The Toronto Globe* referred to in Letter III., on "Colonial Government," as illustrating the question between the two Provinces of Canada respecting the representation :—

"The Opposition party of Upper Canada have had their patience sorely tried during the past ten years. They have seen the Upper Province governed by a minority with reckless tyranny; its trade injured by bad legislation, its resources spent in defiance of its indignant protests, the legislation it needed denied, its institutions tampered with, its westward progress checked, its officials appointed, not on account of merit, but as a reward of treason. They have striven against these evils strenuously, and have accomplished much good by their efforts no doubt. We know that mischief has been done, but we know, also, that much more would have been done but for the activity and watchfulness of the Opposition. The past ten years have put on record a list of injuries inflicted on Upper Canada sufficient to excite indignation in the mind of the most moderate of mankind. We all know from what source these injuries have come. The less numerous and wealthy population of Lower Canada has the same number of representatives in the House of Assembly as that of Upper Canada; and the unity of the French Canadian section of the people does the rest. By favour of Sir Edmund Head, the old French party have retained absolute control of the formation of cabinets; and by the use of the power of the Executive have managed to secure a sufficient number of the representatives of Upper Canada to preserve a preponderance in the Legislature. They have gone as far in the way of offence and injury to the west as their tools from that section dared. The price paid out of the revenue for the assistance of these Upper Canadian traitors has been heavy; not only have the members been bribed, but their constituents also; offices, loans from the treasury never to be repaid, post-offices, custom-houses, contracts, such have been the expensive considerations for which western members have given their votes to Mr. Cartier's Government. Upper Canada, which furnishes seventy per cent. of the revenue of the Province, has been compelled to witness the disbursements of her own money to her own sons for betraying her interests, and has been compelled to find the means for public improvement in Lower Canada besides.

" The leaders of the Lower Canadians have shewn entire unscrupulousness as to the means they have used for carrying on this system. They have corrupted individuals and communities whenever they have found an opportunity. We do not blame them much for endeavouring to secure as great advantages as was possible for their section and their principles; it is natural that they should think their own objects of the greatest importance; but we do blame them for the means they have used to accomplish their end. It is they who are chiefly to blame for the monstrous corruption of the past ten years. We have reason to know that among the better classes of the French Canadians, than whom more honourable men do not exist, the career of Mr. Cartier in this respect is regarded with the utmost indignation. He is considered a disgrace to Lower Canada. These people value their institutions and religion as much as Mr. Cartier; but they see that the corrupt system, when it at last ceases to have power, will exercise an evil effect on all in any degree connected with it, and they feel that it is better to settle affairs with Upper Canada at once, and not jeopardize their interests by delays procured by a frightful system of corruption and injustice. There is no doubt of the correctness of this position. No one in Upper Canada desires to injure the

French people, but we have found that in all the affairs of our common government they, by their unity, obtain the advantage ; we find that they spend on themselves the money which we contribute, and refuse to us what we reasonably demand, and we are determined to obtain a remedy. Had they been less greedy, we should perhaps be less pressing, but, in the end, the result would have been the same. The larger, more wealthy and rapidly progressing Province could not continue for ever dependant upon the liberality of the other.

" Representation by Population is the remedy selected by a large majority of Upper Canadians for the existing state of things. They do not reject other remedies entirely. They are prepared to discuss any proposition made by Lower Canada which promises to be effectual. The French Canadians see in the adoption of this measure a probable reduction of their power. It would still leave to them influence, in proportion to their numbers, and far beyond their wealth and their contributions to the revenue, but they are not satisfied. They must be absolute masters or nothing.

APPENDIX II.

LETTER of "Hochelaga," published in *The Daily News*, July 23, 1862, referred to in Letter IX., on "England and Canada." The liberty has been taken of omitting two or three references to the present writer's name.

"CANADA AND ENGLAND.

"TO THE EDITOR OF THE 'DAILY NEWS.'

" SIR,—If anything more were wanting in support of the arguments for severing the last link—weak as a silken thread for good, but strong as adamant for evil—which connects England with Canada, it would be found in the speech of the Mayor of Montreal at a public dinner recently given by the inhabitants to his Excellency Viscount Monck, the Governor General. The civic functionary, acting as chairman, took the opportunity to make it thoroughly understood what were his own views and those of his French-Canadian compatriots regarding the mutual relations between the Colony and the Mother Country, in case the Governor General might flatter himself, like *The Times* and his Grace of Newcastle, that the rejection of the Militia Bill by the Canadian Legislature was a political and not a financial affair.

"His words were: 'That Canada might esteem herself a most fortunate community in being protected by one of the most powerful nations of the world, which sent them as many soldiers as might be required without rendering them liable in purse or person; that no matter how many red-coats might be required—and the more there might be the better pleased they would be to see them—it would not take one single sous out of their pockets.' The sordid self-complacency and the mocking half-defiant air with which this ignoble sentiment was uttered, and the vociferous applause with which it was hailed, shewed only too truly that it represented the feelings of the audience. His Excellency, in his reply, while he admitted ' that such indeed had hitherto been the case,' ventured to doubt ' whether England, from its unaided resources, could provide red-coats sufficient to defend a frontier so extended and exposed against military forces so formidable as those which could now be brought into the field by the neighbouring States.'

" Every soul present, English and French, was capable of estimating the full value of both these propositions; and while with Monsieur Beaudry, the Mayor, they are willing to make all they can out of John Bull while the opportunity lasts, they also know, with his Lordship, that England, even if she would, cannot successfully defend the Provinces. Knowing all this, they are prepared for separation when it must occur; and not having wasted men or money, and having made the most of the opportunity while anything was to be got, they are willing to defer as long as possible that evil day which is to make a change in arrangements so exclusively profitable to themselves; and they know, too, notwithstanding the vapouring and chiding of *The Times*, that while one red-coat remains in Canada, England is responsible for its defence, and that her national pride and pugnacity would compel her to support the smallest detachment of her military forces with all her means and all her force.

" No sane man here believes that 18,000 British soldiers in North America could defend a frontier extending across half the Continent, hemmed in and opposed by superior forces at every point, from Maine to Minnesota, from the Bay of Fundy to Lake Superior. No sane man here believes that the 20,000 Volunteers of the present Cabinet could have any notable effect, even if the Militia and Volunteers had, or

were ever intended to have, an existence except on paper.
They are both a sham—a bait for more British troops—
a pretence for demanding Imperial aid for railways, roads,
arms, clothing—anything in the shape of money or money's
worth, and to augment or to prolong, in any way, the Imperial stake in the Provinces. To aid in the deception, Bills
may be brought in and rejected, and new ones framed, and
every sort of administrative hocus-pocus gone through ; but
the only Bills which have a real meaning are those which
John Bull will have to pay, for neither sous nor cents will be
contributed by either Province; and there will be neither
men nor supplies except such as are paid for out of Imperial
funds. The British public will open their eyes to this a little
sooner or later; and even the Colonial Minister may be
brought to express vain regrets that his well-founded reliance
on Canadian loyalty has been most unaccountably abused.

" The position of England here is full of danger—threaten-
ing disgrace to herself and disaster to those who so blindly
hang to her, without a single characteristic of dependance,
except imbecility and greediness.   They are not obedient or
helpful. They bear none of the burdens of the Empire.
They add nothing to its strength or resources, but they exact
all they can from the general fund, and they tax to the
utmost point, short of prohibition, the trade of the Mother
Country, in which alone they have an opportunity of shewing
some reciprocity of obligation.   By their fruits ye shall know
them—the fruits being hostile tariffs and rejection of the
Militia Bill.

" A well-arranged separation would release 18,000 British
troops, with their munitions and material, staff and departments, which would be available for home defence, or for
reduction, with a corresponding diminution in the estimates.
There would also be removed the chief incitement to war
with England on the part of the States—their chief and most
reasonable cause of suspicion, rivalry, and distrust, the only
inducement for America and France to league against us.

Above all, with such views, England might come confidently forward as the natural mediator (mediation, mark me, not intervention) between North and South, for it would then be self-evident that her own aggrandisement and influence on this continent was not sought for in the humiliation or weak-ening of the great American Confederacy. If England could say to the North, ' We are prepared to do what we proposed to you to do; and, on condition of your severing the con-nexion with the Southern States, we will withdraw from Canada, and leave it an independent commonwealth,' there could then be no question of her loyalty, no doubt of her disinterestedness. The same scale by which the lack of mutual interest, of national ties and sympathies, between North and South, is ascertained, will shew the incompatibility between English free trade and Canadian tariffs—between races as mutually unsociable as the French Canadian and the English openly were in 1840, and covertly are still. In 1776 a separation, after a violent and bloody struggle, took place between the Mother Country and some of her Colonies, by which both were so greatly gainers that it is hard now to conceive political blindness so complete as was then unhap-pily exhibited in the old country. Can it be supposed that a separation made peacefully, deliberately, with due care for mutual rights and interests, in 186— would prove less mu-tually beneficial?—that nothing would be gained by concen-tration of forces, by diminution of expenditure at home, by leaving the youthful energies of these Colonies untrammelled and unobstructed, above all, by the removal of a temptation to England's enemies, and a snare to herself? If England is to use for herself the same measure with which she would mete to the Americans, there is barely an argument she could honestly use which would not be as applicable to her own case in Canada and New Brunswick, as to the North in her relation with the South.

" One objection which might formerly have been urged has ceased to exist—that for England to withdraw from Canada would be tantamount to its surrender to the States,—as voluntary annexation would have followed, as a matter of course. Of that there is no danger now, as far as Canada is concerned; for she would by no means volunteer to take on herself a share of the burden of the American national debt, still less would she be inclined to connect herself with a democracy so wild and reckless, and which may have to pass through so many phases of suffering—perhaps of revolution—before it settles again into the peaceful, orderly community it once was.

" With its dependent condition as a colony of England, the danger of annexation by force would be at an end. The allegiance due to England might, by conquest, be usurped by the States; but the indefeasible nationality of an independent State has a separate vitality so powerful that it can never be extinguished. If, moreover, the separation were to be made the subject of a treaty, the independence both of Canada and of the Southern States might be guaranteed by both Great Britain and America, and France might be invited to join in the bond, interested as she has a right to be in her descendants in Louisiana and Lower Canada. Thus guaranteed, Canada, during her youth as a nation, would be in the position of Belgium and Switzerland, strong, not by connexion with even the strongest power, but by severance from all.

" The material prosperity and development of Canada would as certainly follow on its independence as it did on that of the States. A nation proud and jealous of its independence, uncompromising in its self-respect, would take the place of the frightened or cunning hanger-on to the skirts of the old country, such as was recently exhibited with sordid unblushing effrontery or abject meanness by the Mayor of Montreal, without encountering a single indignant protest or expression of disgust from either the public or the press.

" HOCHELAGA."

" *Montreal, July 8th,* 1862."